الأسرة المسلمة – الكتاب الرابع

The Muslim Family - 4

أفلاذ أكبادنا

OUR PRECIOUS SPROUTS:

ISLĀMIC REGULATIONS FOR NEWBORNS

مُحَمَّد ٱلجِبالي

MUḤAMMAD AL-JIBĀLĪ

مَنْشُورَاتُ ٱلْكِتَابِ وَٱلسُّنَّةِ

AL-KITAAB & AS-SUNNAH PUBLISHING

Our Precious Sprouts
Islāmic Regulations for Newborns
(The Muslim Family – 4)

26+208 p. 24 × 18 cm
ISBN 1-891229-54-0

Cover Design: ʿAbdullāh al-Jibālī

Printed by:
Al-Maktab al-Islāmī
P.O. Box 11/3771
Beirut, Lebanon
Tel: 961-5-456-280, Fax: 961-5-450-657

Published by:
Al-Kitaab & as-Sunnah Publishing
P.O. Box 2542
Arlington, Texas 76004
Tel & Fax: 1-817-451-2592

TABLE OF CONTENTS

TABLE OF CONTENTS v

PRELUDE xiii

Opening Sermon xiii
Defining Our Mission xv
1. Correcting Our Beliefs and Practices (xvi)
2. Inviting to the True *Dīn* (xvii)
3. Warning Against Deviant Beliefs and Practices (xviii)
4. Purifying the Sunnah (xviii)
5. Liberating the Islāmic Thought (xix)
6. Presenting the Islāmic Solution (xix)
Conclusion (xx)
Technicalities xx
Transliteration (xx)
Translating and Referencing Qur'ān and *Ḥadīth* (xxii)
Notable Utterances (xxiii)
This Book xxiv
Preceding Parts (xxiv)
Current Book (xxv)
Acknowledgements xxvi

CHAPTER 1
PLANTING THE SEED 1

Islām Recommends Seeking Offspring 1
Procreation Is a Main Purpose of Marriage (1)
A Child Is a Favor from Allāh (2)
A child Increases the Number of Muslims (3)
Good Soil is Required for a Good Seed (4)
Reward for Having Children 5
A Guaranteed Reward for True Believers (5)
Children Who Die Young (5)
Children Outliving Their Parents (8)
Invoking Allāh's Blessings and Protection 9

Invoking Allāh's Blessings at Marriage (9)
Invoking Allāh's Protection at Intercourse (10)

CHAPTER 2
EMERGENCE OF THE SPROUT 11
Pregnant Woman's Craving 11
Exposure During Delivery 11
Doctors and Nurses (11)
Videotaping the Delivery (12)
The First Cry 12
Satan's Pang (12)
Condition for Inheritance 13
Applauding the Newborn 14
Announcing the Birth (14)
Congratulations (16)
Giving Presents (17)
No Gender-Based Bias in Islām 17
Submission to Allāh's Decree (17)
Disliking Girls Is a *Jāhilī* Attitude (18)
Merits in Fathering Girls (19)
The Importance of Gratitude 20
Gratitude Is a Quality of the Messengers and Believers (20)
Most People Are Ungrateful (22)
Rewards for Gratefulness and Punishment for Ungratefulness (22)
Gratitude for Having Children 23
A Child Is a Great Favor from Allāh (23)
Raising Children Gratefully (24)

CHAPTER 3
NAMING THE NEWBORN 25
When to Name a Newborn 25
Naming on the Seventh Day (25)
Naming Before the Seventh Day (26)
Conclusion (27)
Who Names the Child? 28
Giving a Good Name 29
Recommended Names 30
Names of *'Ubūdiyyah* (31)

Names with Realistic Meanings (32)
Names of the Prophet Muḥammad (33)
Names of Other Prophets (34)
Names of Righteous People (36)
Ascribing the Child to the Father 37
Ascribing to the Father Is Mandatory (37)
Ascribing to Other than the Father Is a Major Sin (38)
Illegitimate Children (40)
Surnames 42
Definition (42)
Changing the Surname (42)
Carrying the Husband's Last Name (43)
Bearing a *Kunyah* 43
Definition and Recommendation (43)
Bearing a *Kunyah* Before Having Children (44)
Giving *Kunyah* to a Childless Woman (44)
Giving *Kunyah* to Children (45)
The Prophet's *Kunyah* (46)
Prohibited Names 48
Names Expressing Servitude to Other than Allāh (48)
Names and Descriptions Specific to Allāh (48)
Names of Disbelievers and Tyrants (49)
Disliked Names 49
Names Specifically Disapproved by the Prophet (49)
Names with Ugly Meanings (52)
Western and Non-Arabic Names (53)
Names of Singers, Actors, and Other Sinners (53)
Girls' Names Indicating Passion or Bodily Attraction (53)
Combined Names (54)
Names of Angels and Qur'ānic *Sūrah*s (55)
Changing a Name to a Better One 56
The Prophet's Practice (56)
Names That the Prophet Changed (57)
Refusing the Prophet's Recommendation (60)
Calling by a Nickname 60
Calling Adults by Shortened Names (60)
Calling Children by Nicknames or Shortened Names (61)

CHAPTER 4
THE *'AQĪQAH* 63

Meaning of *'Aqīqah* 63
Linguistic and *Shar'ī* Meanings (63)
Is the Name "*'Aqīqah*" Disliked? (63)
Ruling for *'Aqīqah* 64
Is It Disliked? (65)
Evidence that It Is Obligatory (65)
Evidence that It Is Voluntary (68)
'Aqīqah vs. *Ṣadaqah* (70)
Conclusion (70)
Animals that May Be Slaughtered for *'Aqīqah* 71
Animal Type (71)
Number (72)
Sex (73)
Other Qualities (73)
Date of Slaughtering the *'Aqīqah* 74
The Seventh Day (74)
After the Seventh (75)
Offering *'Aqīqah* for Oneself (76)
Method of Slaughtering 76
Sincerity to Allāh (76)
Using a Sharp Knife (77)
Mercy Toward the Animal (78)
Laying the Animal Down (80)
Cutting the Throat (81)
Pronouncing Allāh's Name (82)
Summary (83)
Dispensing of the *'Aqīqah*'s Meat 84
Dividing the Meat (84)
Feeding (84)
Wisdom Behind the *'Aqīqah* 86
Child's Mortgage (86)
Insights into the *'Aqīqah*'s Wisdom (90)
Smearing Blood on a Newborn's Head? 91
Question and Answers 92
Delaying the *'Aqīqah* for Financial Reasons (92)
Buying Meat Instead of Slaughtering (93)

'*Aqīqah* for a Short-Lived Baby (93)
'*Aqīqah* for a Miscarried Fetus? (95)
Storing the '*Aqīqah*'s Meat (95)

CHAPTER 5
CIRCUMCISION 97
Overview 97
Origin of Circumcision (97)
Description of the Process (97)
Circumcision in the Islāmic Texts 98
One of the Characteristics of *Fiṭrah* (98)
A Prophetic Command (100)
A Practice of the Father of Prophets (100)
A Practice of the *Ṣaḥābah* (100)
Ruling 101
Ibn ul-Qayyim's Reasoning (101)
Our Conclusion (102)
Date of Performing Circumcision 102
The Earlier the Better (102)
Narrations Specifying the Seventh (103)
Delaying Circumcision until the Age of Discernment (104)
New Muslims (104)
Benefits and Wisdom 105
Circumcision of Females 106
Description (106)
Excessive Circumcision (106)
Female Circumcision in Islāmic Texts (107)
Ruling (108)
Violations and Innovations 108

CHAPTER 6
OTHER NEWBORN *SUNNAHS* 111
Taḥnīk 111
Definition (111)
Authentic Reports (111)
Discussion and Ruling (113)
Shaving the Head and Giving Charity 114
Authentic Narrations (114)

Both Boys and Girls Should Be Shaved (116)
Date of Shaving (116)
The Whole Head Should Be Shaved (116)
Shaving the Head upon Embracing Islām (118)
Giving Charity (119)
Calling *Athān* and *Iqāmah*? 119

CHAPTER 7
PROTECTING THE BABY FROM EVIL 121
Ruqyah 121
Definition and Ruling (121)
Best *Ruqyah*s (122)
Protecting the Baby 125
The Evil Eye (125)
*Ruqyah*s for Children (126)
Eliminating the "Deterrents" of Good (128)
Protection with Amulets and Talismans? (128)
Blue Beads, Horseshoe, and Other Charms (129)
Making *Duʿāʾ* and *Thikr* on Behalf of the Baby? (130)

CHAPTER 8
DETERRENTS OF GOOD 131
Why It Does Not Work? 131
Dolls and Other Images 131
Modern Children's "Toydom" (131)
Prohibition of Images in Islām (132)
Images Drive The Angels Away (133)
Permission of Dolls and Toy Animals (133)
Conclusion (134)
*Fatwā*s Concerning Images on Clothes (135)
*Fatwā*s Concerning Dolls (136)
Music 137
Bells and Ringing 138
Television 139
Celebrating Birthdays 140

CHAPTER 9
OTHER BABY ISSUES 143
Ṭahārah (Cleanliness and Purity) Issues 143
Babies' Urine (143)
Carrying Babies During the Prayer (144)
Bringing Babies into the *Masjid* (145)
Touching a Baby's Private Parts (146)
Piercing the Ears 147
Changing Allāh's Creation (147)
Inflicting Harm and Pain (149)
Earrings During the Prophet's Time (150)
Conclusion (151)
Kissing Children and Showing Mercy to Them 152
Breast-Feeding 153
Definition and Duration (153)
Historical Background (154)
Importance of Breast-Feeding in Islām (155)
Legislative Texts (156)
Regulations (158)
Advantages of Breast-Feeding (159)
Pregnancy of a Nursing Mother (160)
Concluding Remarks from Ibn ul-Qayyim (161)

APPENDIX I: LIST OF NAMES 163
Introduction 163
General Guidelines (163)
Names of Boys 164
Names of Girls 176

APPENDIX II: ALLĀH'S EXCELLENT NAMES 183
Introduction 183
Rules Concerning Allāh's Names 183
1. All of Allāh's Names Are Excellent (183)
2. Allāh's Names Have Distinctive Meanings (183)
3. Allāh's Names Require Evidence (184)
4. Allāh's Names are Countless (184)
List of Allāh's Authentic Excellent Names 185
Single Names (185)

Combined Excellent Names (190)
Names without Evidence 191

REFERENCES 193
General "Newborn" and "Baby" References 193
ʿ*Aqīqah* and Slaughtering 194
Islāmic Names 194
Allāh's Excellent Names 195

ARABIC TERMS 196
A: Glossary of Common Terms 196
B: Index 205

PRELUDE

Opening Sermon

إِنَّ ٱلْحَمْدَ لِلَّـٰهِ، نَحْمَدُهُ وَنَسْتَعِينُهُ وَنَسْتَغْفِرُهُ،

وَنَعُوذُ بِاللَّـٰهِ مِنْ شُرُورِ أَنْفُسِنَا وَمِنْ سَيِّئَاتِ أَعْمَالِنَا.

مَنْ يَهْدِهِ ٱللَّـٰهُ فَلاَ مُضِلَّ لَهُ، وَمَنْ يُضْلِلْ فَلاَ هَادِيَ لَهُ.

Al-ḥamdu lillāh. Indeed, all praise is due to Allāh. We praise Him and seek His help and forgiveness. We seek refuge with Allāh from our souls' evils and our wrong doings. He whom Allāh guides, no one can misguide; and he whom He misguides, no one can guide.

وَأَشْهَدُ أَنْ لاَ إِلَـٰهَ إِلاَّ ٱللَّـٰهُ، وَحْدَهُ لاَ شَرِيكَ لَهُ.

وَأَشْهَدُ أَنَّ مُحَمَّداً عَبْدُهُ وَرَسُولُهُ.

I bear witness that there is no (true) god except Allāh — alone without any partners. And I bear witness that Muḥammad (ﷺ) is His *ʿabd* (servant) and messenger. [1]

﴿يَا أَيُّهَا ٱلَّذِينَ ءَامَنُوا ٱتَّقُوا ٱللَّهَ حَقَّ تُقَاتِهِ،

وَلاَ تَمُوتُنَّ إِلاَّ وَأَنْتُم مُسْلِمُونَ﴾ آل عمران ١٠٢

«O you who believe! Revere Allāh the right

---

1 The above two paragraphs, together with the following three portions of Qurʾān, are called *Khuṭbat ul-Ḥājah* (the Sermon of Need). Allāh's Messenger (ﷺ) often started his speeches with this sermon, and he was keen to teach it to his companions. The *ḥadīths* in this regard are recorded by Muslim, Abū Dāwūd, an-Nasāʾī, and others, and are narrated by Ibn Masʿūd, Ibn ʿAbbās, and others (ﷺ). A full discussion of the various reports of this sermon is provided by al-Albānī in his booklet, "*Khuṭbat ul-Ḥājah*", published by al-Maktab ul-Islāmī, Beirut.

reverence, and do not die except as Muslims.» [1]

﴿يَا أَيُّهَا ٱلنَّاسُ ٱتَّقُوا رَبَّكُمُ ٱلَّذِي خَلَقَكُم مِنْ نَفْسٍ وَاحِدَةٍ، وَخَلَقَ
مِنْهَا زَوْجَهَا، وَبَثَّ مِنْهُمَا رِجَالاً كَثِيرًا وَنِسَآءً، وَٱتَّقُواْ ٱللَّهَ ٱلَّذِي
تَسَآءَلُونَ بِهِ وَٱلأَرْحَامَ، إِنَّ ٱللَّهَ كَانَ عَلَيْكُمْ رَقِيبًا۝﴾ النساء ١

«O people! Revere your Lord who has created you from a single soul, created from it its mate, and dispersed from both of them many men and women. Revere Allāh through whom you demand things from one another, and (cherish the ties of) the wombs. Indeed, Allāh is ever-watchful over you.» [2]

﴿يَٰٓأَيُّهَا ٱلَّذِينَ ءَامَنُواْ ٱتَّقُواْ ٱللَّهَ وَقُولُواْ قَوْلاً سَدِيدًا۝ يُصْلِحْ
لَكُمْ أَعْمَٰلَكُمْ، وَيَغْفِرْ لَكُمْ ذُنُوبَكُمْ، وَمَن يُطِعِ ٱللَّهَ وَرَسُولَهُ فَقَدْ
فَازَ فَوْزًا عَظِيمًا۝﴾ الأحزاب ٧٠-٧١

«O you who believe! Revere Allāh and say just words. He will then rectify your deeds and forgive your sins. He who obeys Allāh and His Messenger has certainly achieved a great victory.» [3]

أَمَّا بَعْدُ، فَإِنَّ خَيْرَ ٱلْحَدِيثِ كِتَابُ ٱللَّهِ،
وَخَيْرَ الهَدْيِ هَدْيُ مُحَمَّدٍ (ﷺ)، وَشَرَّ الأُمُورِ مُحْدَثَاتُهَا،
وَكُلَّ مُحْدَثَةٍ بِدْعَةٌ، وَكُلَّ بِدْعَةٍ ضَلاَلَةٌ، وَكُلَّ ضَلاَلَةٍ فِي ٱلنَّارِ.

Verily, the best speech is Allāh's (ﷻ) speech; the best guidance is Muḥammad's (ﷺ) guidance; and the worst matters (in creed or worship) are those innovated (by the people), for every innovated matter is a *bid'ah* (prohibited innovation), and every *bid'ah* is an act

---

1 *Āl 'Imrān* 3:102.

2 *An-Nisā'* 4:1.

3 *Al-Aḥzāb* 33:70-71.

of misguidance that (whoever initiated it) will reside in the Fire. [1]

Defining Our Mission

Our goal in our works is propagating the true *Daʿwah* that derives from Allāh's (ﷻ) Book and His Messenger's (ﷺ) *Sunnah*. This is a duty that every Muslim should cherish. Allāh (ﷻ) says:

﴿وَلْتَكُن مِّنكُمْ أُمَّةٌ يَدْعُونَ إِلَى ٱلْخَيْرِ وَيَأْمُرُونَ بِٱلْمَعْرُوفِ وَيَنْهَوْنَ عَنِ ٱلْمُنكَرِ، وَأُوْلَـٰٓئِكَ هُمُ ٱلْمُفْلِحُونَ۝﴾ آل عمران ١٠٤

«Let there arise from you a group of people inviting to the good, enjoining the right and forbidding the wrong. Those will be the successful.» [2]

This *Daʿwah* has two fundamental aspects:

(a) *Taṣfiyah*: Cleansing and purifying the Islāmic beliefs and practices.

(b) *Tarbiyah*: Guiding and educating the people according to the purified teachings.

Allāh (ﷻ) indicates that this was the Prophet's (ﷺ) message:

﴿هُوَ ٱلَّذِي بَعَثَ فِي ٱلْأُمِّيِّـۧنَ رَسُولاً مِّنْهُمْ، يَتْلُواْ عَلَيْهِمْ ءَايَـٰتِهِ وَيُزَكِّيهِمْ وَيُعَلِّمُهُمُ ٱلْكِتَـٰبَ وَٱلْحِكْمَةَ وَإِن كَانُواْ مِن قَبْلُ لَفِي ضَلَـٰلٍ مُّبِينٍ۝﴾ الجمعة ٢

«It is He who has sent among the unlettered a Messenger from themselves reciting to them His *āyāt*,

---

1 Muslim and others have recorded from Jābir Bin ʿAbdillāh (ﷺ) that Allāh's Messenger (ﷺ) used to start his speeches with this paragraph.

2 *Āl ʿImrān* 3:104.

purifying them, and teaching them the Book and Wisdom — although they were before in clear deviation.» [1]

This is also an obligation on every Muslim according to his ability, as Allāh (ﷻ) commands:

﴿وَتَعَاوَنُوا۟ عَلَى ٱلْبِرِّ وَٱلتَّقْوَىٰ، وَلَا تَعَاوَنُوا۟ عَلَى ٱلْإِثْمِ وَٱلْعُدْوَٰنِ﴾ المائدة ٢

«Help one another in righteousness and piety; and do not help one another in sinning and transgression.» [2]

Our mission is then to propagate the Islāmic teachings in various areas as follows:

1. Correcting Our Beliefs and Practices

We should revere, study, comprehend, and implement the noble Qur'ān and the Prophet's authentic Sunnah in accordance with the understanding and practice of the righteous *salaf*: the *ṣaḥābah* and their true followers, who are described in the following:

﴿وَٱلسَّـٰبِقُونَ ٱلْأَوَّلُونَ مِنَ ٱلْمُهَـٰجِرِينَ وَٱلْأَنصَارِ وَٱلَّذِينَ ٱتَّبَعُوهُم
بِإِحْسَـٰنٍ رَّضِيَ ٱللَّهُ عَنْهُمْ وَرَضُوا۟ عَنْهُ وَأَعَدَّ لَهُمْ جَنَّـٰتٍ تَجْرِي تَحْتَهَا
ٱلْأَنْهَـٰرُ خَـٰلِدِينَ فِيهَا أَبَدًا، ذَٰلِكَ ٱلْفَوْزُ ٱلْعَظِيمُ۝﴾ التوبة ١٠٠

«The first to embrace Islām among the *Muhājirūn* and the *Anṣār*, and also those who followed them in the best way — Allāh is pleased with them and they with Him. He has prepared for them gardens beneath which rivers flow: They will abide therein forever. This is the supreme success.» [3]

---

1 *Al-Jumuʿah* 62:2.

2 *Al-Māʾidah* 5:2.

3 *At-Tawbah* 9:100.

Thus, the guidance of the *salaf* is the only true guidance. Furthermore, the beliefs of the *ṣaḥābah* are the only acceptable beliefs:

﴿فَإِنْ آمَنُوا بِمِثْلِ مَا آمَنْتُم بِهِ فَقَدِ ٱهْتَدَوا﴾ البقرة ١٣٧

«So if they believe as you believe [1], they are indeed truly guided.» [2]

Allāh warns against following any guidance other than the Messenger's (ﷺ) and his companions (ﷺ):

﴿وَمَن يُشَاقِقِ ٱلرَّسُولَ مِن بَعْدِ مَا تَبَيَّنَ لَهُ ٱلْهُدَىٰ، وَيَتَّبِعْ غَيْرَ سَبِيلِ ٱلْمُؤْمِنِينَ، نُوَلِّهِ مَا تَوَلَّىٰ، وَنُصْلِهِ جَهَنَّمَ، وَسَآءَتْ مَصِيرًا۝﴾ النساء ١١٥

«Whoever opposes the Messenger, after guidance has become clear to him, and follows other than the way of the believers [3], We will give him what he has chosen and let him into Hell: What an evil destination!» [4]

2. Inviting to the True *Dīn*

We should contribute to educating and guiding the Muslims to adopt the true *Dīn*, act according to its teachings, and adorn themselves with its virtues and ethics.

We should also contribute to inviting the non-Muslims to the unadulterated truth of Islām.

This is the only way for any person to attain Allāh's acceptance and achieve happiness and glory. Allāh (ﷻ) says:

---

1 The address here is to the *ṣaḥābah* (ﷺ).

2 *Al-Baqarah* 2:137.

3 The description "believers" here applies first and foremost to the *ṣaḥābah* (ﷺ).

4 *An-Nisā'* 4:115.

﴿وَٱلْعَصْرِ ۝ إِنَّ ٱلإِنسَـٰنَ لَفِي خُسْرٍ ۝ إِلاَّ ٱلَّذِينَ ءَامَنُوا۟ وَعَمِلُوا۟
ٱلصَّـٰلِحَـٰتِ وَتَوَاصَوْا۟ بِٱلْحَقِّ وَتَوَاصَوْا۟ بِٱلصَّبْرِ ۝﴾ العصر ١-٣

«By time, the human being is surely in loss, except for those who believe, do righteous deeds, enjoin upon one another the keeping to truth, and enjoin upon one another patience (in adversity).» [1]

3. Warning Against Deviant Beliefs and Practices

We should caution the Muslims and exhort them against any beliefs or practices alien to the pure teachings of Islām, such as *shirk* and *bidʿahs*.

4. Purifying the Sunnah

We should contribute to cleansing the Sunnah of weak and fabricated narrations. Wrong beliefs and practices deriving from weak reports have marred the beauty of Islām and prevented the Muslims' advancement.

The duty of purifying the Sunnah is so vital that the Messenger (ﷺ) praised those who perform it by saying:

«يحمل هذا العلم من كل خلف عدوله، ينفون عنه
تحريفَ الغالين، وانتحالَ المبطلين، وتأويلَ الجاهلين.»

‹This knowledge will be carried by the trustworthy ones of every generation — they will expel from it the alterations made by those going beyond bounds, the false claims of the liars, and the false interpretations of the ignorant.› [2]

---

1 *Al-ʿAṣr* 103:1-3.

2 Recorded by Ibn ʿAdiyy, al-Khaṭīb al-Baghdādī, Ibn ʿAsākir, and others. It is reported from a number of *ṣaḥābah* including Abū Hurayrah, Ibn Masʿūd, and Anas (رضي الله عنهم). All of its reports have various levels of weakness, but they add up collectively to make this *ḥadīth ḥasan*, as is indicated by al-Albānī in *Mishkāt ul-*

5. Liberating the Islāmic Thought

Guided by the Islāmic principles, we should contribute to reviving the unobstructed Islāmic thought and opposing stubborn adherence to *mat͟hhab*s and prejudiced loyalty to parties. Neglecting this in the past has caused rust to dwell on the hearts and minds of Muslims, diverting them from the pure original sources of Islām, and causing them to deviate from the honest Islāmic brotherhood called to by Allāh (ﷻ):

﴿وَٱعْتَصِمُوا۟ بِحَبْلِ ٱللَّهِ جَمِيعًا وَلَا تَفَرَّقُوا۟﴾ آل عمران ١٠٣

«And hold fast, all together, by the rope of Allāh, and be not divided among yourselves.» [1]

And by His Messenger (ﷺ):

«وكونوا، عبادَ اللّه، إخواناً»

‹Be, worshippers of Allāh, brothers.› [2]

6. Presenting the Islāmic Solution

We should contribute to providing realistic Islāmic solutions to contemporary problems, and strive toward resuming a true Islāmic way of life and establishing a true Islāmic society governed by Allāh's law. Allāh (ﷻ) says:

﴿وَأَنِ ٱحْكُم بَيْنَهُم بِمَا أَنزَلَ ٱللَّهُ وَلَا تَتَّبِعْ أَهْوَآءَهُمْ﴾ المائدة ٤٩

«Hence, judge between them in accordance with what Allāh has revealed, and do not follow their errant views.» [3]

We call upon all the Muslims to support us in carrying out this

---

Maṣābīḥ (no. 248), and as expressed by al-Ḥalabī in *al-Ḥiṭṭah* (p. 70).

1 *Āl ʿImrān* 3:103.

2 Recorded by al-Bukhārī and Muslim.

3 *Al-Māʾidah* 5:49.

noble trust. This will surely elevate and honor them and spread the eternal message of Islām all over the earth, as is Allāh's true promise:

﴿هُوَ ٱلَّذِي أَرْسَلَ رَسُولَهُۥ بِٱلْهُدَىٰ وَدِينِ ٱلْحَقِّ لِيُظْهِرَهُۥ عَلَى ٱلدِّينِ كُلِّهِۦ وَلَوْ كَرِهَ ٱلْمُشْرِكُونَ﴾ الصف ٩

«It is He who has sent His Messenger with Guidance and the Religion of Truth, in order to make it prevail over all (false) religion, however hateful this may be to the pagans.» [1]

CONCLUSION

This work is, therefore, a humble response to our realization of a great responsibility: the responsibility to help bring forth before the English-speaking public writings that refine Islām and present it pure and simple, as close as possible to the way it was understood and practiced by its early righteous pioneers — the *salaf.*

Technicalities

TRANSLITERATION

We make a serious attempt to limit the use of transliterated Arabic terms to the following two situations:

a) There is no English expression that can reflect the same meaning as the original term.

b) The Arabic term is of such importance that it is essential to familiarize the readers with it.

At the end of this book, we have included a glossary defining common Arabic terms that fulfill the above criteria. In addition, we

1 *Aṣ-Ṣaff* 61:9.

have included an index of the Arabic terms that are more pertinent to this current work, indicating the page on which they have been defined.

Except for proper nouns, transliterated Arabic terms are *italic*ized. In general, the rules of English pronunciation can be applied. The following table includes additional symbols employed in this book to help pronounce the Arabic terms.

Symbol	Stands for	English Equivalent Sounds
ā, Ā	(ا) *Alif* (long vowel a)	Mostly: Man, sad. At times: Father, hard, god.
ū, Ū	(و) *Wāw* (long vowel u)	Root, soup, flute.
ī, Ī	(ي) *Yā'* (long vowel i)	Seed, lean, piece, receive.
'	(ء) *Hamzah*	The first consonant vocal sound uttered when saying: at, it or oh.
Th, th	(ث) *Thā'*	Three, moth.
Ḥ, ḥ	(ح) *Ḥā'*	No equivalent. Produced in the lower throat, below "h". Resembles the sound produced after swallowing.
Kh, kh	(خ) *Khā'*	No equivalent. Produced in the back of the mouth and top of the throat.
Th, th	(ذ) *Thāl*	There, mother.
Ṣ, ṣ	(ص) *Ṣād*	A deeper "s" sound. Somewhat close to the "sc" in "muscle".
Ḍ, ḍ	(ض) *Ḍād*	Sounds deeper than a "d". Produced by touching the tongue to the mouth's roof.
Ṭ, ṭ	(ط) *Ṭah*	Similar but deeper than a "t".

Symbol	Stands for	English Equivalent Sounds
Ẓ, ẓ	(ظ) *Ẓah*	A deeper *th̲āl*, produced by touching the tip of the tongue to the back of the front teeth.
ʿ	(ع) *ʿAyn*	Produced in the bottom of the throat, underneath "ḥ".
Gh, gh	(غ) *Ghayn*	A gurgling sound produced in the back of the mouth, just above the *khāʾ*. Similar to the "R" in some french accents.
Q, q	(ق) *Qāf*	Somewhat similar to the "c" in "c̲offee".

TRANSLATING AND REFERENCING QURʾĀN AND *ḤADĪTH*

The Qurʾān contains Allāh's exact words. These words cannot be exactly translated into other languages because of possible misinterpretations and limited human understanding. It is best to translate the meanings as understood by the Muslim scholars. This is what is attempted here. When an *āyah* is cited, the Arabic text is quoted first, followed, between double angle quotation marks («»), by the English meaning in **boldface**. The meaning is extracted from books of *tafsīr* and from accessible translations.

The location of a Qurʾānic citation is specified in a footnote. It provides the name of the *sūrah* followed by its number and the number(s) of the *āyah*(s) cited.

Similarly, when we cite a *ḥadīth*, we provide the Arabic text for the Prophet's (ﷺ) words, and follow that by its meaning, in **boldface**, between single angle quotation marks (‹›).

A footnote normally specifies the location of a cited *ḥadīth* in the *Ḥadīth* compilations. The footnote indicates as well its degree of authenticity and the names of scholars who made such judgement. A *ḥadīth* narrated by al-Bukhārī or Muslim is automatically considered authentic.

NOTABLE UTTERANCES

Out of love, appreciation, gratitude and other noble feelings, a Muslim is encouraged to utter certain phrases at the mention of Allāh, His messengers, the angels, the *ṣaḥābah*, or other righteous Muslims. We present these phrases in condensed Arabic calligraphy as follows:

Phrase	Mentioned with	Transliteration	Meaning
سبحانه وتعالى	Allāh's Name	*Subḥānahū wa taʿālā.*	He is exalted above weakness and indignity.
عز وجل	Allāh's Name	*ʿAzza wa-jall.*	He is exalted and glorified.
جل جلاله	Allāh's Name	*Jalla jalāluh.*	Exalted is His glory.
صلى الله عليه وسلم	Muḥammad and other prophets	*Ṣalla 'Llāhu ʿalayhi wa sallam* [1].	May Allāh's peace and praise be on him.
عليه السلام	Prophets and angels	*ʿAlayh is-Salām.*	Peace be on him.
رضي الله عنه	A male companion	*Raḍiya 'Llāhu ʿanhu.*	May Allāh be pleased with him.
رضي الله عنها	A female companion	*Raḍiya 'Llāhu ʿanhā.*	May Allāh be pleased with her.
رضي الله عنهما	Two companion	*Raḍiya 'Llāhu ʿanhumā.*	May Allāh be pleased with them.

1 Uttering this is sometimes described as, "saying *ṣalāh* upon the Messenger".

Phrase	Mentioned with	Transliteration	Meaning
رضي الله عنهم	More than two companions	*Raḍiya 'Llāhu ʿanhum.*	May Allāh be pleased with them.
رحمه الله	A past scholar or righteous Muslim.	*Raḥimahu 'Llāh.*	May Allāh have mercy on him.

When coming across any of these symbols, the reader is advised to utter the complete phrase in order to obtain the reward of saying the appropriate *thikr* or *duʿā'*.

This Book

Preceding Parts

This is the fourth book of the Muslim Family Series. The first three books dealt with various aspects of marriage as follows:

1. ﴿وَجَعَلَ بَيْنَكُم مَّوَدَّةً وَرَحْمَةً﴾

" The Quest for Love & Mercy"

Fiqh of Marriage & Wedding in *Islām*

Covers the importance and advantages of marriage, selecting a spouse, the courting process, the marriage contract, marriage consummation, celebrating the wedding and the *walīmah*, and forbidden marriages; provides a practical procedure for performing the marriage contract; and includes a sample marriage certificate.

2. ﴿هُنَّ لِبَاسٌ لَّكُمْ، وَأَنتُمْ لِبَاسٌ لَّهُنَّ.﴾

"Closer than a Garment"

Marital Intimacy According to the Pure *Sunnah*

Covers the proper etiquettes of marital intimacy, forbidden acts of intimacy, the perils of *zinā*, and birth control; answers many frequently-asked questions about various acts of intimacy.

3. «رفقاً بالقوارير»

"The Fragile Vessels"

Rights and Obligations between the Spouses in *Islām*

Covers the obligations of the two spouses, the wife's rights, and the husband's rights; contains biographies of the Mothers of the Believers; paints very realistic pictures from the life of the Prophet (ﷺ) with his wives; and presents a complete discussion of the *ḥadīth* of Umm Zar'.

Current Book

As a logical continuation to the first three books, this sequel deals with the normal fruit of marriage: babies. It covers the Islāmic regulations relating to a newborn. This includes welcoming the baby, naming it, shaving its hair, circumcising it, and slaughtering the sacrificial *'aqīqah*.

The discussion of naming the newborn covers recommended and prohibited names, nicknames, and *kunyah*s. It is further enhanced with two appendices. The first appendix provides a list of suggested names for both boys and girls. The second appendix discusses Allāh's excellent names and includes a list of authentic names that have evidence from the Qur'ān and Sunnah.

The discussion of *'aqīqah* includes its ruling, animals to be slaughtered, dispensing of the meat, the *'aqīqah*'s feast, and the *'aqīqah*'s wisdom.

The discussion of circumcision includes the circumcision process, its ruling for boys and girls, its benefits, and excessiveness and other violations.

Other discussions include *taḥnīk*, shaving the baby's head, piercing the ears, breast-feeding, protection from the evil eye, babies' toys and clothes, birthdays, and so on.

We intended and we believe that we largely succeeded in making this book a complete reference covering the correct Islāmic acts that parents need to perform for their newborn during its first few weeks.

Acknowledgements

All praise and thanks are due to our Lord (ﷻ) who facilitated completing this work. May He further reward all the Muslims who helped and supported this effort in various ways. In particular, may Allāh (ﷻ) reward my *shaykh* and teacher, Muḥammad Nāṣir ud-Dīn al-Albānī whose works have benefited us in ways beyond description, my wife Umm ʿAbdullāh whose continued support and encouragement have been vital for completing this and other works, ʿAbdullāh al-Jibālī who designed the cover, and Sakīnah Towery and Ālāʾ al-Jibālī who proof-read the manuscript and made valuable suggestions.

We ask Allāh (ﷻ) to make this humble effort helpful and fruitful to the Muslims, forgive our shortcomings, purify our work from hypocrisy and conceit, and accept it from us.

Our Lord, forgive us and all of the believers, and bestow Your peace and praise upon our Prophet Muḥammad (ﷺ).

Muhammad al-Jibāli
29 *Shawwāl* 1422 H
13 January 2002

CHAPTER 1

PLANTING THE SEED

Muslims are urged to have children and raise them righteously according to the Islāmic teachings. This involves selecting a righteous spouse to help in this most important cultivation process. It also involves understanding the great rewards that Allāh (ﷻ) has promised to those Muslims who handle their parenting responsibility seriously. These issues are the subject of discussion in this chapter.

Islām Recommends Seeking Offspring

Procreation Is a Main Purpose of Marriage

Procreation is one of the main goals of marriage. We should realize that Allāh (ﷻ) has ordained for us the channel of marriage in order to correctly produce more people who seek to obey Him and live by His commands. Allāh (ﷻ) says:

﴿فَٱلْـَٔـٰنَ بَـٰشِرُوهُنَّ وَٱبْتَغُوا۟ مَا كَتَبَ ٱللَّهُ لَكُمْ.﴾ البقرة ١٨٧

> **«So now (during *Ramaḍān*'s nights), have relations with them (your wives) and seek that which Allāh has decreed for you (offspring).»** [1]

"Seeking that which Allāh has decreed for you" means the "offspring" as asserted by Mujāhid, al-Ḥakam, ʿIkrimah, al-Ḥasan al-Baṣrī, as-Suddī, and aḍ-Ḍaḥḥāk. [2]

Ibn ul-Qayyim (رحمه الله) said:

---

1 *Al-Baqarah* 2:233.

2 *Tuḥfat ul-Mawdūd* p. 9.

"Allāh (ﷻ) has facilitated things for the (Muslim) *Ummah* by permitting intercourse until dawn during the nights of fasting. But a person involved in intercourse is so much overwhelmed by lust and the need to fulfill his desire that nothing else occurs to his heart. Because of this, Allāh (ﷻ) guided them (the Muslims) to seek His pleasure while under the influence of this desire. They should not pursue it under the mere influence of lust, but should seek through it what Allāh has decreed for them of rewards, as well as the offspring that would issue from this to become a worshiper of Allāh ..." [1]

A Child Is a Favor from Allāh

Children are among the boundless favors from Allāh (ﷻ) upon the people in this worldly life. He (ﷻ) says:

﴿وَٱللَّهُ جَعَلَ لَكُم مِّنْ أَنفُسِكُمْ أَزْوَٰجًا، وَجَعَلَ لَكُم مِنْ أَزْوَٰجِكُم بَنِينَ وَحَفَدَةً، وَرَزَقَكُم مِّنَ ٱلطَّيِّبَٰتِ﴾ النحل ٧٢

«Allāh has given you spouses from yourselves, has granted you, from your spouses, children and grandchildren, and has provided you with good things for your sustenance.» [2]

Allāh (ﷻ) has favored His messengers with children. He (ﷻ) says:

﴿وَلَقَدْ أَرْسَلْنَا رُسُلاً مِّن قَبْلِكَ وَجَعَلْنَا لَهُمْ أَزْوَاجًا وَذُرِّيَّةً﴾ الرعد ٣٨

«And We have surely sent messengers before you (O Muḥammad) and granted them wives and offspring.» [3]

---

1 *Tuḥfat ul-Mawdūd* p. 9.

2 *An-Naḥl* 16:72.

3 *Ar-Ra'd* 13:38.

A CHILD INCREASES THE NUMBER OF MUSLIMS

It is recommended for a Muslim to seek offspring and thereafter raise them according to Islām.

Maʿqil Bin Yasār (ﷺ) reported that a man came to Allāh's Messenger (ﷺ) and said, "I have encountered a woman of honor and beauty, but she cannot bear children. Should I marry her?" Allāh's Messenger (ﷺ) indicated disapproval by saying:

«تزوجوا الودود الولود، فإني مكاثر بكم.»

‹Marry a woman who is loving and can bear many children, because I will boast of your numbers (on the Day of Resurrection).› [1]

Similarly, ʿĀ'ishah (ﷺ) reported that Allāh's Messenger (ﷺ) said:

«النكاح سنتي، فمن لم يعمل بسنتي فليس مني. وتزوجوا فإني مكاثرٌ بكم الأمم يوم القيامة.»

‹Marriage is a *sunnah* (way) of mine; and whoever does not follow my Sunnah is not of my followers. Get married because I will display your outnumbering of the other nations on the Day of Resurrection.› [2]

Also, Abū Hurayrah (ﷺ) reported that Allāh's Messenger (ﷺ) said:

«انكِحوا فإني مكاثرٌ بكم.»

‹Get married, because I will be exhibiting your large numbers (on Judgment Day).› [3]

---

1 Recorded by Abū Dāwūd and an-Nasā'ī. Verified to be authentic by al-Albānī (*Ṣaḥīḥ ul-Jāmiʿ* no. 2940 & *Irwā'ul-Ghalīl* no. 1784).

2 Recorded by Ibn Mājah. Verified to be authentic by al-Albānī (*aṣ-Ṣaḥīḥah* no. 2383).

3 Recorded by Ibn Mājah. Verified to be authentic by al-Albānī (*Ṣaḥīḥ ul-Jāmiʿ* no.

And Abū Umāmah (ﷺ) reported that Allāh's Messenger (ﷺ) said:

«تزوجوا فإني مكاثر بكم الأمم، ولا تكونوا كرهبانية النصارى.»

‹Marry so that (on Judgment Day) I will be delighted by your outnumbering other nations. Do not practice monasticism like the Christians.› [1]

Good Soil is Required for a Good Seed

Mere numbers do not count in the scale of Islām. The number of good Muslims, however, is very important. Good Muslims are the only ones among the creation who elect to live by Allāh's (ﷻ) commands and follow His Messenger's (ﷺ) guidance. Such are the people who should increase and multiply so as to establish Allāh's religion in this life and enter His gardens in the next.

A Muslim should try to increase the number of righteous Muslims. He should strive to raise his family upon the true religion. Only then, would they be among the numbers of Muslims who will please and delight Allāh's Messenger (ﷺ) on Judgment Day.

Because of this, a Muslim is required to seek a good and righteous spouse who is capable of playing a positive and constructive part in nesting and raising the children.

ʿĀʾishah (رضي الله عنها) reported that Allāh's Messenger (ﷺ) said:

«تخيروا لنُطَفِكم، فأنكِحوا الأكفاءَ وأنكِحوا إليهم.»

‹Make a (good) choice for your sperm (i.e. offspring): marry worthy (women), and marry (your daughters) to them (worthy men).› [2]

1514).

1 Recorded by al-Bayhaqī and others. Verified to be authentic by al-Albānī (*Ṣaḥīḥ ul-Jāmiʿ* no. 2941 & *aṣ-Ṣaḥīḥah* no. 1782).

2 Recorded by Ibn Mājah, al-Ḥākim, and others. Verified to be authentic by al-Albānī (*Ṣaḥīḥ ul-Jāmiʿ* no. 2928 & *aṣ-Ṣaḥīḥah* no. 1067).

Reward for Having Children

A Guaranteed Reward for True Believers

The believers are rewarded for the children they beget, even if they die before puberty. Abū Tharr (ﷺ) reported that the Prophet (ﷺ) said:

«أرأيتَ لو كان لك ولدٌ فأدركَ ورجوتَ خيره فمات، أكُنتَ تحتسبُه؟»

‹If you had a child who reached puberty, and you expected good from him, but he died, would you seek Allāh's reward for that?›

Abū Tharr replied, "Yes!" The Prophet (ﷺ) asked: «فأنتَ خلقتَه؟» **‹Are you the one who created him?›** Abū Tharr replied, "No, it is Allāh who created him." The Prophet (ﷺ) asked: «فأنت هديتَه؟» **‹Are you the one who guided him?›** Abū Tharr replied, "No, it is Allāh who guided him!" The Prophet (ﷺ) asked: «فأنت ترزقُه؟» **‹Are you the One Who sustains him?›** Abū Tharr replied, "No, it is Allāh who would have sustained him!" The Prophet (ﷺ) then said:

«كذلك، فضعهُ في حلالهِ وجنِّبهُ حرامَه، فإن شاء اللهُ
أحياه، وإن شاء أماتهُ، ولك أجرٌ.»

‹Thus, put it (your seed) in the lawful (intercourse with your wife), and avert it from the prohibited (*zinā*). If Allāh wills, He would then give it life; and if He wills, He would make him die. And you will be rewarded (in both cases).› [1]

Children Who Die Young

As indicated above, when a believer loses a child and shows patience and submission to Allāh's will, he will be immensely rewarded.

One of the *tābiʿūn* known as Abū Ḥassān reported that he lost two

---

1 Recorded by Aḥmad, Ibn Ḥibbān, and an-Nasāʾī. Verified to be authentic by al-Albānī (*aṣ-Ṣaḥīḥah* no. 575).

young sons. He met Abū Hurayrah and asked him, "Can you relate to us something that you heard from Allāh's Messenger (ﷺ) to appease our souls in regard to the ones that we have lost?" Abū Hurayrah (ﷺ) then reported that he heard the following from Allāh's Messenger (ﷺ):

«صغارُهم دعاميص الجنة. يتلقَّى أحدُهُم أباه فيأخذ بناحية ثوبه أو يده، كما آخُذُ أنا بِصَنِفَةِ ثوبِكَ هذا، فلا يتناهى حتى يُدخِلَهُ اللهُ وأباهُ الجنةَ.»

‹**Their young ones (who die) are the free roamers of Jannah. When one of them meets its parent, it holds on to the edge of his (or her) garment like I hold your garment, and does not desist until Allāh admits it with its parent into Jannah.**› [1]

Abū Hurayrah (ﷺ) also reported that Allāh's Messenger (ﷺ) said:

«ما من مسلمين يموت لهما ثلاثةٌ من الولد لم يبلغوا الحِنْثَ إلا أدخلهم اللهُ وأبويهم الجنةَ بفضل رحمته. ويكونون على باب من أبواب الجنة، فيقال لهم: ادخلوا الجنة. فيقولون: حتي يجيءَ أبوانا. فيقال لهم: أُدخلوا الجنة أنتم وأبواكم بفضل رحمة الله.»

‹**When three of a Muslim couple's children die before reaching puberty, Allāh will admit the parents into Jannah by virtue of His mercy. They (the children) will be standing by one of the gates of Jannah, and will be told, "Enter Jannah." They will say, "Not until our parents come." They will be told, "Enter Jannah, together with your parents, by virtue of Allāh's mercy!"**› [2]

Qurrah al-Muzanī (ﷺ) reported that when Allāh's Prophet (ﷺ) sat

---

1　Recorded by Muslim and Aḥmad.

2　Recorded by an-Nasāʾī, al-Bayhaqī, and others. Verified to be authentic by al-Albānī (*Aḥkām ul-Janāʾiz* p. 34).

(in the *Masjid* for teaching) a group of his companions would sit with him. Among them was a man who had a little son that would come from behind him and sit in front of him. The Prophet (ﷺ) asked him, «تحبه؟» **‹Do you love him?›** He replied, "O Allāh's Messenger! May Allāh love you like I love him!" Later on, the boy passed away, and the father was so sad that he stopped coming to the *ḥalqah*. Allāh's Messenger (ﷺ) missed him and asked, «ما لي لا أرى فلاناً؟» **‹Why don't I see so-and-so?›** He was told, "O Allāh's Messenger! His son that you saw has died." So the Prophet (ﷺ) summoned him, consoled him, and asked him:

«يا فلان، أيُّما كان أحبَّ إليك؟ أن تُمتَّعَ به عمرَك، أو لا تأتي غداً إلى باب من أبواب الجنة إلاّ وجدتَه قد سبقك إليه يفتحُه لك؟»

‹O so-and-so! What would you like better — enjoying your child during this life, or that tomorrow (in the hereafter) you would not reach a gate of *Jannah* but find that he has preceded you to open it for you?›

He replied, "Rather, his preceding me to the *Jannah*'s gate to open it for me is dearer to me." He told him, «فذاك لك.» **‹This will be yours!›** A man of *al-Anṣār* asked, "O Allāh's Messenger — may Allāh make me a ransom for you, is that specifically for him, or is it for all of us (who lose their children)?" He replied, «بل لكلِّكم.» **‹Rather, it is for all of you.›** [1]

Buraydah Bin al-Ḥaṣīb (ﷺ) reported that Allāh's Messenger (ﷺ) used to look after the *Anṣār*, visit them, and inquire about them. One day he was told that an *Anṣārī* woman was extremely sad because she had lost her only child. So Allāh's Messenger (ﷺ) went with some of his companions to visit and console her. He said:

«أما إنه بلغني أنكِ جزعتِ على ٱبنِك، فٱتقي الله وٱصبري.»

‹I have been informed that you are sorrowful for

---

1 Recorded by an-Nasā'ī, Aḥmad, and others. Verified to be authentic by al-Albānī (*Aḥkām ul-Janā'iz* p. 205).

your son. Have *taqwā* of Allāh, and be patient.›

She replied, "How can I not be sorrowful when I am now a childless woman, having no other children?" He said:

«الرقوب الذي يبقى ولدُها . ما من آمرئٍ أو آمرأةٍ مسلمة

يموت لهما ثلاثة أولاد يحتسبانهم إلا أدخلهما اللهُ بهم الجنةَ. »

‹**A truly childless women is that whose children remain alive (not offering them for Allāh's cause)! Whenever three children of a Muslim man or woman die and they seek Allāh's reward for that, Allāh will admit them into *Jannah* because of them (their children).›**

'Umar (⌾), who was sitting on the Messenger's (⌾) right, asked, "May my father and mother be a ransom for you! How about two children dying?" He replied, «وآثنان.» ‹**Also two!›** [1]

CHILDREN OUTLIVING THEIR PARENTS

A righteous child who outlives his parents can contribute to their record of good deeds after their death. Abū Hurayrah (⌾) reported that Allāh's Messenger (⌾) said:

«إذا مات الإنسانُ أنقطع عملُه إلا من ثلاثٍ: صدقةٍ جاريةٍ،

أو علمٍ يُنتفعُ به، أو ولدٍ صالحٍ يدعو له. »

‹**When a human being dies, his (good) deeds come to an end, except for three things: ongoing charity, beneficent knowledge, or a righteous child supplicating for him.›** [2]

---

1   Recorded by al-Bazzār and al-Ḥākim. Verified to be authentic by al-Albānī (*Aḥkām ul-Janāʾiz* p. 208).

2   Recorded by Muslim.

Invoking Allāh's Blessings and Protection

Invoking Allāh's Blessings at Marriage

A couple should start their marriage by invoking Allāh's (ﷻ) blessings for themselves and their offspring.

ʿAbdullāh Bin ʿAmr (ﷺ) reported that Allāh's Messenger (ﷺ) said:

«إذا أفاد أحدُكم امرأةً فليأخذ بناصيتها، وليسم الله، وليدع بالبركة، وليقل: "بسم الله، اللهم بارك لي فيها. اللهم إني أسألك من خيرها وخيرِ ما جبلتَها عليه، وأعوذ بكَ من شرِّها وشرِّ ماجبلتَها عليه."»

> **‹When one of you marries a woman, he should put his hand on her forehead, invoke Allāh's blessing, and say:**
> ***"Bismillāh, allāhumma bārik lī fīhā. Allāhumma innī as'aluka min khayrihā wa-khayri mā jabaltahā ʿalayhi, wa-aʿūthu bika min sharrihā wa-sharri mā jabaltahā ʿalayh —***
> **With Allāh's name. O Allāh, bless her for me. O Allāh, I ask You to grant me of her good, and the good upon which You created her; and I ask You to protect me from her evil and any evil upon which You created her."›** [1]

Shaqīq reported that ʿAbdullāh Bin Masʿūd (ﷺ) said:

> "Indeed, love between the two spouses is from Allāh and dislike is from Satan. Satan wants you to loathe what Allāh made lawful for you. When your wife first comes to you, lead her in praying two *rakʿāt*, then say:

"اللهم بارِك لي في أهلي، وبارِك لهم فيَّ. اللهم اْجمع

1 A combined report recorded by al-Bukhārī, Ibn Abī Shaybah, and others.

بيننا ما جمعتَ بخير، وفرِّق بيننا إذا فرَّقتَ إلى خير. "

'Allāhumma bārik lī fī ahlī, wa-bārik lahum fiyya. Allāhumm ajma' baynanā ma jama'ta bikhayr, wa-farriq baynanā ithā farraqta ilā khayr — O Allāh, bless my wife for me, and bless me for her. O Allāh, let our joining be upon what is good, and let our separation, when you separate between us, be to what is good.'" [1]

INVOKING ALLĀH'S PROTECTION AT INTERCOURSE

One of the noble goals of intercourse is producing righteous progeny. Thus, it is important for the spouses to supplicate to Allāh asking him to keep Satan away from their progeny.

Ibn 'Abbās (🙼) reported that the Messenger (🙼) said:

«لو أن أحدَكم إذا أراد أن يأتيَ أهلهُ قال: "بسم الله، اللّهم جنِّبنا الشيطانَ، وجنِّب الشيطانَ ما رزقتنا، " فإنه إن قُضيَ بينهما ولدٌ من ذلك لم يضرّه الشيطانُ أبداً. »

‹When one of you who wants to approach his wife (with intercourse) says:
"*Bismillāh. Allāhumma jannib nash-Shayṭān, wa-jannib ish-Shayṭāna mā razaqtanā* — With Allāh's name (I perform intercourse). O Allāh, keep Satan away from us, and from what You grant us,"
If it is then decreed that they have a child (from that intercourse), Satan will never harm it.› [2]

---

1   Recorded by Ibn Abī Shaybah and 'Abd ur-Razzāq. Verified to be authentic by al-Albānī (*Ādāb uz-Zifāf* p. 96).

2   Recorded by al-Bukhārī, Muslim, and others.

CHAPTER 2

EMERGENCE OF THE SPROUT

Pregnant Woman's Craving

During pregnancy, especially in the early stages, some women develop strong craving for specific food items or other things. They feel that those craved things can reduce their morning sickness.

A common belief is that the woman must have what she craved. If she does not, a mark similar to the craved item will appear on the baby's body after birth. All of this has no basis in Islām.

Exposure During Delivery

Doctors and Nurses

Pregnancy often requires regular checkups by an obstetrician. Delivery is usually handled by the obstetrician and a number of nurses. Thus, a woman is expected to expose the most private part of her body to several individuals during the course of her pregnancy and delivery.

Islām demands limiting this exposure to the bare minimum. [1] To fulfill this, a woman should apply guidelines like the following:

1. She should make sure that her physicians and nurses be Muslim females. If this is not possible, they should at least be all females (not necessarily Muslim). Exposure in the presence of male doctors or nurses should be a highly exceptional case. A Muslim family should only allow it for an absolute necessity.

2. She should limit her doctor's checkups (even if the doctor is

---

1 A detailed discussion of *ʿawrah* (private parts) is presented in the Authors, "Closer than a Garment".

female) without endangering herself or her baby.

3. She should limit the number of nurses and hospital staff members present during her delivery.

4. She should not expose any part of her body beyond the minimum amount required for checkup or delivery.

VIDEOTAPING THE DELIVERY

An ugly practice related to the above is for the husband or some other individual to photograph or videotape the delivery process and the emergence of the baby to life. This appalling practice is one of the ways of the disbelievers that a Muslim should never imitate.

The First Cry

The first indication of a live birth is the baby's cry. This cry falls upon the ears of the impatient parents and relatives as the sweetest sound in the world.

Did we ever ask ourselves why the baby starts its worldly presence with a cry rather than a laugh? The important answer to this interesting question is given by the Prophet (ﷺ).

SATAN'S PANG

Satan's extreme jealousy and hatred of the human race has no limit. He does not hesitate to direct his attacks on every human being from birth. Abū Hurayrah (ﷺ) reported that Allāh's Messenger (ﷺ) said:

«صياح المولودِ حين يقعُ (أو يولدُ) نزغةٌ من الشيطان.»

‹A baby's crying when it is born is because of a poking by Satan.› [1]

---

1 Recorded by al-Bukhārī, Muslim, and others.

Abū Hurayrah (圖) also reported that Allāh's Messenger (圖) said:

«ما من مولودٍ يولدُ إلا نَخَسَه الشيطانُ، فيستهلُّ صارخاً

من نَخْسةِ الشيطان، إلا ابنُ مريمَ وأُمُّه.»

‹There is no baby but is poked by Satan when it is
born, so it starts off by crying from Satan's pang —
except for the Son of Maryam and his mother.›

Abū Hurayrah (圖) then added, "Recite if you wish Allāh's saying:

﴿وَإِنِّى أُعِيذُهَا بِكَ وَذُرِّيَّتَهَا مِنَ ٱلشَّيْطَـٰنِ ٱلرَّجِيمِ ۞﴾ آل عمران ٣٦

«(Maryam's mother supplicated to Allāh saying,)
"And I seek Your protection for her and her
progeny from Satan, the outcast."» [1,] [2]

Thus, a child who has not yet encountered anything in this life is
first received with a poking from man's worst enemy: Satan.

As the child grows into an adult who understands and appreciates
various worldly pleasures, Satan will have more chances to seduce
him. The human being will then be in serious need of a shield in the
face of Satan's seduction and misguidance. This is where the Message
from Allāh (圖) plays an important role: It provides the human being
with a survival kit capable of protecting him from his archenemy —
from his first to his last days on earth.

Condition for Inheritance

The condition for a fetus to inherit is that it is born alive — even for
a brief moment. Abū Hurayrah (圖) reported that Allāh's
Messenger (圖) said:

---

1   *Āl 'Imrān* 3:36.

2   Recorded by al-Bukhārī, Muslim, and others.

«إذا استهل المولود وَرِثَ.»

‹As soon as a baby cries (at birth), it inherits.› [1]

An exception to the above is an illegitimate child of *zinā*. Such a child would not inherit from the biological father. Ibn 'Umar (☺) reported that Allāh's Messenger (☺) said:

«أيُّما رجلٍ عاهَرَ بِحُرَّةٍ أو أمةٍ، فالولد ولد زناً، لا يرثُ ولا يورِّث.»

‹**Whichever man commits *zinā* with a free or slave woman, the child (that she bears) is a child of *zinā*. It neither inherits (from him) nor gives him inheritance.**› [2].

The reason for this is that a child from *zinā* may not be attributed to the biological father. 'Ā'ishah, Abū Hurayrah, and other *ṣaḥābah* (☺) reported that Allāh's Messenger (☺) said:

«الولد للفراش، وللعاهر الحَجَر.»

‹**A child belongs to the mattress (where it was born), and the one who committed adultery receives the stones (as punishment).**› [3]

This *ḥadīth* will be discussed further in the next chapter.

Applauding the Newborn

ANNOUNCING THE BIRTH

It is recommended to announce a child's birth to the parents and those

---

1   Recorded by Abū Dāwūd and al-Bayhaqī. Verified to be authentic by al-Albānī (*Irwā'ul-Ghalīl* no. 1707).

2   Recorded by at-Tirmithī. Verified to be authentic by al-Albānī (*Ṣaḥīḥ ul-Jāmi'* no. 2723).

3   Recorded by al-Bukhārī, Muslim, and others.

who would appreciate the news. This brings pleasure and happiness to the believers, which is a recommended act in Islām. Allāh (ﷻ) tells us that He sent angels to give the good tidings to Ibrāhīm (ﷺ) and Zakariyyā (ﷺ).

Allāh (ﷻ) gave Ibrāhīm (ﷺ) the good news of the impending birth of his first son Ismāʿīl (ﷺ):

﴿فَبَشَّرْنَاهُ بِغُلَٰمٍ حَلِيمٍ ۝﴾ الصافات ١٠١

«So We gave him the good tidings of a tolerant Boy.» [1]

Allāh (ﷻ) also gave Ibrāhīm (ﷺ) and his wife the good news of the forthcoming birth of their son Isḥāq (ﷺ), which would consequently be followed by the birth of Isḥāq's son, Yaʿqūb (ﷺ):

﴿وَلَقَدْ جَآءَتْ رُسُلُنَآ إِبْرَٰهِيمَ بِٱلْبُشْرَىٰ، قَالُواْ سَلَٰمًا، قَالَ سَلَٰمٌ، فَمَا لَبِثَ أَن جَآءَ بِعِجْلٍ حَنِيذٍ ۝ فَلَمَّا رَءَآ أَيْدِيَهُمْ لَا تَصِلُ إِلَيْهِ نَكِرَهُمْ وَأَوْجَسَ مِنْهُمْ خِيفَةً، قَالُواْ لَا تَخَفْ إِنَّآ أُرْسِلْنَآ إِلَىٰ قَوْمِ لُوطٍ ۝ وَٱمْرَأَتُهُ قَآئِمَةٌ فَضَحِكَتْ، فَبَشَّرْنَٰهَا بِإِسْحَٰقَ وَمِن وَرَآءِ إِسْحَٰقَ يَعْقُوبَ ۝﴾ هود ٦٩-٧١

«Our messengers (the angels) have surely come to Ibrāhīm with good tidings. They said, "Peace." He replied, "Peace." And he hastened to bring them a roasted calf. But when he saw their hands not reaching for it, he deemed their conduct strange and became apprehensive of them. They said, "Fear not. We have been sent to the people of Lūṭ." His wife was standing, and she smiled. Then We gave her good tidings of (the birth of) Isḥāq and, after Isḥāq, of (his son) Yaʿqūb.» [2]

---

1 *Aṣ-Ṣāffāt* 37:101.

2 *Hūd* 11:69-71.

Allāh (ﷻ) also says in regard to this:

﴿فَأَوْجَسَ مِنْهُمْ خِيفَةً قَالُوا۟ لَا تَخَفْ وَبَشَّرُوهُ بِغُلَـٰمٍ عَلِيمٍ ۝﴾ الذاريات ٢٨

«He conceived fear of them. They said, "Fear not!" And they gave him good news of a knowledgeable boy.» [1]

And Allāh (ﷻ) gave Zakariyyā the good news of Yaḥyā's (ﷺ) birth:

﴿يَا زَكَرِيَّآ إِنَّا نُبَشِّرُكَ بِغُلَـٰمٍ ٱسْمُهُۥ يَحْيَىٰ
لَمْ نَجْعَل لَّهُۥ مِن قَبْلُ سَمِيًّا ۝﴾ مريم ٧

«(He was told,) "O Zakariyyā, indeed We bring you good tidings of a son whose name will be Yaḥyā. We have never given this name to anyone before him."» [2]

CONGRATULATIONS

As stated above, when a pleasant event occurs to a Muslim, it is recommended that some of his relatives or friends give him the good news. As for those who miss giving the good tidings, it is still possible for them to bring pleasure to that Muslim by offering congratulations.

Thus, *bishārah* (giving good tidings) is the deliverance of pleasant information. *Tahni'ah* (congratulation), on the other hand, is sharing the pleasure and making supplications for one who has already received the good tidings.

When Allāh (ﷻ) revealed that He has accepted the repentance of Kaʿb Bin Mālik and his other two companions [3], a man rushed to Kaʿb and gave him the good news. Later on, when Kaʿb entered into the *Masjid*, the other people congratulated him. [4]

1 *Ath-Thāriyāt* 51:28.

2 *Maryam* 19:7.

3 *At-Tawbah* 9:118.

4 The full story of Kaʿb's repentance is recorded by al-Bukhārī, Muslim, and others.

Tahni'ah may only be made with Islāmically acceptable terms, such as asking Allāh to bless the child and give it a righteous life.

Abū Bakr Bin al-Mun<u>th</u>ir reported that a man who was granted a male baby was sitting with al-Ḥasan al-Baṣrī when another man came in and said to the new father, "May you be pleased with your newly-born knight." Al-Ḥasan interjected, "How do you know whether it will be a knight or a donkey?" They asked, "What should we say then?" He replied, "Say, 'May what you have been granted be blessed for you, may you be able to show gratitude to the Giver, may it (the newborn) attain adulthood, and may it be good to you.'" [1]

GIVING PRESENTS

Giving presents to Muslims is a good practice in all occasions. Abū Hurayrah (﷛) reported that Allāh's Messenger (ﷺ) said:

«تهادُوا تَحَابُّوا.»

‹Exchange presents: that will make you love each other.› [2]

Thus It is permissible to give a present to a newborn's family as a token of help and support for the added responsibility. However, the present should be given without extravagance or show-off. Furthermore, it should not be given with the understanding that it is a required and consistent obligation upon all relatives and acquaintances.

No Gender-Based Bias in Islām

SUBMISSION TO ALLĀH'S DECREE

We should be pleased with the children that Allāh grants us, regardless of whether they are boys or girls. We must understand that whatever

---

1 *Tuḥfat ul-Mawdūd* p. 21.

2 Recorded by Abū Yaʿlā, al-Bayhaqī and al-Bukhārī in *al-Adab ul-Mufrad*. Verified to be *ḥasan* by al-Albānī (*Irwāʾ ul-Ghalīl* no. 1601).

Allāh (ﷻ) decrees for us is part of His great knowledge and wisdom. Nothing happens haphazardly in Allāh's dominion. Allāh (ﷻ) says:

﴿لِّلَّهِ مُلْكُ ٱلسَّمَٰوَٰتِ وَٱلْأَرْضِ، يَخْلُقُ مَا يَشَآءُ، يَهَبُ لِمَن يَشَآءُ إِنَٰثًا، وَيَهَبُ لِمَن يَشَآءُ ٱلذُّكُورَ ۝ أَوْ يُزَوِّجُهُمْ ذُكْرَانًا وَإِنَٰثًا وَيَجْعَلُ مَن يَشَآءُ عَقِيمًا، إِنَّهُۥ عَلِيمٌ قَدِيرٌ ۝﴾ الشورى ٤٩-٥٠

«To Allāh belongs the dominion of the heavens and earth. He creates what He wills. He gives to whom He wills females, and He gives to whom He wills males. Or He couples them as males and females, and He renders whom He wills childless. Indeed, He is Knowing and Capable.» [1]

DISLIKING GIRLS IS A *JĀHILĪ* ATTITUDE

It is prohibited to favor boys over girls or dislike the birth of girls. Allāh (ﷻ) condemns this as being one of the traits of *Jāhiliyyah*. He says:

﴿وَإِذَا بُشِّرَ أَحَدُهُمْ بِالْأُنثَىٰ ظَلَّ وَجْهُهُۥ مُسْوَدًّا وَهُوَ كَظِيمٌ ۝ يَتَوَارَىٰ مِنَ ٱلْقَوْمِ مِن سُوٓءِ مَا بُشِّرَ بِهِۦ، أَيُمْسِكُهُۥ عَلَىٰ هُونٍ أَمْ يَدُسُّهُۥ فِي ٱلتُّرَابِ؟ أَلَا سَآءَ مَا يَحْكُمُونَ ۝﴾ النحل ٥٨-٥٩

«And when one of them is informed of a female (born to him), his face darkens with suppressed anger. He hides himself from the people because of the ill of which he has been informed. Should he keep it in humiliation or bury it in the ground? Unquestionable, evil is what they decide.» [2]

The pagans of *Jāhiliyyah* hated to have girls and considered them

1 *Ash-Shūrā* 42:49-50.

2 *An-Naḥl* 16:58-59.

a source of shame and scorn. They often killed them or buried them alive to get rid of the disgrace associated with them. At the same time, they believed that the angels were female and that they were Allāh's daughters! Allāh (ﷻ) mocks this contradiction in the following:

﴿وَإِذَا بُشِّرَ أَحَدُهُم بِمَا ضَرَبَ لِلرَّحْمَـٰنِ مَثَلاً ظَلَّ وَجْهُهُ مُسْوَدًّا وَهُوَ كَظِيمٌ ۝﴾ الزخرف ١٧

«And when one of them is given tidings of (the birth of) that which he so readily attributes to the Most Merciful (i.e. a daughter), his face darkens with suppressed anger.» [1]

Merits in Fathering Girls

A believer is pleased with whatever Allāh grants him. He realizes that one girl could often be better than many boys.

When Maryam's mother gave birth to her, she thought that Maryam would not be as good as a boy. However, Maryam grew up to be better than most men, and the best of women who ever lived. Anas and Jābir (ﷺ) reported that Allāh's Messenger (ﷺ) said:

«خيرُ نساء العالمين أربعٌ: مريمُ بنتُ عِمرانَ، وخديجةُ بنتُ خويلدٍ، وفاطمة بنتُ محمدٍ، وآسية امرأةُ فرعونَ.»

‹The best of the people's women are four: Maryam Bint ʿImrān, Khadījah Bint Khuwaylid, Fāṭimah Bint Muḥammad, and Āsiyah the wife of Pharaoh.› [2]

Raising girls righteously is a great deed. It makes one worthy of close company with the Messenger (ﷺ) in *Jannah*. Anas (ﷺ) reported that Allāh's Messenger (ﷺ) said:

---

1 *Az-Zukhruf* 43:17.

2 Recorded by Aḥmad, at-Tirmiṯhī, and others. Verified to be authentic by al-Albānī (*Ṣaḥīḥ ul-Jāmiʿ* no. 3328 & 3143).

«مَنْ عَالَ جَارِيتَيْنِ حَتَّى تَبْلُغَا جَاءَ يَوْمَ الْقِيَامَةِ أَنَا وَهُو هَكَذَا.»

‹Whoever nurtures two girls until they reach puberty, he will be with me on the Day of Resurrection like this.›

Here, the Prophet (ﷺ) brought together his index and middle finger. [1]

We know that a number of the prophets only fathered females. This applies, for instance, to Lūṭ (عليه السلام) and Muḥammad (ﷺ).

Ṣāliḥ, the son of Imām Aḥmad Bin Ḥanbal, reported that when his father or others whom he knew had female babies, Aḥmad (رحمه الله) would say, "The prophets have fathered girls. And Allāh has revealed in regard to females what you know." [2]

The Importance of Gratitude

Those who receive a favor should show gratitude for it. And who deserves our gratitude more than our greatest benefactor: Allāh (عز وجل)?

Gratitude to Allāh (ﷻ) is a main objective of worship. A true believer acknowledges Allāh's favors with gratitude, contentment and love.

One should strive to be grateful to Allāh (عز وجل) in all situations and circumstances. Gratitude is rendered to Him with the tongue through words of praise, dedication, and glorification. It is also rendered with the body and limbs through actions of submission and obedience.

GRATITUDE IS A QUALITY OF THE MESSENGERS AND BELIEVERS

Gratitude is a quality that Allāh (ﷻ) praises, and to which He calls His messengers and their followers. Allāh praises His *Khalīl* (close confidant) Ibrāhīm (عليه السلام) for being grateful to Him:

﴿إِنَّ إِبْرَاهِيمَ كَانَ أُمَّةً قَانِتًا لِلَّهِ حَنِيفًا، وَلَمْ يَكُ مِنَ ٱلْمُشْرِكِينَ﴾ ۝

---

1   Recorded by Muslim.

2   *Tuḥfat ul-Mawdūd* p. 19.

﴿شَاكِرًا لِأَنْعُمِهِ، ٱجْتَبَاهُ وَهَدَاهُ إِلَى صِرَاطٍ مُسْتَقِيمٍ ۝﴾

النحل ١٢٠-١٢١

«Verily, Ibrāhīm was an *ummah* (a comprehensive leader), devoutly obedient to Allāh, inclining toward the truth, and was not of those who join partners with Allāh. He was grateful for His (Allāh's) favors. He (Allāh) chose him and guided him to a Straight Path.» [1]

Similarly, Allāh (ﷻ) praises His prophet Nūḥ's (ﷺ) gratefulness:

﴿ذُرِّيَّةَ مَنْ حَمَلْنَا مَعَ نُوحٍ، إِنَّهُ كَانَ عَبْدًا شَكُورًا ۝﴾ الإسراء ٣

«The offspring of those whom we carried with Nūḥ — Indeed, he was a grateful servant (to Us).» [2]

Allāh (ﷻ) commands all of the believers to adorn themselves with the virtue of gratitude. He says:

﴿يَاأَيُّهَا ٱلَّذِينَ ءَامَنُوا۟ كُلُوا۟ مِنْ طَيِّبَاتِ مَا رَزَقْنَاكُمْ، وَٱشْكُرُوا۟ لِلَّهِ إِنْ كُنْتُمْ إِيَّاهُ تَعْبُدُونَ ۝﴾ البقرة ١٧٢

«Oh you who believe, eat of the good things which We have provided for you, and be grateful to Allāh — if it is indeed Him that you worship.» [3]

And He (ﷻ) says:

﴿فَٱذْكُرُونِي أَذْكُرْكُمْ، وَٱشْكُرُوا۟ لِي وَلَا تَكْفُرُونِ ۝﴾ البقرة ١٥٢

«So, remember Me — I will then remember you;

---

1 *An-Naḥl* 16:120-121.

2 *Al-Isrā'* 17:31.

3 *Al-Baqarah* 2:172.

and be grateful to Me, and do not deny Me .» [1]

MOST PEOPLE ARE UNGRATEFUL

Despite Allāh's boundless favors upon us, most people are ungrateful to Him. He (ﷻ) says:

﴿وَجَعَلَ لَكُمُ ٱلسَّمْعَ وَٱلْأَبْصَـٰرَ وَٱلْأَفْـِٔدَةَ، قَلِيلاً مَّا تَشْكُرُونَ ۝﴾

السجدة ٩

«And it is He Who gave you hearing, eyesight, and hearts. But little are you grateful (to Him).» [2]

Allāh (ﷻ) also says:

﴿وَقَلِيلٌ مِّنْ عِبَادِيَ ٱلشَّكُورُ ۝﴾ سبأ ١٣

«Only few among My servants are the grateful.» [3]

REWARDS FOR GRATEFULNESS AND PUNISHMENT FOR UNGRATEFULNESS

Allāh (ﷻ) promises prosperity and abundance for those who are grateful to Him. On the other hand, He (ﷻ) condemns those who are ungrateful and promises severe punishment for them. He (ﷻ) says:

﴿وَإِذْ تَأَذَّنَ رَبُّكُمْ لَئِن شَكَرْتُمْ لَأَزِيدَنَّكُمْ، وَلَئِن كَفَرْتُمْ إِنَّ عَذَابِي لَشَدِيدٌ ۝﴾ إبراهيم ٧

«And (remember) when your Lord proclaimed, "If you are grateful (to Me), I will surely give you more (of My favors). But if you are ungrateful, indeed, My punishment is surely severe."» [4]

---

1 *Al-Baqarah* 2:152.

2 *As-Sajdah* 32:9.

3 *Saba'* 34:13.

4 *Ibrāhīm* 14:7.

Similarly, Allāh (ﷻ) tells us that He punished the tribe of Saba' for their ingratitude:

﴿ذَٰلِكَ جَزَيْنَٰهُم بِمَا كَفَرُواْ ۖ وَهَلْ نُجَٰزِيٓ إِلَّا ٱلْكَفُورَ ۝﴾ سبأ ١٧

«That was their punishment because of their ingratitude — and do We thus punish except the ungrateful?» [1]

Gratitude for Having Children

A Child Is a Great Favor from Allāh

One of Allāh's great favors on us is the granting of offspring. Allāh (ﷻ) says:

﴿وَٱتَّقُواْ ٱلَّذِيٓ أَمَدَّكُم بِمَا تَعْلَمُونَ ۝ أَمَدَّكُم بِأَنْعَٰمٍ وَبَنِينَ ۝
وَجَنَّٰتٍ وَعُيُونٍ ۝﴾ الشعراء ١٣٢-١٣٤

«So revere and fear the One who provided you with that which you know: He provided you with cattle and children, and gardens and springs.» [2]

And Allāh (ﷻ) says:

﴿وَٱللَّهُ جَعَلَ لَكُم مِّنْ أَنفُسِكُمْ أَزْوَٰجًا وَجَعَلَ لَكُم مِّنْ أَزْوَٰجِكُم
بَنِينَ وَحَفَدَةً وَرَزَقَكُم مِّنَ ٱلطَّيِّبَٰتِ﴾ النحل ٧٢

«Allāh has given you spouses from yourselves, has granted you, from your spouses, children and grandchildren, and has provided you with good things for your sustenance.» [3]

1 *Saba'* 34:17.

2 *Ash-Shu'arā'* 26:132-134.

3 *An-Naḥl* 16:72.

Raising Children Gratefully

The best way of utilizing a favor that Allāh (ﷻ) grants us is by making that favor a source of obedience and a show of gratitude. This applies to our children.

The believers must strive to make their offspring pious, submissive to Allāh, consistent in their prayers, and responsible bearers of the *daʿwah* to Islām. If they do so, they contribute to their children's life-long well-being and eternal salvation. If, on the other hand, they neglect this important duty, they contribute to their children's possible eternal ruin.

Abū Hurayrah and al-Aswad Bin Sarīʿ reported that Allāh's Messenger (ﷺ) said:

«كل مولود يولد على الفطرة حتى يُعرب عن لسانه.
فأبواه يهودانه أو ينصّرانه أو يمجّسانِه أو يشرّكانِه.
كالشاة تولد جمعاء، هل ترى فيها من جدعاء؟»

‹Every child is born with the pure *fiṭrah* (nature) — until he becomes able to express himself. It is his parents who then turn him into a Jew, a Christian, a Magian, or a pagan. The is like baby goats: they are born intact — can you find any of them (at birth) with a cut ear?› [1]

From the moment a child is born, we should exhibit deep gratitude to Allāh for this great favor. We should demonstrate our gratitude by slaughtering *ʿaqīqah*, performing various *sunnah*s pertaining to a newborn, avoiding violations and *bidʿah*s committed by the ignorant, and striving to raise our child to be a righteous individual who will show gratitude to his Lord (ﷻ) as well.

---

1 This is a combined report recorded by al-Bukhārī, Muslim, and others.

CHAPTER 3

NAMING THE NEWBORN

When to Name a Newborn

NAMING ON THE SEVENTH DAY

Some authentic *ḥadīths* require for a newborn to be named on its
seventh day. Samurah Bin Jundub (﷼) reported that Allāh's
Messenger (ﷺ) said:

«كل غلام رهينة بعقيقته، تُذبح عنه يومَ سابعه
ويُسمّى فيه ويُحلَقُ رأسُه.»

‹Every child is mortgaged with its *'aqīqah*, which is
to be slaughtered for it on its seventh day. On that
day, it should also be named, and its head should be
shaved.› [1]

And 'Abdullāh Bin 'Amr (﷼) reported:

"أمر النبيُّ بتسميةِ المولودِ يومَ سابعِه،
ووضعِ الأذى عنهُ، والعقَّ."

"The Prophet (ﷺ) commanded us to name a newborn
on its seventh day, and to remove filth off it and
perform its *'aqīqah*." [2]

---

1 Recorded by Aḥmad, Abū Dāwūd, and others. Verified to be authentic by al-Albānī
   (*Ṣaḥīḥ ul-Jāmi'* no. 4541 and *Irwā'ul-Ghalīl* no. 1165).

2 Recorded by at-Tirmithī and Ibn Abī Shaybah. Verified to be *ḥasan* by al-Albānī
   (*Ṣaḥīḥ at-Tirmithī* no. 2269).

On the other hand, there are authentic reports indicating that the Prophet (ﷺ) named some newborns before the seventh day.

Anas (ﷺ) reported that on the morning following the birth of the Prophet's (ﷺ) son Ibrāhīm, the Prophet (ﷺ) said:

«وُلد لِيَ الليلةَ غلامٌ فسمّيتُه باسم أبي إبراهيم.»

‹A baby-boy was born for me this past night. So I named him with my father's [1] name, Ibrāhīm.› [2]

Anas (ﷺ) also reported that as soon as his mother, Umm Sulaym, gave birth to his young brother, ʿAbdullāh, she told him, "O Anas, take these dates, and do not let the baby eat anything until you first hand him to Allāh's Messenger (ﷺ) in the morning."

In the morning, Anas took the baby to Allāh's Messenger (ﷺ). He found him wearing a striped cloak and marking some cattle that he had received. When he saw the baby he asked Anas, «أَوَلَدَتْ بِنْتُ مِلْحَانٍ؟» ‹Did Milḥān's daughter deliver?› He replied, "Yes!" He said, «رُوَيْدكَ أَفْرُغْ لك.» ‹Wait until I finish what I am doing.›

He then put away what he had in his hand, held the baby, and asked, «أمعه شيءٌ؟» ‹Did you bring anything with him?› He replied, "Yes, some dates."

The Prophet (ﷺ) took some dates, chewed on them, mixing them with his saliva, opened the baby's mouth, and rubbed the chewed dates inside his mouth. The baby began to hungrily suck the sweetness of the dates together with Allāh's Messenger's (ﷺ) saliva. Thus the first thing to enter the baby's stomach was the saliva of Allāh's Messenger (ﷺ). He then said:

«انظروا إلى حب الأنصار التمر.»

‹Watch how the *Anṣār* love dates!›

---

1   Meanaing, "great grandfather".

2   Recorded by al-Bukhārī, Muslim, and others.

Anas then said, "O Allāh's Messenger! Give him a name." The Prophet (ﷺ) rubbed the baby's face and named him ʿAbdullāh. [1]

Abū Mūsā al-Ashʿarī (رضي الله عنه) reported:

"وُلد لي غلام، فأتيتُ به النبي، فسماه إبراهيم،
فحنّكه بتمرةٍ، ودعا له بالبركة، ودفعه إلي."

> "A baby-boy was born for me. I took him to the Prophet (ﷺ) who named him Ibrāhīm, chewed on a date and made him suck it, invoked blessings for him, and then gave him back to me." [2]

Sahl (رضي الله عنه) reported that when al-Mun<u>th</u>ir Bin Abī Usayd was born, he was brought to the Prophet. The Prophet (ﷺ) asked, «ما اسمُه.» **‹What is his name?›** His father, Abū Usayd, replied, "So-and so." The Prophet (ﷺ) said, «لا، لكن اسمُه الْمُنذر.» **‹No. Rather, his name is al-Mun<u>th</u>ir.›** [3]

CONCLUSION

From the above, we see that the Prophet (ﷺ) commanded naming a newborn on the seventh day. However, his practice shows that he named some newborns as soon as they were born.

A few among the *ʿulamāʾ*, such as al-Ḥasan al-Baṣrī (رحمه الله) and Imām Mālik (رحمه الله), hold the opinion that it is not permissible to name a child before the seventh.

Most of the *ʿulamāʾ*, however, are of the opinion that it is permissible to name a newborn as soon as it is born, but naming it should not be delayed past the seventh day.

We find the latter opinion more appropriate for the following

---

1 This is a combined report from al-Bukhārī, Muslim, Aḥmad, and others (*Aḥkām ul-Janāʾiz* p. 35-38). The full narration of the birth of ʿAbdullāh Bin Abī Talḥah is presented in the Author's, "Funerals, Regulations & Exhortations", pp. 44-47.

2 Recorded by al-Bukhārī, Muslim, and others.

3 Recorded by al-Bukhārī, Muslim, and others.

reasons:

1. It is not clear from the Prophet's (ﷺ) above commands that he prohibited naming a newborn before the seventh day. In other words, we do not have a text saying, for example, "Do not name a baby before the seventh day."

2. The best way to reconcile between the Prophet's (ﷺ) statements and actions is by allowing both of them to hold simultaneously — if possible. This reconciliation is possible in this case, and there is no need to assume that either of the two forms of evidence abrogates the other.

Thus we conclude —Allāh knows best— that a newborn should be named no later than the seventh day from birth.

Who Names the Child?

The *'ulamā'* agree that the father has the first right to name the newborn. This is because Allāh appointed him for the responsibility of leading the family. Allāh (ﷻ) says:

﴿ٱلرِّجَالُ قَوَّٰمُونَ عَلَى ٱلنِّسَآءِ بِمَا فَضَّلَ ٱللَّهُ بَعْضَهُمْ عَلَىٰ بَعْضٍ وَبِمَآ أَنفَقُوا۟ مِنْ أَمْوَٰلِهِمْ.﴾ النساء ٣٤

«Men are in charge of women by (right of) what (qualities) Allāh has given one over the other and what they spend (in support) from their wealth.» [1]

Ibn 'Umar (ﷺ) reported that the Messenger (ﷺ) said:

«كُلّكم راعٍ، وكُلّكم مسؤولٌ عن رعيّته. فالإمامُ راعٍ، وهو مسؤول عن رعيته؛ والرجل راع في أهله، وهو مسؤول عن رعيته؛ والمرأة

1 *An-Nisā'* 4:34.

راعية في بيت زوجها، وهي مسؤولةٌ عن رعيتها؛ والخادم راعٍ في مال سيده، وهو مسؤول عن رعيته؛ والرجل راعٍ في مال أبيه، وهو مسؤولٌ عن رعيته. فكلكم راعٍ، وكلكم مسؤول عن رعيته.»

‹Each one of you is entrusted with a responsibility, and each one of you is accountable for his responsibility. The ruler is responsible (for his people), and is accountable for his responsibility. The man is responsible for his family, and is accountable for his responsibility. The women is responsible for her husband's house, and is accountable for her responsibility. The servant is responsible for his master's property, and is accountable for his responsibility. And a man is responsible for his father's wealth, and is accountable for his responsibility. Thus, each one of you has a responsibility, and each one of you is accountable for his responsibility.› [1]

However, it is recommended for the father to show kindness to his wife by consulting with her and seriously considering her suggested names, especially if they are within the guidelines of good names that we discuss below.

It is also recommended for the parents to consult with individuals of knowledge and wisdom who can help them find the most suitable names for their offspring.

Giving a Good Name

The parents are required to choose a good name for their newborn. A good name is a name that is known to be pleasing to Allāh (ﷻ), approved by His Messenger, or acceptable to the righteous *'ulamā'* of Islām.

Bakr Abū Zayd says:

1 Recorded by al-Bukhārī, Muslim, and others.

> "The *'ulamā'* agree that it is obligatory to name both men and women …
>
> If the parent violates this *shar'ī* reality, and selects (for the newborn) a name disapproved by the *Shar'* or not possible to accommodate by the Arabic language, this choice would produce a conflict and contradiction between its (the child's) dignity as a human being and a Muslim and its improperly chosen title …
>
> A name is the first thing that faces a newborn when it exits from the darkness of the womb. A name is the first description that distinguishes it from other human beings. A name is the first long-lasting act that a parent does for the newborn. A name is the first process through which a newborn enters into the nation's record. …
>
> Thus we see, as stated by Ibn ul-Qayyim (رحمه الله), that most of the lowly people have names suitable to their status, and most of the honorable and decent people have names suitable to their status …
>
> Indeed, the names affect the named ones: in terms of beauty or ugliness, cheerfulness or repulsion, and kindness or harshness.
>
> Thus, O Muslim —May Allāh bless what He granted you— be good toward your newborn, yourself, and your nation by selecting a name that is pleasant in utterance and in meaning." [1]

Therefore, the parents should carefully appraise the name that they want to give to their child. They should make sure that it has a good meaning and that it sounds well.

Recommended Names

There is a number of guidelines to be considered when looking for a name for one's child. These guidelines are discussed in the following

1 *Tasmiyat ul-Mawlūd* pp. 20-24.

subsections. In Appendix I, we present lists of names for boys and girls that mostly fulfill these guidelines.

NAMES OF *'UBŪDIYYAH*

The best and most beloved names to Allāh (ﷻ) are 'Abdullāh and 'Abd ur-Raḥmān. Ibn 'Umar, Abū Hurayrah, Anas, and others (ﷺ) reported that the Prophet (ﷺ) said:

«إن أحبَّ (خير) الأسماءِ إلى اللهِ: عبد اللهِ وعبدُ الرحْمٰن،
وأصدقها الحارثُ وهمّامُ، وأقبحُها حربٌ ومُرّة.»

‹Indeed, the best and most beloved names to Allāh are: 'Abdullāh and 'Abd ur-Raḥmān. The most truthful names are: al-Ḥārith (cultivator) and Hammām (planner). And the ugliest are: Ḥarb (war) and Murrah (bitter).› [1]

The first two names mentioned in this *ḥadīth* describe their bearers as being *'ibād* (servants and worshipers) of Allāh. They reflect the true purpose of a person's existence: *'ubūdiyyah* or servitude to Allāh, as Allāh (ﷻ) says:

﴿وَمَا خَلَقْتُ ٱلْجِنَّ وَٱلْإِنسَ إِلَّا لِيَعْبُدُونِ ۝﴾ الذاريات ٥٦

«I have only created *jinns* and the humans to worship Me.» [2]

These two names ('Abdullāh and 'Abd ur-Raḥmān) declare servitude to Allāh through His two foremost excellent names: Allāh and ar-Raḥmān, which are mentioned in the following:

﴿قُلِ ٱدْعُوا۟ ٱللَّهَ أَوِ ٱدْعُوا۟ ٱلرَّحْمَـٰنَ، أَيًّا مَا تَدْعُوا۟

1 Recorded by Muslim, Ibn Mājah, and others.

2 *Surat at͟h-T͟haariyaat* 51:56.

فَلَهُ ٱلْأَسْمَآءُ ٱلْحُسْنَىٰ. ﴾ الإسراء ١١٠

«Say, "Call upon Allāh or call upon ar-Raḥmān. Whichever (name) you call (is acceptable, because) to Him belong the best names."» [1]

The first name, 'Abdullāh, is the most common among the *ṣaḥābah*, with about 300 of them having borne it. The very first child that was born for the *muhājirīn* in al-Madīnah was named 'Abdullāh Bin az-Zubayr (☸).

We can see from the above *āyah* that it is also recommended to give names expressing servitude to any of Allāh's other authentic excellent names. A full list of Allāh's excellent names is included in Appendix II.

Note that one may not rely on fabricated and baseless narrations in order to demonstrate the recommendation of names of servitude. The following narration, for example, is fabricated:

> "The most beloved names to Allāh are those expressing servitude." [2]

And the following is another often-mentioned narration that has absolutely no basis in any of the books of *ḥadīth*:

"أحب الأسماء إلى الله ما عُبّد وحُمّد."

"The most beloved names to Allāh are those containing ''abd' or 'ḥamd'." [3]

NAMES WITH REALISTIC MEANINGS

The other two good names mentioned in Ibn 'Umar's above *ḥadīth* are al-Ḥārith (cultivator) and Hammām (planner). They both reflect true

---

1   *Al-Isrā* 17:110.

2   Recorded by aṭ-Ṭabarānī. Verified to be fabricated by al-Albānī (*aḍ-Ḍa'īfah* no. 408).

3   Verified by al-Albānī to be baseless (*aḍ-Ḍa'īfah* no. 411).

qualities that are within human nature. Every human is a cultivator in this life — even though some of them cultivate good crops and others evil crops. And every human is a planner and maker of decisions.

Bearing these two names would not constitute exaggeration or lying. Because of this, they are beloved to Allāh as well.

Similarly, other names that fulfill the same criteria of being truthful and modest would be good.

Names of the Prophet Muḥammad

It is indeed recommended to bear the name of Allāh's Messenger (ﷺ), because he is our example and the pick of humanity. Furthermore, he invited the Muslims to use his name.

Jābir, Abū Hurayrah, and Anas (ﷺ) reported that the Prophet (ﷺ) said:

«تَسمُّوا باسمي ولا تَكنُّوا بكنيتي.»

‹Bear my name, but do not use my *kunyah*.› [1]

This permission, however applies to the Prophet's (ﷺ) name, "Muḥammad", or its synonyms, "Aḥmad", "Maḥmūd", "Ḥumayd", and so on. It does not apply to other names describing specific acts of the Prophet (ﷺ), as in the following *ḥadīth*.

Jubayr Bin Muṭʿim (ﷺ) reported that Allāh's Messenger (ﷺ) said:

«إن لي أسماءً: أنا مُحمد، ,أنا أحمدُ، وأنا الْماحي الذي يمحي اللّهُ بيَ الكفرَ، وأنا الحاشرُ الذي يُحشرُ الناسُ على قدميَّ، وأنا العاقبُ الذي ليس بعده نبي.»

‹I have several names:

1. **I am Muḥammad (the often-praised);**
2. **I am Aḥmad (the highly praised);**
3. **I am al-Māḥī (the eraser) because Allāh erases disbelief by means of me;**

---

1 Recorded by al-Bukhārī, Muslim, and others.

> **4. I am al-Ḥāshir (the gatherer) because Allāh gathers all people after me (on Judgment Day);**
> **5. And I am al-ʿĀqib (the succeeder) because there is no prophet after me.›** [1]

It should be noted that naming a child Muḥammad is recommended but not obligatory. One should beware of excessive fabricated *ḥadīth*s in this regard, such as the following:

> "Anyone who was granted three sons and did not name any of them Muḥammad has indeed acted ignorantly." [2]

Another baseless *ḥadīth* in this regard is the one mentioned earlier:

> "The most beloved names to Allāh are those containing 'ʿabd' or 'ḥamd' (praise)." [3]

And still another one:

> "Whoever is granted a baby-boy and names him Muḥammad for the sake of the blessing in this name, He and his newborn will be admitted into *Jannah.*" [4]

Names of Other Prophets

It is recommended to bear names of prophets because they are the most righteous of humanity, and Allāh (ﷻ) chose them as His envoys to the people. In some cases, Allāh specifically mentions that He directly named some of His prophets, as in the case of Yaḥyā and ʿĪsā. Allāh (ﷻ) says:

---

1 Recorded by al-Bukhārī, Muslim, and others.

2 Recorded by aṭ-Ṭabarānī from Ibn ʿAbbās. Verified to be fabricated by al-Albānī (*aḍ-Ḍaʿīfah* no. 437).

3 Verified by al-Albānī to be baseless (*aḍ-Ḍaʿīfah* no. 411).

4 Recorded by Ibn Bakīr. Verified to be fabricated by al-Albānī (*aḍ-Ḍaʿīfah* no. 171).

﴿يا زَكَرِيَّآ إِنَّا نُبَشِّرُكَ بِغُلَٰمٍ ٱسْمُهُۥ يَحْيَىٰ
لَمْ نَجْعَل لَّهُۥ مِن قَبْلُ سَمِيًّا ۝﴾ مريم ٧

«(He was told,) "O Zakariyyā, indeed We bring you good tidings of a son whose name will be Yaḥyā. We have never given this name to anyone before him."» [1]

And He (ﷻ) says:

﴿إِذْ قَالَتِ ٱلْمَلَٰٓئِكَةُ يَٰمَرْيَمُ إِنَّ ٱللَّهَ يُبَشِّرُكِ بِكَلِمَةٍ مِّنْهُ
ٱسْمُهُ ٱلْمَسِيحُ عِيسَى ٱبْنُ مَرْيَمَ.﴾ آل عمران ٤٥

«And when the angels said, "O Maryam, indeed Allāh gives you tidings of a word from Him whose name will be the Messiah, ʿĪsā, the son of Maryam."» [2]

Furthermore, on some occasions the Prophet (ﷺ) named newborns after prophets. Abū Mūsā al-Ashʿarī (ﷺ) reported:

"وُلد لي غلام، فأتيتُ به النبي، فسماه إبراهيم،
فحنّكه بتمرةٍ، ودعا له بالبركة، ودفعه إلي."

"A baby-boy was born for me. I took him to the Prophet (ﷺ) who named him Ibrāhīm, chewed on a date and made him suck it, invoked blessings for him, and then gave him back to me." [3]

Yūsuf Bin ʿAbdillāh Bin Salām reported:

---

1 *Maryam* 19:7.

2 *Āl ʿImrān* 3:45.

3 Recorded by al-Bukhārī, Muslim, and others.

"سماني النبيُّ يوسفَ، وأقعدني على حِجره، ومسح على رأسي."

"The Prophet (ﷺ) named me Yūsuf, sat me on his lap, and rubbed his hand over my head." [1]

Anas (ﷺ) reported that on the morning following the birth of Ibrāhīm, Allāh's Messenger (ﷺ) said:

«ولد ليَ الليلةَ غلامٌ فسمّيتُه باسم أبي إبراهيم.»

‹A baby-boy was born for me this past night. So I named him with my father's [2] name. Ibrāhīm.› [3]

Naming individuals after prophets and righteous people was an old practice among the earlier nations. Al-Mughīrah Bin Shuʿbah (ﷺ) reported that when he went to Nijrān (in Yemen) he was asked by the Christians there, "You recite in your book regarding Maryam (Mary), ﴿يَٰٓأُخۡتَ هَٰرُونَ﴾ **«O Sister of Hārūn (Aaron) ...»** even though Hārūn and Mūsā (Moses) preceded ʿIsā (Jesus) by numerous years." So when he came back to al-Madīnah, he asked the Prophet (ﷺ) about this, and the Prophet (ﷺ) explained to him:

«إنهم كانوا يُسَمُّون بأنبيائهم والصالحين قبلهم.»

‹Indeed, they used to bear names of their prophets and righteous men who preceded them.› [4]

Names of Righteous People

Next to the prophets, the most esteemed individuals to us are other righteous scholars of Islām, headed by the Prophet's companions (ﷺ). They are the inheritors of the knowledge of prophethood, and the

1 Recorded by Aḥmad, at-Tirmithī (in *ash-Shamāʾil*), and al-Bukhārī (in *al-Adab ul-Mufrad*). Verified to be authentic by al-Albānī (*Mukhtaṣar ush-Shamāʾil* no. 292 and *Ṣaḥīḥ ul-Adab il-Mufrad* no. 834).

2 Meaning, "forefather Ibrāhīm (ﷺ)".

3 Recorded by al-Bukhārī, Muslim, and others.

4 Recorded by Muslim (no. 2135).

teachers of goodness. Their favors and benefits are tremendous to all people. Thus, they are the best examples to take, and it would honor a person to carry one of their names.

With this understanding, we find that az-Zubayr Bin al-ʿAwwām (ﷺ) named his nine sons after *shuhadā'* (martyrs) of Badr: ʿAbdullāh, al-Munthir, ʿUrwah, Ḥamzah, Jaʿfar, Muṣʿab, ʿUbaydah, Khālid, and ʿUmar.

Therefore, it is recommended to give to one's children names of the Four Rightly Guided Successors (Abū Bakr, ʿUmar, ʿUthmān, ʿAlī), the Mothers of the Believers [1], other *ṣaḥābah*, scholars of Islām, and so on.

Ascribing the Child to the Father

Ascribing to the Father Is Mandatory

A child should be ascribed to his (or her) true father, and not to the mother or some other person. Thus, if the child's name is Zayd and the father's is ʿAmr, the child is called Zayd Bin ʿAmr (Zayd son of ʿAmr). Allāh (ﷻ) says:

﴿ٱدْعُوهُمْ لِآبَآئِهِمْ هُوَ أَقْسَطُ عِندَ ٱللَّهِ، فَإِن لَّمْ تَعْلَمُوٓا۟
ءَابَآءَهُمْ فَإِخْوَانُكُمْ فِى ٱلدِّينِ وَمَوَالِيكُمْ.﴾ الأحزاب ٥

«Ascribe them to their fathers; it is more just in the sight of Allāh. But if you do not know their fathers — then they are still your brothers in religion and your allies.» [2]

Even on Judgment Day, the people will be ascribed to their fathers. Ibn ʿUmar (ﷺ) reported that Allāh's Messenger (ﷺ) said:

1 The names and biographies of the Mothers of the Believers are covered in the Author's, "The Fragile Vessels".

2 *Al-Aḥzāb* 33:5.

«إن الغادرَ يُرفعُ له لواءٌ يوم القيامةِ، يقالُ:
"هذه غدرةُ فُلانِ ابنِ فُلانٍ."»

‹On the Day of Resurrection, a banner will be reaised over a traitor saying, "This is for the treachery of so-and-so son of so-and-so (man).› [1]

Note that this *ḥadīth* refutes the claim made in a fabricated *ḥadīth*:

"On Judgment Day, the people will be called by (ascribing to) their mothers." [2]

Ascribing to Other than the Father Is a Major Sin

In Islām, ascribing a child to other than the true father is a major sin. Its punishment is denial of Jannah in the hereafter.

Saʿd Bin Abī Waqqāṣ and Abū Bakrah (ﷺ) reported that Allāh's Messenger (ﷺ) said:

«من ادّعى إلى غير أبيه، وهو يعلم أنه غيرُ أبيه، فالجنةُ عليه حرام.»

‹Anyone who relates himself to other than his (true) father, knowing that he is not his father, *Jannah* will then be prohibited for him.› [3]

Abū Tharr (ﷺ) reported that Allāh's Messenger (ﷺ) said:

«ليس من رجلٍ ادّعى لغير أبيه، وهو يعلم،إلاّ كفر. ومن ادّعى
ما ليس له فليس منّا، وليتبوّأ مقعده من النار. ومن دعا رجلاً
بالكفر أو قال:"عدوُّ الله،" وليس كذلك، إلاّ حار عليه.»

---

1 Recorded by al-Bukhārī, Muslim, and others.

2 Recorded by Ibn ʿAdiyy from Anas and by aṭ-Ṭabarānī from Ibn ʿAbbās. Verified to be fabricated by al-Albānī (*aḍ-Ḍaʿīfah* no. 433,434).

3 Recorded by al-Bukhārī, Muslim, and others.

‹Any man who knowingly assigns himself to other than his father is a *kāfr* (by this). And anyone who claims ownership of something not belonging to him is not one of us, and he will have a seat in the Fire. And anyone who calls a man *kāfir* or enemy of Allāh when he is not so, this turns back to him.› [1]

ʿAlī Bin Abī Ṭālib, Ibn ʿAbbās, and Anas (ﷺ) reported that Allāh's Messenger (ﷺ) said:

«من ٱدّعى إلى غير أبيه، أو ٱنتمى إلى (تولّى) غير مواليه، فعليه لعنة الله والملائكة والناس أجمعين.»

‹Anyone who relates himself to other than his (true) father, or associates himself with other than his (true) masters, then upon him will be the curse of Allāh, the Angels, and all people.› [2]

ʿAbdullāh Bin ʿAmr (ﷺ) reported that Allāh's Messenger (ﷺ) said:

«كفرٌ تبرّؤٌ من نسبٍ، وإن دقَّ، وٱدّعاءُ نسبٍ لا يُعرَف.»

‹It is an act of disbelief to deny a (true) relationship — slight though it might be, as well as to claim an untrue relationship.› [3]

ʿAbdullāh Bin ʿAmr (ﷺ) also reported that Allāh's Messenger (ﷺ) said:

«من ادّعى إلى غير أبيه، لم يرُح رائحة الجنة، وإن ريحَها

---

1 Recorded by al-Bukhārī and Muslim.

2 Recorded by al-Bukhārī, Muslim, and others.

3 Recorded by Aḥmad and aṭ-Ṭabarānī (in aṣ-Ṣaghīr). Verified to be authentic by al-Albānī (*Ṣaḥīḥ ut-Targhīb wat-Tarhīb* no. 1987).

لیوجدُ من مسیرة سبعین عاماً .»

‹Anyone who relates himself to other than his (true) father, he will not smell the fragrance of *Jannah*, even though its fragrance can be found from a seventy-years travel distance.› [1]

Illegitimate Children

The above rule has an exception in the case of an illegitimate child who is conceived as a result of a *zinā* relationship. An illegitimate child may not be ascribed to the biological father — even if the father is known beyond doubt.

Abū Hurayrah and more than twenty [2] other companions (ﷺ) narrated that Allāh's Messenger (ﷺ) said:

«الولد لصاحب الفراش، وللعاهر الحجرُ.»

‹The child belongs to (the owner of) the mattress; and the adulterer deserves a stone (i.e., is a loser).› [3]

More specifically, ʿĀ'ishah (ﷺ) reported that, after the conquest of Makkah, Saʿd Bin Abī Waqqāṣ (ﷺ) and ʿAbd Bin Zamʿah [4] (ﷺ) went to Allāh's Messenger (ﷺ) to resolve a dispute between them.

Saʿd (ﷺ) said, "O Allāh's Messenger, this child is my nephew. My brother ʿUtbah Bin Abī Waqqāṣ testified to me that he is his son, and you can see his resemblance to him."

ʿAbd Bin Zamʿah (ﷺ) said, "O Allāh's Messenger! This is my brother, from my father's slave woman. He was born on my father's mattress."

Inspecting the child, the Prophet (ﷺ) observed an obvious

1 Recorded by Aḥmad. Verified to be authentic by al-Albānī (*Ṣaḥīḥ ut-Targhīb wat-Tarhīb* no. 1988).

2 This is stated by Ibn Ḥajar (ﷺ) in *Fatḥ ul-Bārī*.

3 Recorded by al-Bukhārī, Muslim, and others.

4 He was the brother of Sawdah Bint Zamʿah , one of the Prophet's wives.

resemblance between him and ʿUtbah [1]. Yet, he (ﷺ) said:

«هو لكَ يا عبدُ بنُ زَمْعةَ. الولدُ للفراشِ، وللعاهرِ الحجرُ.»

‹He is yours, O ʿAbd Bin Zamʿah. The child belongs to (the owner of) the mattress; and the adulterer deserves a stone (i.e., is a loser).›

Turning to his wife Sawdah, the Prophet (ﷺ) added, «احتجبي منه يا سَودة.» **‹Keep your *ḥijāb* in his presence, O Sawdah.›** So the disputed child never saw Sawdah after that." [2]

This *ḥadīth* indicates that an illegitimate child belongs to the owner of the mattress on which it was conceived, or to the legitimate husband (or master) of the mother at the time of conception, regardless of other claims or chances. This holds whether the concerned individuals were Muslim or not when the child was conceived.

This is the most correct opinion in regard to this issue. [3] All laws of inheritance, family relations, etc, should follow this understanding.

As for the Prophet's (ﷺ) command to Sawdah to cover herself from ʿAbd ur-Raḥmān, despite the fact that he is considered her brother, it is out of precaution and protection for the Mothers of the Believers, because of the great similarity that the Prophet (ﷺ) found between him and ʿUtbah.

Note that this does not condone the great sin that the two partners committed in their illegitimate contact, for which they deserve a severe punishment under the *Islām*ic law and incur a great burden of sin on Judgment Day. [4]

---

1 This child, whose name was ʿAbd ur-Raḥmān Bin Zamʿah, was born as a result of a *zinā* relationship that was accepted during *Jāhiliyyah* as a form of marriage. A woman would have intercourse with different men. Should she deliver a child, they would attribute him to the man that it resembled the most. More information on this is provided in the Author's, "The Quest for Love and Mercy".

2 Recorded by al-Bukhārī, Muslim, and others.

3 Review *fatḥ ul-Bārī, ḥadīth* no. 6741,6750.

4 For more discussion on the subject of *zinā*, review the Author's, "Closer than a Garment".

From the above *ḥadīth* we also conclude that a child conceived by a free (non-slave) single woman should carry her name. For example, if her name was Lubnā Bint Charles Johnson and his name was Sāmī, his full name would then be Sāmī Bin Lubnā Bint Charles Johnson.

Surnames

Definition

A last name, family name, or surname is a name borne in common by members of a family.

Surnames have mostly started from tribe names or nicknames. A nickname is a descriptive name usually given instead of, or in addition to, the one belonging to a person, place, or thing, and is derived from occupation or other circumstance.

In recent times, most countries have adopted surnames as a means of differentiating between families and keeping track of family lineage. This is important for marriage, custody, inheritance, and other purposes.

In many Muslim countries, the use of surnames has led to dropping the Islāmic way of nomenclature whereby a man is ascribed to his father with the term *ibn* or *bin* (son), and a woman with *bint* (daughter).

Regardless of what government and legal requirements are, a Muslim should continue to present himself using the Islāmic naming method in correspondence, introductions, and so on. Thus, if his name is Sālim, his father's is Rafīq, and his surname is ʿAbdullāh, he should introduce himself as Sālim Bin Rafīq ʿAbdullāh.

Changing the Surname

We have shown earlier that it is prohibited to ascribe oneself to other than one's true father. This does not necessarily apply to changing one's last name. As is discussed later above, the last name is different from the father's name. Changing the last name is only permissible if it does not cause confusion in regard to one's lineage — whether legally or in the minds of some people.

Assume, for example, that a woman's name before she accepted Islām was Christina, and her father's was Charles Johnson. Thus, her full name was Christina Bint Charles Johnson. After embracing Islām, she wanted to change her first name to Lubnā and her last name to ʿAbdullāh. Her new name would then be Lubnā ʿAbdullāḥ Bint Charles Johnson, which is often shortened to Lubnā ʿAbdullāh. This is permissible if it does not result in losing her lineage to her father or cause confusion in her relationships.

Carrying the Husband's Last Name

A common practice in many countries nowadays, including some Muslim countries, is to legally change a woman's last name to her husband's last name upon marriage.

The same discussion of the previous subsection applies here as well. However, we'd like to add that if a woman has the option of keeping her maiden last name, she should do so rather than following this non-Islāmic practice.

Bearing a *Kunyah*

Definition and Recommendation

A *kunyah* is a combined term consisting of a name preceded by the word *Abū* (father) or *Umm* (mother). Depending on its position in a sentence, *Abū* may appear as *Abā* or *Abī*. Most often, the name used in the *kunyah* is the bearer's eldest child. But, as we will show below, this is not a necessary condition.

Bearing a *kunyah* and addressing people by their *kunyahs* is an old Arab etiquette that was condoned by Islām. It was practiced by the Prophet (ﷺ), his companions, and the righteous Muslims through the ages. Addressing a person with his *kunyah* is a show of respect and esteem. Thus, it is recommended for a Muslim to bear a *kunyah* and to address others by their *kunhahs*.

BEARING A *KUNYAH* BEFORE HAVING CHILDREN

Contrary to common understanding, it is recommended for a Muslim to bear a *kunyah* even without having offspring.

Hamzah Bin Ṣuhayb reported that 'Umar (⁕) said to Ṣuhayb, "How come you use Abū Yaḥyā as your *kunyah* even though you do not have a son (called Yaḥyā)?" Ṣuhayb (⁕) replied:

$$\text{"كنّاني رسولُ اللهِ بأبي يحيى."}$$

"Allāh's Messenger (⁕) gave me this *kunyah* of Abū Yaḥyā." [1]

Furthermore, a person's *kunyah* should not necessarily contain the name of one of his (or her) children. Many of the companions (⁕) were known with a *kunyah* that did not derive from a child's name. Examples: Abū Bakr, Abū Ḥafṣ ('Umar), Abū Hurayrah, Abū Tharr, Abū Sulaymān (Khalid Bin al-Walīd), Abū Salamah, etc.

GIVING *KUNYAH* TO A CHILDLESS WOMAN

Further to the above discussion, it is also recommended for a woman to take on a *kunyah*, even if she does not have any offspring.

'Ā'ishah (⁕) reported that she once said to the Prophet (⁕), "O Allāh's Messenger, why do you not give me a *kunyah*?" He replied:

$$\text{«تَكَنِّي بابنِ أختِك: عبد الله. فأنتِ أم عبد الله.»}$$

‹Take a *kunyah* after your sister's son 'Abdullāh. So you are Umm 'Abdillāh.› [2]

Commenting on this *hadīth*, al-Albānī (⁕) said:

---

1   Recorded by Ibn Mājah, al-Ḥākim, and others. Verified to be authentic by al-Albānī (*aṣ-Ṣaḥīḥah* no. 44).

2   Recorded by Aḥmad, Abū Dāwūd, and others. Verified to be authentic by al-Albānī (*aṣ-Ṣaḥīḥah* no. 132 and *Ṣaḥīḥ ul-Adab il-Mufrad* nos. 850,851).

"This indicates that it is recommended to have a *kunyah*, even for those who do not have children. This is an Islāmic etiquette that, as far as I know, is unparalleled by other nations. Thus, all Muslims, men and women, should adhere to it and drop what has invaded them of foreign customs …" [1]

GIVING *KUNYAH* TO CHILDREN

It is also permissible to give *kunyahs* to children and address them by their *kunyahs*. This is part of the Arab and Islāmic tradition that the Prophet (ﷺ) approved and practiced.

Anas (رضي الله عنه) reported that Allāh's Messenger (ﷺ) often visited Anas's family. On one of his visits, he saw a young brother of Anas sad. The Messenger (ﷺ) asked, «ما شأنه؟» **‹What is his problem?›** He was told that he had a small bird that died. So he said to him:

«يا أبا عمير، ما فعل النُّغير؟»

‹O Abū 'Umayr, what happened to the birdie?› [2]

Umm Khālid Bint Khālid (رضي الله عنها) reported that once the Prophet (ﷺ) was brought some garments among which was a small black *khamīṣah* [3] with green or yellow impressions. He asked his companions, «من ترون نكسوها هذه الخميصة؟» **‹To which girl do you think we should give this *khamīṣah*?›** They all remained silent. So he said, «ائتوني بأم خالد.» **‹Bring me Umm Khālid.›** She was carried before the Prophet (ﷺ) wearing a yellow dress, and he put the garment on her with his own hand while saying:

«أبلي وأخلقي. هذا سنا يا أمَّ خالد، هذا سنا يا أم خالد.»

‹May you wear it out and replace it. This is pretty,

---

1 *Aṣ-Ṣaḥīḥah* vol..1.1 p. 257.

2 Recorded by al-Bukhārī, Muslim, and others.

3 *Khamīṣah*: A light black or red garment made of silk or wool with little colored impressions.

O Umm Khālid! This is pretty, O Umm Khālid!› [1]

THE PROPHET'S *KUNYAH*

It is not permissible to bear the Prophet's (ﷺ) *kunyah*: Abul-Qāsim. It is further preferable to avoid naming one's eldest son as Qāsim because, by common tradition, the father would be called Abul-Qāsim.

Jābir Bin ʿAbdillāh (ﷺ) reported that a boy was born for a man from among the Anṣār, so he named him Qāsim. The Anṣār said to him, "We will not address you as Abul-Qāsim, and will not please your eye with this." When the Prophet (ﷺ) heard about this he said:

«أحسنت الأنصار! تسموا باسمي ولا تكنوا بكنيتي، فإنما جُعلتُ قاسماً أقسمُ بينكم. تسموا بي ولا تكنوا بكنيتي.»

‹The Anṣār have done well! Bear my name, but do not use my *kunyah*. I have only been made a Qāsim (distributor) because I distribute and judge among you. So, bear my name but do not use my *kunyah*.›

The Prophet (ﷺ) then said to the man, «سم ابنَك عبدَ الرحْمٰن.» **‹Name your son ʿAbd ur-Raḥmān.›** [2]

Similarly, Abū Hurayrah and Anas (ﷺ) reported that the Prophet (ﷺ) said:

«تسمُّوا باسمي ولا تكنُّوا بكنيتي.»

‹Use my name, but do not use my *kunyah*.› [3]

Some reports of this *ḥadīth* from Anas indicate that the Prophet (ﷺ) said this when a man was calling another man saying, "O Abul-Qāsim!" The Prophet (ﷺ) thought that he meant him and turned to look at him. The man then explained, "I did not mean you, O

---

1 Recorded by al-Bukhārī.

2 Recorded by al-Bukhārī, Muslim, and others.

3 Recorded by al-Bukhārī, Muslim, and others.

Allāh's Messenger." [1]

'Alī (⬥) reported that he said to the Prophet (⬥), "O Allāh's Messenger, if I am granted a son after you, may I give him your name and your *kunyah*?" The Prophet (⬥) replied, «نعم.» ‹Yes.› [2]

Commenting on the various views regarding this issue, Ibn ul-Qayyim said:

"The dislike (of using the Prophet's (⬥) *kunyah*) has three reasons:

1. Giving the meaning of the name (Qāsim) to those who do not deserve it ... because he (⬥) divided among the people according to Allāh's command, and not the division of kings who give and deny according to desire.

2. Concern about confusing (between the Prophet (⬥) and someone else) when addressing or calling ... as was the case when a caller said to the Prophet (⬥), 'I did not mean you.' ...

3. Using both of the Prophet's (⬥) name and *kunyah* removes the benefit of having a distinction (in name) for him ...

The first reason makes it prohibited to use the Prophet's (⬥) *kunyah* during his life and after his death. The second reason limits the prohibition to his lifetime. The third reason only prohibits bearing both his name and his *kunyah* (by the same person) ..."

---

1   Recorded by al-Bukhārī, Muslim, and others.

2   Recorded by Abū Dāwūd, at-Tirmithī, and others. Verified to be authentic by al-Albānī (*aṣ-Ṣaḥīḥah* vol. 6.2, pp. 1081-1082).

Prohibited Names

Names Expressing Servitude to Other than Allāh

There is a consensus among the Muslim *'ulamā'* [1] that it is prohibited to use a name expressing servitude to other than Allāh by means of terms such as *'abd* (slave), *ghulām* (servant), and the likes. Examples: 'Abd ur-Rasūl (Messenger's slave), 'Abd 'Alī, 'Abd ul-Ḥusayn, 'Abd ul-Ka'bah, 'Abd ul-'Uzzā, 'Abd Shams (Sun's slave), Ghulām Rasūl, Ghulām Muḥammad, and so on.

It is also prohibited to use a name expressing servitude to an unauthentic name of Allāh, such as 'Abd ul-Maqṣūd or 'Abd us-Sattār. A list of the most common names without evidence is presented at the end of Appendix II.

Names and Descriptions Specific to Allāh

Among Allāh's excellent names, there are some that may be applied to people. For example, Allāh is al-Baṣīr (the Seeing) and a human is *baṣīr* (seeing). Obviously, the human's sight is limited whereas Allāh's is not.

On the other hand, there are some excellent names that are unique and specific to Allāh. They may not be applied to any of His creation. Among these are the following: Allāh, ar-Raḥmān, al-Aḥad, al-Khallāq, al-Bāri', aṣ-Ṣamad, al-Qayyūm, ar-Razzāq, al-Jabbār, and al-Mutakabbir.

The reader is referred to Appendix II for a complete list of Allāh's names together with their meanings.

It is also prohibited to apply to a human being a description that is Allāh's sole right, such as King of Kings or Judge of Judges, Supreme Owner of the Dominion, Knower of the *Ghayb*, and so on. Abū Hurayrah (ﷺ) reported that Allāh's Messenger (ﷺ) said:

«أخنعُ اسمٍ عند الله يوم القيامة رجلٌ تسمّى ملِكَ الأملاك».

1 Review Ibn Taymiyyah's *al-Fatāwā* 1:378.

لا مَلِكَ إلا الله.»

‹On the Day of Resurrection, the most degraded name before Allāh will be that of a man who called himself King of Kings. There is no (true) king except Allāh.› [1]

NAMES OF DISBELIEVERS AND TYRANTS

It is prohibited to use names of known disbelievers, tyrants, and other deviant individuals. Examples: Shayṭān (Satan), Khinzib (a devil), Firʿawn (Pharaoh), Hāmān (Pharaoh's general), Qārūn, Cleopatra, Qayṣar (Caesar), Kisrā, and so on.

Disliked Names

NAMES SPECIFICALLY DISAPPROVED BY THE PROPHET

There are other names that the Prophet (ﷺ) specifically disapproved of. Some of these disapproved names constituted self-praise or glorification; ex. Rabāḥ (winner). Others reflect bad meanings when put in certain contexts. For example, if a person called Barakah (blessing) departs from someplace, one would say, "The blessing has departed." This would bring pessimism and gloom to some ignorant people.

Samurah Bin Jundub (ﷺ) reported that the Prophet (ﷺ) said:

«لا تُسَمِّ غُلامَك رباحَ ولا أفلحَ ولا يسارَ ولا نجيح،
يقال: "أثمَّ هو؟" فيقال: "لا." »

‹Do not name your servant Rabāḥ (winner) or Aflaḥ (successful) or Yasār (facilitation) or Najīḥ (successful), because it would be said, "Is he there?" And the answer would be (if he is not), "No!"› [2]

---

1 Recorded by al-Bukhārī, Muslim, and others.

2 Recorded by Abū Dāwūd and at-Tirmiṯhī. Verified to be authentic by al-Albānī

Thus, one would think that the negation does apply to the person bearing one of these names but to the good quality itself. It is as if one is asking, "Do you have facilitation, success, and victory?" And the answer would be, "No!"

In another report from Samurah (⌐), he said:

"نهى رسول الله أن نسمي رقيقنا أربعة أسماء:

أفلح ونافع ورباح ويسار."

"Allāh's Messenger (⌐) prohibited us from naming our slaves as Aflaḥ (successful), Nāfi' (useful), Rabāḥ (winner), or Yasār (facilitation)." [1]

Jābir (⌐) reported from 'Umar (⌐) that the Prophet (⌐) said:

«لَأُنهِيَنّ أن يُسَمّى رافعٌ وبركةُ ويسارٌ.»

⟨**I will surely prohibit naming Rāfi' (lifter), Barakah (blessing), or Yasār.**⟩ [2]

In another report, 'Umar (⌐) said that Allāh's Messenger (⌐) said:

«لئن عشتُ لأَنهِيَنّ أن يُسَمّى: رباحٌ، ونجيحٌ، وأفلحُ، ونافعٌ، ويسارٌ.»

⟨**If I live long enough, I will prohibit naming Rabāḥ, Najīḥ (successful), Aflaḥ, Nāfi', and Yasār.**⟩ [3]

And Jābir Bin 'Abdillāh (⌐) said:

(Ṣaḥīḥ ul-Jāmi' no. 7328).

1   Recorded by Ibn Mājah. Verified to be authentic by al-Albānī (Irwā' ul-Ghalīl no. 1177 and Ṣaḥīḥ Ibn Mājāh no. 3006).

2   Recorded by at-Tirmithī. Verified to be authentic by al-Albānī (Ṣaḥīḥ ul-Jāmi' no. 5056).

3   Recorded by at-Tirmithī, Ibn Mājāh, and others. Verified to be authentic by al-Albānī (aṣ-Ṣaḥīḥah no. 2143).

"أراد النبي أن ينهى عن أن يُسَمَّى بيعلى وببركة وبأفلح وبيسار وبنافع وبنحو ذلك، ثم رأيتُه سكت بعدُ عنها فلم يفعل شيئاً. ثم قُبِض رسول الله ولم ينه عن ذلك. ثم أراد عمرُ أن ينهى عن ذلك ثم تركه.»

"The Prophet (ﷺ) intended to prohibit naming Yaʿlā (high), Barakah, Aflaḥ, Yasār, Nāfiʿ, and so on. But he did not say or do anything in this regard until he passed away. ʿUmar then intended to prohibit this, but he later stopped." [1]

Al-Albānī commented on Jābir's statement saying:

"According to Jābir's knowledge, the Prophet (ﷺ) passed without prohibiting these names. However, Samurah Bin Jundub recorded his prohibition of them." [2]

The *ʿulamāʾ* agree [3] that the names mentioned in the above *ḥadīth*s are merely disliked but not fully prohibited. The reason for this is that they have been used by numerous knowledgeable people during and after the Prophet's (ﷺ) time. One important example is the Prophet's (ﷺ) own servant whose name was Rabāḥ.

ʿUmar (ﷺ) reported:

"لَمّا اعتزل النبيُّ نساءَه، فإذا أنا برباحٍ، غلام رسول الله، فناديت: يا رباحُ! استأذِن لي على رسول الله."

"When Allāh's Messenger (ﷺ) abandoned his wives [4], I saw his servant Rabāḥ and told him, 'O Rabāḥ, take

1 Recorded by Muslim and others.

2 *Aṣ-Ṣaḥīḥah* vol. 5 p. 177.

3 As in *Sharḥ Muslim* by an-Nawawī (ﷺ).

4 A detailed discussion of this incident is presented in the author's, "The Fragile Vessels".

permission for me to see Allāh's Messenger.'" [1]

The same ruling of dislike would probably apply to other names that have meanings similar to the disliked ones. Ibn ul-Qayyim said:

> "... Similar to this are: Mubrak (blessed), Mufliḥ (successful), Khayr (goodness), Surūr (happiness), Ni'mah (bounty), and the like. The reason for which the Prophet (ﷺ) disliked the four (above) names applies to these as well ..." [2]

Names with Ugly Meanings

Islām disapproves of using ugly names that would repulse the heart with their meaning or pronunciation. Such names could cause mockery and bring awkwardness to their bearers. In addition, they conflict with the Prophet's (ﷺ) recommendation of using good names.

In the *ḥadīth* that we cited earlier from Ibn 'Umar and others (ﷺ), the Prophet (ﷺ) said:

«... وأقبحها حربٌ ومُرّة.»

> **‹... And indeed, the ugliest names are: Ḥarb (war) and Murrah (bitter).›** [3]

We will see below that, on many instances, the Prophet (ﷺ) changed ugly names to good names. For example, he changed Shihāb (a burning comet) because it represent fire and destruction; he changed Ḥazan because it represents gloom and sadness; and so on.

Aṭ-Ṭabarī (ﷺ) said:

> "One should not use a name of ugly meaning, a name that constitutes self-praise, or a name that reflects a curse — even if those names were proper nouns for

---

1 Recorded by al-Bukhārī, Muslim, and others.

2 *Taḥfat ul-Mawdūd* p. 74.

3 Recorded by Muslim, Ibn Mājah, and others.

individuals and were not intended for the literal meaning they represent. The reason for the dislike is that on hearing such a name, one would think that it is a description of its bearer. Because of this, the Prophet (ﷺ) transformed some people's names to names that truly described their bearers." [1]

Western and Non-Arabic Names

It is disliked for a Muslim to give his child a name coming from cultures outside the Islāmic culture. Such names express glorification of those cultures. Furthermore, when some of those names are traced to their roots, it is often found that they have ugly original meanings.

Examples: Jacklyn, Julie, Diana, Susan, Victoria, Emily, Gloria, Lara, Linda, Maya, Heidy, Yara, Mervat, Shīrīn, Nīvīn, Narimān, Jihān, etc.

Many Muslims use names of Arabic origins that were transferred to some crooked derivations from other languages, such as the Turkish and Persian. Examples: Jawdat, Midḥat, Najdat, Ṣafwat, ʿIṣmat, Raʾfat, Ḥaqqī, Fawzī, Majdī, Ramzī, Rajāʾī, Rushdī, etc.

And among the ugliest names that have entered into some Muslim countries are names that have no meaning in any language and are more like names of dogs and cats. Examples: Zūzū, Fīfī, Mīmī, etc.

Names of Singers, Actors, and Other Sinners

It is disliked to bear names of movie stars, singers, musicians, sports champions, and other celebrities. Such individuals do not present good role models in Islām. Therefore, they do not deserve to be given a position of importance in our lives or the lives of our offsprings.

Girls' Names Indicating Passion or Bodily Attraction

Parents often give their daughters names that indicate love, attraction, seduction, and so on. In addition to being away from the way of the *salaf*, such names carry an implicit invitation to sin and corruption.

---

1 Reported by al-Ḥāfiẓ in *fatḥ ul-Bārī* 10:476.

Al-Albānī (رحمه الله) said:

"And among the ugliest names that have become widespread in our time, and that should be immediately changed because of their ugly meaning ... are names such as: Wiṣāl (lovers' union), Sihām (arrows of love), Nāhid (full-breasted woman), Ghādah (sensual woman), Fitnah (temptation), and so on." [1]

Bakr Abū Zayd says:

"... And those infatuated, mushy, and silly names: Aḥlām (dreams), Arīj (fragrance), Taghrīd (chirping), Ghādah, Fātin (temptress), Nāhid, Huyām — which means insanity caused by extreme infatuation ... and so on, in a list that would be too long to mention." [2]

COMBINED NAMES

It is also disliked to use names that are made up by combining two or more words. The only exception to this are the names of servitude to Allāh that we discussed earlier.

Many of the combined names consist of a descriptive word combined with the words "*dīn* (religion)", "Islām", Allāh, or "*ḥaqq* (truth)". They usually constitute excessive praise for their bearers. Examples: Khayr ud-Dīn (goodness of the Religion), Ḍiyā' ud-Dīn (light of the Religion), Sayf ud-Dīn (sword of the Religion), Naṣr ud-Dīn (victory of the Religion), Fakhr ud-Dīn (glory of the Religion), Sharaf ud-Dīn (honor of the Religion), Shihāb ud-Dīn (comet of the Religion), Bahā' ud-Dīn (beauty of the Religion), Sa'd ud-Dīn (happiness of the Religion), Taqiyy ud-Dīn (pious in Religion), Ṣalāḥ ud-Dīn (Righteousness of the Religion), 'Alā' ud-Dīn (highness of the Religion), Nūr ud-Dīn (light of the Religion), Nūr ul-Islām (light of Islām), Nūr ul-Ḥaq (light of truth), Raḥmat ul-Lāh (Allāh's mercy), and so on.

---

1 *Aṣ-Ṣaḥīḥah* vol. 1.1, p. 427.
2 *Tasmiyat ul-Mawlūd* p. 8.

Such names were never used by the *ṣaḥābah* or the early righteous Muslims, and mostly came to Islām from non-Arab cultures. And even some of the great 'Ulamā' who were given such names by their parents later declared their disapproval of them, as in the case of Muḥy id-Dīn an-Nawawī, Taqiyy ud-Dīn Ibn Taymiyyah, and Nāsir ud-Dīn al-Albānī.

Al-Albānī (ﷺ) said:

> "Thus, it is not permissible to use names such as 'Izz ud-Dīn (honor ot the Religion), Muḥy id-Dīn (revivor of the Religion), Nāṣir ud-Dīn (protector of the Religion), and so on." [1]

There are many other forms of disliked combined names. One of these forms consists of the name Muḥammad preceding other boys' names. Thus, instead of 'Alī or Māhir, for example, some people would make up the combined names Muḥammad 'Alī or Muḥammad Māhir. Except for official records, the bearer of such a name would usually be addressed by his second name. The first name (Muḥammad) is only included for blessings. This is another unacceptable innovation in naming children. It was only introduced among the later generations of Muslims, and should therefore be avoided.

Names of Angels and Qur'ānic *Sūrahs*

Many of the *'ulamā'* dislike naming with Angels' names, such as Jibrīl, Mīkā'īl, and Isrāfīl, because this was not the practice of the *salaf*. For the same reason, it is disliked to name a girl Malak or Malāk (both mean angel).

Similarly, it is disliked to name a child Ṭāhā, Yāsīn, Ḥāmīm, or other names of Qur'ānic *sūrahs*. Many people think that the first two of these are names of the Prophet (ﷺ). However, there is no ground for this claim.

---

1 *Aṣ-Ṣaḥīḥah* vol. 1.1, p. 427.

Changing a Name to a Better One

The Prophet's Practice

If one finds that one's name is improper or disapproved in Islām, one should try to change it to a better name.

It was the Prophet's (ﷺ) practice to change bad names to good ones. ʿĀʾishah (رضي الله عنها) reported:

"كان النبي يغير الاسم القبيح إلى الاسمِ الحسن."

> "The Prophet (ﷺ) used to change a bad name to a good name." [1]

Similarly, ʿĀʾishah (رضي الله عنها) reported:

"كان النبي إذا أتاه الرجل وله اسمٌ لا يحبّه حوّلَه."

> "When a man came to the Prophet (ﷺ) with a name that he disliked, he would change it." [2]

ʿĀʾishah (رضي الله عنها) also reported:

"كان النبي إذا سمع اسماً قبيحاً غيّره. فمر على قرية يُقالُ لها عَفِرة فسماها خضِرة."

> "When the Prophet (ﷺ) heard a bad name, he would change it. Thus, when he passed by a village called ʿAfirah (infertile), he named it Khaḏirah (green)." [3]

And both Abū Ḥamīd and Jābir Bin Samurah (رضي الله عنه) reported that the

---

1 Recorded by at-Tirmithī and Ibn ʿAdiyy. Verified to be authentic by al-Albānī (*aṣ-Ṣaḥīḥah* no. 207).

2 Recorded by aṭ-Ṭabarānī and al-Khallāl. Verified to be authentic by al-Albānī (*aṣ-Ṣaḥīḥah* no. 209).

3 Recorded by aṭ-Ṭabarānī, Abū Yaʿlā, and others. Verified to be authentic by al-Albānī (*aṣ-Ṣaḥīḥah* no. 208).

Prophet (ﷺ) changed al-Madinah's old name of Yathrib (corruption and condemnation) to Ṭābah (goodness). [1]

Names That the Prophet Changed

There are many examples of names that the Prophet (ﷺ) changed for children and adults, males and females.

Zaynab Bint Abī Salamah (ﷺ) also reported that her name was Barrah, but Allāh's Messenger (ﷺ) told Umm Salamah (ﷺ):

«لا تزكوا أنفُسكم، فإن الله هو أعلمُ بالبرَّةِ منكنَّ والفاجرة. سمِّيها زينب.»

‹Do not magnify yourselves. Indeed, only Allāh knows the righteous and the corrupt among you. Name her Zaynab.› [2]

Abū Hurayrah (ﷺ) reported the same:

"كان اسم زينبَ برّة، فقيل: تُزكّي نفسَها. فسماها النبيّ زينب."

"The name of Zaynab (Bint Abī Salamah) was Barrah (righteous), and it was said that this constituted self-praise. So the Prophet (ﷺ) changed it to Zaynab (nice smelling and good looking tree)." [3]

Ibn ʿAbbās (ﷺ) reported:

"كانت جُويريةُ اسمُها برة، فحوّل رسول الله اسمَها جويريةَ. وكان يكرهُ أن يُقالَ: خرج من عندِ برّةَ."

"Juwayriyah's name was Barrah (righteous), but Allāh's Messenger (ﷺ) changed it to Juwayriyah (little friend

---

1 Recorded by al-Bukhārī, Muslim, and others.

2 Recorded by al-Bukhārī, Muslim, and others.

3 Recorded by al-Bukhārī, Muslim, and others.

or wife). The reason was that he hated to be said about him (when leaving her house), 'He departed from the righteous.'" [1]

Ibn 'Umar (&) reported that he had a sister called 'Aṣiyah (disobedient) [2] but the Prophet (&) changed it and told her, «أنتِ جميلة.» ‹You are Jamīlah (the good one).› [3]

Hishām Bin 'Āmir (&) reported that the Prophet (&) asked him about his name. He replied, "Shihāb (comet)." The Prophet (&) said, «بل أنت هشام.» ‹Rather, you are Hishām (an expert camel milker or a destroyer (of enemy)).› [4]

'Ā'ishah (&) reported that an old woman came to the Prophet (&) while he was in her house. Allāh's Messenger (&) asked the old woman, «من أنتِ؟» ‹Who are you?› She replied, "Juthāmah (nightmare) from the tribe of Muzan." He said, «بل أنت حسّانة الْمُزَنيّة.» ‹Rather, you are Ḥassānah (the good or pretty one) from the Muzan.› (Having recognized her,) the Prophet (&) added:

«كيف أنتم؟ كيف حالُكُم؟ كيف كنتُم بعدَنا؟»

‹How are you? How are your affairs? And how have you been after we last met?›

The woman replied, "We are all well — may my father and mother be a ransom for you, O Allāh's Messenger!"

After the old woman left, 'Ā'ishah (&) said, "O Allāh's Messenger, why did you give this old woman so much attention?" He replied:

---

1   Recorded by Muslim, Aḥmad, and others.

2   Note that this is different from Āsiyah, which is a good name that we have included in the list of recommended names in Appendix I.

3   Recorded by Muslim, Aḥmad, and others.

4   Recorded by Abū Dāwūd, al-Ḥākim, and others. Verified to be authentic by al-Albānī (as-Ṣaḥīḥah no. 215).

«إنها كانت تأتينا زمنَ خديجة، وإن حُسنَ العهد من الإيمان.»

‹She used to visit us during the time of Khadījah. And indeed, keeping the old trusts is part of *īmān*.› [1]

Sahl (ﷺ) reported that when al-Munthir Bin Abī Usayd was born, he was brought to the Prophet. The Prophet (ﷺ) asked, «ما اسمه.» **‹What is his name?›** His father, Abū Usayd, replied, "So-and so." The Prophet (ﷺ) said, «لا، لكن أسمه الْمُنذر.» **‹No. Rather, his name is al-Munthir.›** [2]

Hāni' Bin Yazīd (ﷺ) reported that when he visited the Prophet (ﷺ) with some of his people, the Prophet (ﷺ) heard them call him Abul-Ḥakam. The Prophet (ﷺ) summoned him and said:

«إن الله هو الحَكَم، وإليه الحُكْمُ. فلم تكنيتَ بأبي الحكم؟»

‹Indeed, Allāh is the Ḥakam (Judge) and to Him belongs the judgment. Why then did you use this *kunyah* of Abul-Ḥakam?›

He replied, "It is only that when my people had a dispute, they would come to me for arbitration, and my judgment would appease both sides." The Prophet (ﷺ) commented, «ما أحسَنَ هذا!» **‹How good is this!›** Then he asked him, «ما لك من الولد؟» **‹What male children do you have?›** He replied, "Shurayḥ, ʿAbdullāh, and Muslim." He asked him, «فمن أكبرُهُم؟» **‹Who is the eldest among them?›** He replied, "Shurayḥ." The Prophet (ﷺ) then said, «فأنت أبو شُرَيح.» **‹You are Abū Shurayḥ then.›** And he made supplications for him and his children.

Hāni' added that the Prophet (ﷺ) also heard some people calling one of them, "ʿAbd ul-Ḥajar (stone-slave or worshiper)." He asked that man, «ما اسمُكَ؟» **‹What is your name?›** He replied, "ʿAbd ul-Ḥajar." The Prophet (ﷺ) said, «لا. أنت عبدُ الله.» **‹No! You are ʿAbdullāh.›**

When it was time for Hāni' to return to his land, he asked the

---

1 Recorded by al-Hākim, al-Bayhaqī, and others. Verified to be authentic by al-Albānī (*aṣ-Ṣaḥīḥah* no. 216).

2 Recorded by al-Bukhārī, Muslim, and others.

Prophet (ﷺ), "Tell me what thing would admit me to *Jannah*." The Prophet (ﷺ) replied:

«عليك بحسن الكلام وبذل الطعام.»

‹Say good things, and generously offer food (to the needy).› [1]

REFUSING THE PROPHET'S RECOMMENDATION

It is never right to oppose a command or a recommendation by the Prophet (ﷺ), even when it only deals with changing a name.

Saʿīd Bin al-Musayyib (رحمه الله) reported that his grandfather went to the Prophet (ﷺ) who asked him about his name. He replied, "Ḥazan (sadness)." The Prophet (ﷺ) said, «أنتَ سهل.» **‹You are Sahl (easy or field).›** He responded, "But a field is stepped on and subjugated, and I do not like changing a name given to me by my father." Saʿīd concluded, "Thus, sadness remained in our family from that time on." [2]

Calling by a Nickname

CALLING ADULTS BY SHORTENED NAMES

It is permissible to call adults by reduced versions of their names. This is usually done as a show of love, kindness, friendliness, or intimacy.

ʿĀʾishah (رضي الله عنها) reported that Allāh's Messenger (ﷺ) once said to her:

«يا عائشُ! هذا جبريل يقرأُ عليكِ السلام.»

‹O ʿĀʾish [3], This is Jibrīl giving you *salām*.›

She replied, "And upon him be *salām* and Allāh's mercy and blessings.

1 Recorded by al-Bukhārī, al-Ḥākim, and others.

2 Recorded by al-Bukhārī, Abū Dāwūd, and others.

3 A nickname with which Allāh's Messenger (ﷺ) sometimes called his wife.

O Allāh's Messenger, you see that which we cannot see." [1]

Similarly, ʿĀʾishah (🌸) reported that, when she followed the Prophet (🌸) to al-Baqīʿ and then ran back to her bed, he entered and exclaimed, «ما لَكِ يا عائشُ حَشيًا رابِيَة؟» ‹What is wrong with you, O ʿĀʾish, panting and your abdomen rising and falling?› [2]

CALLING CHILDREN BY NICKNAMES OR SHORTENED NAMES

It is conventional to call children by nicknames or reduced versions of their names. This seems to please and delight them, and there is nothing against it in Islām. Rather, the Prophet (🌸) practiced this on some occasions.

Anas (🌸) reported that the Prophet (🌸) used to play with Zaynab, Umm Salamah's daughter, repeatedly saying to her:

«يا زُوَينِبُ، يا زُوَينِب.»

‹O Zuwaynib, O Zuwaynib.› [3]

---

1   Recorded by al-Bukhārī, Muslim, and others. ʿĀʾishah's response is recorded by al-Bukhārī in *al-Adab ul-Mufrad* (no. 827) and verfifed to be authentic by al-Albānī.

2   Recorded by Muslim, Aḥmad, and others. The full narration of this *ḥadīth* in presented in the Author's, "The Fragile Vessels".

3   Recorded by aḍ-Ḍiyāʾ ul-Maqdisī. Verified to be authentic by al-Albānī (*aṣ-Ṣaḥīḥah* no. 2141).

CHAPTER 4

THE ʿ*AQĪQAH*

Meaning of ʿ*Aqīqah*

Linguistic and *Sharʿī* Meanings

The root of "ʿ*aqīqah*" derives from the Arabic verb ʿ*aqqa*, which means split or cut. "ʿ*Aqīqah*" refers to cutting the throat of the animal that is sacrificed for a child's birth. This understanding was adopted by Aḥmad, Ibn ʿAbd il-Barr, al-Khaṭ ṭābī, and others. [1]

According to al-Aṣmaʿī, az-Zamakhsharī, and others, "ʿ*aqīqah*" originally referred to the baby's hair at birth. Subsequently, it was applied to the sacrificed animal because the sacrifice was offered at the same time as when the hair was shaved.

According to Ibn ul-Qayyim, both meanings are acceptable and correct.

Therefore, in Islāmic terminology, ʿ*aqīqah* refers to the animal slaughtered as a sacrifice for a newborn child. It is so named because the animal's throat is cut during the sacrifice.

Is the Name "ʿ*Aqīqah*" Disliked?

Some scholars dislike calling this sacrifice "ʿ*aqīqah*" because the Prophet (ﷺ) showed dislike of this name in the following *ḥadīth*. They believe that it is preferable to call it *nasīkah* (sacrifice).

ʿAmr Bin al-ʿĀṣ (ﷺ) reported that Allāh's Messenger (ﷺ) was asked about ʿ*aqīqah*. As if he (ﷺ) disliked the name, he replied:

«لا يحب الله العقوق (لا أحب العقوق).»

‹Allāh does not like (or I do not like) ʿ***uqūq***

1 Review *Fatḥ ul-Bārī* 9:501.

(ungratefulness).›

He was told, "This is not what we meant. We are referring to that associated with having a baby." He said:

«من أحب أن ينسِكَ عن ولده فلينسِك عنه، عن الغلامِ شاتان مكافئتان، وعن الجاريةِ شاةٌ.»

‹Whoever wishes to perform a sacrifice for (the birth of) his child, let him do so — two comparable goats for a boy, and one goat for a girl.› [1]

In this *ḥadīth*, it appears that the Prophet (ﷺ) disliked using the term "*ʿaqīqah*" because of its connection with "*ʿuqūq*" [2] which means "ungratefulness to parents and relatives". Instead of *ʿaqīqah*, the Prophet (ﷺ) used the verb *nasaka* for sacrificing.

However, we will see below many other *ḥadīth*s in which the Prophet (ﷺ) called this sacrifice "*ʿaqīqah*" without showing any dislike of the name. Thus, it appears that when *ʿuqūq* was mentioned in the above *ḥadīth*, the Prophet (ﷺ) took the opportunity to warn against ungratefulness, without truly disapproving of the term "*ʿaqīqah*" itself — and Allāh knows best.

Ruling for *ʿAqīqah*

Most of the *ʿulamāʾ* recognize *ʿaqīqah* as being voluntary (*nafl*). Some *ʿulamāʾ* consider it compulsory (*wājib*). And some go to the extreme of considering it disliked! In this section, we discuss each one of these views and show that the correct view is that it is obligatory upon those who can afford it.

---

1 Recorded by Abū Dāwūd, an-Nasāʾī, and others. Verified to be *ḥasan* by al-Albānī (*Irwāʾ ul-Ghalīl* no. 1166).

2 Both words derive from the same root past-tense verb *ʿaqqa* means cut.

Is It Disliked?

A small number of scholars believe that the *ʿaqīqah* is one of the practices of *Jāhiliyyah* that Islām censored or disapproved. They base their opinion on what the Prophet (ﷺ) said in the above *ḥadīth* of Ibn ʿAmr, «لا أحب العقوق.» **‹I do not like *ʿuqūq*.›** However, we have shown that this word "*ʿuqūq*" could mean "slaughtering a *ʿaqīqah*" or "ungratefulness". We have shown that the Prophet (ﷺ) referred to the second meaning, as is clear from the rest of this *ḥadīth*.

Ibn ul-Munthir (رحمه الله) [1] said:

> "Among those who believed in *ʿaqīqah* (as a correct practice) are: ʿAbdullāh Bin ʿAbbās, ʿAbdullāh Bin ʿUmar, ʿĀʾishah—Mother of the Believers, Fāṭimah—Allāh's Messenger's daughter, Buraydah al-Aslamī, al-Qāsim Bin Muḥammad, ʿUrwah Bin az-Zubayr, ʿAṭāʾ Bin Abī Rabāḥ, az-Zuhrī, Abū az-Zanād, Mālik, the people of al-Madīnah, ash-Shāfiʿī and his followers, Aḥmad, Isḥāq, Abū Thawr, and a large-numbered groups of learned people. By this, they follow Allāh's Messenger's (ﷺ) Sunnah. When a *sunnah* is authenticated, one's view must agree with it, regardless of those who reject it. The followers of opinions (the *Ḥanafī*s) denied that the *ʿaqīqah* is a *sunnah*, thereby violating authentic narrations from Allāh's Messenger (ﷺ), his companions (رضي الله عنهم), and whoever reported them from the *tābiʿīn*." [2]

Evidence that It Is Obligatory

Those who hold the position that the *ʿaqīqah* is *wājib* base their opinion on the following *ḥadīth*s:

1. Salmān Bin ʿĀmir aḍ-Ḍabbī reported that Allāh's Messenger (ﷺ)

---

1 Author of "*Al-Fatḥ ur-Rabbānī*".

2 Reported by Ibn ul-Qayyim in *taḥfat ul-Mawdūd* (p. 27).

said:

« مع َ (في) الغلام ِ عقيقة، فأهْريقوا عنهُ دماً، وأميطوا عنه الأذى. »

‹A ʿaqīqah is prescribed for every child. Thus shed
blood on its behalf, and remove the harm off it.› [1]

2. ʿĀʾishah, Umm Kurz, and Salmān Bin ʿĀmir (﴿) reported that
Allāh's Messenger (ﷺ) said:

« عن الغلام شاتان مكافأتان، وعن الجارية شاة.

لا يضركم ذكراناً كنّ أو إناثاً. »

‹(Slaughter) for a boy two compatible sheep, and for
a girl just one. It does not matter whether they (the
sheep) are male or female.› [2]

3. Ibn ʿAbbās (﴿) reported that Allāh's Messenger (ﷺ) said:

« عن الغلام عقيقتان، وعن الجارية عقيقةٌ. »

‹Two ʿaqīqahs (should be slaughtered) for a boy and
one for a girl.› [3]

4. Asmāʾ Bint Yazīd (﴿) reported that Allāh's Messenger (ﷺ) said:

« العقيقة حق، عن الغلام شاتان متكافئتان، وعن الجارية شاةٌ. »

‹The ʿaqīqah is a right (upon you). (Slaughter) for a

---

1   Recorded by at-Tirmithī, an-Nasāʾī, and others. Verified to be authentic by al-Albānī
    (Ṣaḥīḥ ul-Jāmiʿ no. 4253 & 5877, and Irwāʾ ul-Ghalīl no. 1171).

2   This is a combined report recorded by Aḥmad, Abū Dāwūd, others. Verified to be
    authentic by al-Albānī (Ṣaḥīḥ ul-Jāmiʿ no. 4105 & 4106, and Irwāʾ ul-Ghalīl no.
    1166).

3   Recorded by aṭ-Ṭabarānī (in al-Kabīr). Verified to be authentic by al-Albānī (Ṣaḥīḥ
    ul-Jāmiʿ no. 4107, and Irwāʾ ul-Ghalīl no. 1166).

boy two compatible sheep, and for a girl just one.⟩ [1]

5. Samurah Bin Jundub (⌘) reported that Allāh's Messenger (⌘) said:

«كل غلام رهينة بعقيقته، تُذبح عنه يومَ سابعه

ويُسمّى فيه ويُحلَقُ رأسُه.»

⟨**Every child is mortgaged** [2] **by its 'aqīqah. It should be slaughtered for him (or her) on its seventh day, the child's hair should be shaved, and he (or she) should be named.**⟩ [3]

6. Ibn 'Abbās, 'Ā'ishah, Anas, 'Alī, and others (⌘) reported:

"عق رسول اللّه عن الحسن والحسين كبشاً كبشاً (بكبشين كبشين)."

"**Allāh's Messenger (⌘) offered 'aqīqah for al-Ḥasan and al-Ḥusayn: a ram, a ram (two rams, two rams).**" [4]

It should be noted that some reports of this *ḥadīth* express that the Prophet (⌘) slaughtered one ram for each grandson while others mention two rams. Commenting on this, al-Albānī (⌘) indicated that "two rams" should be the correct number for two reasons:

"a. (The reports with this number) include an addition over the other reports. And additions from trustworthy reporters are acceptable …

b. This agrees with the other *ḥadīths* in this regard in which (the Prophet ⌘) requires slaughtering two

---

1 Recorded by Aḥmad and others. Verified to be authentic by al-Albānī (*Ṣaḥīḥ ul-Jāmi'* no. 4133, and *Irwā' ul-Ghalīl* no. 1166).

2 The meaning of this "mortgage" is discussed in depth near the end of this chapter.

3 Recorded by an-Nasā'ī, Abū Dāwūd, and others. Verified to be authentic by al-Albānī (*Ṣaḥīḥ ul-Jāmi'* no. 4541, and *Irwā' ul-Ghalīl* no. 1165).

4 Recorded by an-Nasā'ī, Abū Dāwūd, and others. Verified to be authentic by al-Albānī (*Irwā' ul-Ghalīl* no. 1164).

sheep for a boy ... "[1]

From the above reports, it is clear that Allāh's Messenger (ﷺ) commanded the people to slaughter a *ʿaqīqah*, indicated that it is compulsory for the newborn, and performed it himself for his grandsons al-Ḥasan and al-Ḥusayn.

It is well established in the Islāmic *fiqh* that a command from Allāh (ﷻ) or His Messenger (ﷺ) indicates an obligation — unless there is an additional evidence to reduce it from being obligatory to being voluntary.

In the case of *ʿaqīqah*, the above reports clearly classify it as an obligation. In what follows, we discuss the counter evidence.

EVIDENCE THAT IT IS VOLUNTARY

Many scholars believe that the following reports reduce the *ʿaqīqah* from the level of *wujūb* (obligation) to the level of *istiḥbāb* (recommendation):

1. In the previously cited *ḥadīth* of ʿAbdullāh Bin ʿAmr (رضي الله عنه), Allāh's Messenger (ﷺ) said:

   «من أحب أن ينسُكَ عن ولده فلينسِك عنه، عن الغلامِ
   شاتان مكافئتان، وعن الجاريةِ شاةٌ.»

   ‹Whoever wishes to perform a sacrifice for (the birth of) his child, let him do so — two comparable goats for a boy, and one goat for a girl.› [2]

The scholars who believe that the *ʿaqīqah* is voluntary argue that this *ḥadīth* makes it dependant on the person's wish or inclination.

Our response is that, in light of the earlier evidence (in the previous subsection), the choice given in this *ḥadīth* should be understood to

---

1 *Irwāʾ ul-Ghalīl* vol 1, p. 384.

2 Recorded by Abū Dāwūd, an-Nasāʾī, and others. Verified to be *ḥasan* by al-Albānī (*Irwāʾ ul-Ghalīl* no. 1166).

mean, "Whoever wishes to sacrifice because he can afford it ..."

Another possible explanation is that, similar to any other Islāmic obligation, the ʿaqīqah is not enforced on a person. Rather, it is subject to his choice, and he has the option of complying or refusing (for which he would be subject to either reward or punishment). Ibn Ḥazm () said:

> "If this ḥadīth were authentic, it would be an evidence for us against them, because it requires it (the ʿaqīqah) for the boy and girl. It further indicates that this obligation does not bind the father against his will. This is the text and outcome of the ḥadīth. It makes it (the ʿaqīqah) similar to zakāh and zakāt ul-fiṭr in this regard, without any difference." [1]

2. Abū Rāfiʿ () reported that when Fāṭimah () gave birth to al-Ḥasan (), she asked Allāh's Messenger (), "Shouldn't I sacrifice blood (as ʿaqīqah) for my son?" He replied:

«لا تَعُقِّي عنه، ولكن أَحْلِقِي شعرَ رأسِه، وتصدقي بزنةِ شعره فضةً.»

‹No, do not slaughter a ʿaqīqah for him. Just shave the hair of his head, and give ṣadaqah (charity) equal to its weight in silver.›

She did this; and when al-Ḥusayn was born, she did the same. [2]

The argument here is that the Prophet () prevented his daughter from offering the ʿaqīqah. He would not have done so had the ʿaqīqah been obligatroy.

However, the earlier report by Ibn ʿAbbās and other ṣaḥābah, including Fāṭimah's husband ʿAlī (), is clear in that the Prophet () himself had slaughtered two rams for each of his two grandsons. Therefore, there was no reason for Fāṭimah or ʿAlī to slaughter. Al-

---

1   Al-Muḥallā 6:241.

2   Recorded by Aḥmad, al-Bayhaqī, and others. Verified to be ḥasan (good) by al-Albānī (Irwāʾ ul-Ghalīl no. 1175).

Bayhaqī (ﷺ) said:

> "It is as if he (the Prophet ﷺ) wanted to perform the *ʿaqīqah* himself, as we have narrated, so he commanded her (Fāṭimah) to do another thing instead, which was to give charity ..." [1]

ʿ*Aqīqah* vs. *Ṣadaqah*

Some people may ask, "Is it permissible to give charity in place of slaughtering *ʿaqīqah*?" The answer is that it is not permissible to do so, even if the amount of charity was more than the cost of the *ʿaqīqah*. Each act of worship in Islām has its own time, place, or conditions that would not normally allow other acts to replace it.

Imām Aḥmad (ﷺ) was asked, "Would you prefer for a person to slaughter *ʿaqīqah* or give its value to the needy?" He replied, "The *ʿaqīqah* (is better)." [2]

Ibn ul-Qayyim said:

> "Slaughtering for a specific requirement is better than giving its value or more in charity — similar to the *hady* (*Ḥajj* sacrifice) and *uḍḥiyah*. This is because the slaughter and spilling of blood are specifically required in these cases ... " [3]

Conclusion

We clearly conclude from the above that the *ʿaqīqah* is *wājib* (obligatory) upon the father or those who are in immediate custody of the newborn — and Allāh (ﷻ) knows best.

Ibn Ḥazm (ﷺ) said:

> "The Prophet's (ﷺ) command concerning *ʿaqīqah* makes it a *farḍ* (obligation). It is not permissible for

---

1 Reported by al-Albānī in *Irwāʾ ul-Ghalīl* vol. 1, p. 404.

2 Reported by al-Khallāl in *al-Jāmiʿ*.

3 *Tuḥfat ul-Mawdūd* p. 44.

anyone to understand that any of his (⬥) commands are elective unless there is an additional text in that regard. Otherwise, saying such a thing would be lying … " [1]

A well-founded rule in Islām is that accountability is based on capability. Thus, the ʿaqīqah obligation drops off those who cannot afford it. This does not mean that they would then be prohibited from performing, but merely that it becomes optional for them. They may find relatives or friends willing to help with its cost, or may borrow money for this purpose.

Imām Aḥmad's (⬥) son Ṣāliḥ asked him concerning a man to whom a child is borne. The man has no money to offer a ʿaqīqah; should he borrow and offer it or wait until he has the money? The Imām's response was:

> "The greatest warning that we heard in regard to ʿaqīqah is Samurah's ḥadīth that every child is mortgaged by its ʿaqīqah. Indeed, I hope that if this man borrows money, Allāh (⬥) will quickly enrich him because he revives a sunnah of the Prophet's (⬥) and follows his guidance." [2]

Animals that May Be Slaughtered for ʿAqīqah

ANIMAL TYPE

In the ḥadīths concerning ʿaqīqah, the Prophet (⬥) referred to the animal to be slaughtered as shāh (or "shāt"). In the above, we have translated "shāh" as "sheep" or "goat". According to Ibn Manẓūr:

> "Shāh means one sheep; it can be male or female … And it is believed (by some) that shāh can be a sheep, a goat, a deer, a cow, a farm animal, or a zebra." [3]

---

1   Al-Muḥallā 6:237.
2   Reported by al-Khallāl in al-Jāmiʿ.
3   Lisān ul-ʿArab under "shawaha".

As for the Prophet's (ﷺ) practical Sunnah, we have seen in an earlier report by Ibn ʿAbbās (ﷺ) that the Prophet (ﷺ) slaughtered two rams for each of his grandsons.

The common and accepted practice among the *salaf* has been to only slaughter sheep or goats for *ʿaqīqah* — even though, as we have shown, the texts of the *ḥadīth*s do not exclude slaughtering larger animals.

As for slaughtering camels, there is a clear text from ʿĀʾishah (ﷺ) rejecting this. Abū Mulaykah reported that ʿAbd ur-Raḥmān Bin Abī Bakr (ﷺ) had a male baby. His sister ʿĀʾishah (ﷺ) was told, "O Mother of the believers, slaughter a camel for his *ʿaqīqah*." She replied:

"معاذ اللهِ، ولكن ما قال رسولُ اللّهِ: شاتان مُكافِئتان."

"I seek refuge with Allāh! Only what Allāh's Messenger had said, **‹Two comparable *shāh*s.›**" [1]

This shows that it is not permissible to slaughter camels for the *ʿaqīqah* — even though one of the companions, namely, Anas (ﷺ) had done it. [2]

NUMBER

We have cited earlier a number of reports indicating that a *ʿaqīqah* consists of two animals for a boy and one for a girl. For example, Ibn ʿAbbās (ﷺ) reported that Allāh's Messenger (ﷺ) said:

«عن الغلام عقيقتان، وعن الجارية عقيقةٌ.»

‹(Slaughter) two *ʿaqīqah*s (or animals) for a boy and one for a girl.› [3]

---

1 Recorded by aṭ-Ṭaḥāwī and al-Bayhaqī. Verified to be *ḥasan* by al-Albānī (*Irwāʾ ul-Ghalīl* no. 1166).

2 Recorded by Ibn Abī Shaybah and aṭ-Ṭabarānī with an authentic *isnād*.

3 Recorded by aṭ-Ṭabarānī (in *al-Kabīr*). Verified to be authentic by al-Albānī (*Ṣaḥīḥ ul-Jāmiʿ* no. 4107, and *Irwāʾ ul-Ghalīl* no. 1166).

According to some scholars, the difference between male and female newborns in terms of the number of ʿ*aqīqah* animals is comparable to the difference between males and females in matters of testimony, inheritance, blood ransom, etc. It arises from the difference in social rights and liabilities, and gives no guarantee of additional merit or better rewards for either side, the latter being only based on piety.

Sex

The sex of the animals slaughtered for ʿ*aqīqah* is immaterial. We again cite the *ḥadīth* reported by Umm Kurz (ﷺ) that Allāh's Messenger (ﷺ) said:

«عن الغلام شاتان وعن الجارية شاة. لا يضركم ذكرانا كنّ أو إناثا.»

‹(Slaughter) for a boy two sheep, and for a girl just one. It does not matter whether they (the sheep) are male or female.› [1]

Other Qualities

There is no authentic text requiring other qualities for a ʿ*aqīqah*, such as size, age, color, etc. Some scholars hold the opinion that it should have similar qualities to the *uḍḥiyah* [2]. This has no proof, and acts of worship cannot be subjected to *qiyās* (analogy).

Yet it is to be noted that, similar to the *uḍḥiyah*, the ʿ*aqīqah* is a sacrifice offered to Allāh (ﷻ) as an expression of servitude and gratitude. Therefore, in both cases, one should try to sacrifice animals of good quality and appearance.

---

1 Recorded by Aḥmad, Abū Dāwūd, and others. Verified to be authentic by al-Albānī (*Irwāʾ ul-Ghalīl* no. 1166).

2 The sacrifice offered on the ʿ*Īd* of *al-Aḍḥā*.

Date of Slaughtering the *ʿAqīqah*

THE SEVENTH DAY

The *ʿaqīqah* should be slaughtered on the seventh day from birth (counting the birthday). We site again two *ḥadīths* in this regard.

Samurah Bin Jundub (ﷺ) reported that Allāh's Messenger (ﷺ) said:

«كل غلامٍ رهينة بعقيقته، تُذبح عنه يومَ سابعه ويُسمّى فيه ويُحلَقُ رأسُه.»

‹Every child is mortgaged by its *ʿaqīqah*. It should be slaughtered for it on its seventh day, its (the child's) hair should be shaved, and it should be named.› [1]

ʿAbdullāh Bin ʿAmr (ﷺ) reported:

"أمر النبيُّ بتسميةِ المولودِ يومَ سابعِه، ووضعِ الأذى عنهُ، والعقِّ."

"The Prophet (ﷺ) commanded that a newborn be named on the seventh day and that the harm be removed off it and its *ʿaqīqah* be slaughtered." [2]

Since the Prophet (ﷺ) has set the timing for this act of worship, it is not permissible to slaughter the *ʿaqīqah* prior to the seventh day — just like prohibiting to slaughter the *ʿīd* sacrifice before the *ʿīd* prayer.

Ibn Ḥazm (ﷺ) said:

"Slaughtering should be performed on the seventh day from birth, and is not acceptable before the seventh. If

1 Recorded by an-Nasāʾī, Abū Dāwūd, and others. Verified to be authentic by al-Albānī (*Ṣaḥīḥ ul-Jāmiʿ* no. 4541, and *Irwāʾ ul-Ghalīl* no. 1165).

2 Recorded by at-Tirmithī and Ibn Abī Shaybah. Verified to be *ḥāsan* by al-Albānī (*Ṣaḥīḥ at-Tirmithī* no. 2269).

the slaughter is not done on the seventh, it is mandatory to do it whenever it becomes possible after that." [1]

Waliyy Ullāh id-Dahlawī (رحمه الله) said:

"The ʿaqīqah is slaughtered on the seventh day so as to give the family enough time to recover from the pains and hardship of childbirth, and to enable them to find the animals needed for ʿaqīqah." [2]

AFTER THE SEVENTH

If the ʿaqīqah is not slaughtered on the seventh, it may still be slaughtered on the fourteenth or twenty-first day from birth.

Buraydah (رضي الله عنه) reported that the Prophet (ﷺ) said:

«العقيقة تُذبح لسبع، أو لأربعَ عشرةَ، أو لإحدى وعشرين.»

‹**The ʿaqīqah should be slaughtered on the seventh, the fourteenth, or the twenty-first day (after birth).**› [3]

If the ʿaqīqah is not slaughtered on one of these three dates for a legitimate reason, it should be slaughtered as soon as possible after that. Legitimate reasons include: inability to find an animal, forgetting, ignorance, poverty, and so on.

Deliberately neglecting to slaughter the ʿaqīqah on the specified days is a sin that requires repentance. In addition, as indicated above by Ibn Ḥazm, the ʿaqīqah would still need to be slaughtered after repentance.

It is important to note that these dates are set for the actual slaughtering of the ʿaqīqah. As for cooking and eating it, it may be done at any later date.

---

1   *Al-Muḥallā* 6:234.

2   *Ḥujjat Ullāh il-Bālighah.*

3   Recorded by aṭ-Ṭabarānī (in *al-Awsaṭ*) and aḍ-Ḍiyāʾ. Verified to be authentic by al-Albānī (*Ṣaḥīḥ ul-Jāmiʿ* no. 4132 and *Irwāʾ ul-Ghalīl* no. 1170).

OFFERING ʿAQĪQAH FOR ONESELF

Offering the *ʿaqīqah* is an obligation upon the parents or those who are in custody of the newborn. It is not the newborn's obligation or responsibility.

However, if no one performed this obligation for an individual, it is permissible for him to perform it when he reaches adulthood. The Prophet (ﷺ) did this for himself.

Anas (ﷺ) reported:

"عق رسول الله عن نفسه بعدما بُعث نبياً."

> "Allāh's Messenger (ﷺ) performed *ʿaqīqah* for himself after he was appointed as prophet." [1]

Muḥammad Ibn Sīrīn (ﷺ) said:

> "If I know that the *ʿaqīqah* was not performed for me, I would perform it for myself." [2]

Al-Ḥasan al-Baṣrī (ﷺ) said:

> "If no one performed *ʿaqīqah* for you, perform it for yourself — even if you are a full grown man." [3]

Method of Slaughtering

SINCERITY TO ALLĀH

The *ʿaqīqah* must be offered purely and sincerely to Allāh (ﷻ).

---

1 Recorded by ʿAbd ur-Razzāq, aṭ-Ṭaḥāwī, and others. Verified to be authentic by al-Albānī (*aṣ-Ṣaḥīḥah* no. 2726).

2 Recorded by Ibn Ibn Abī Shaybah in *al-Muṣannaf*. Verified to be authentic by al-Albānī (*aṣ-Ṣaḥīḥah* vol. 6.1 p. 506).

3 Recorded by Ibn Ḥazm in *al-Muḥallā*. Verified to be *ḥasan* by al-Albānī (*aṣ-Ṣaḥīḥah* vol. 6.1 p. 506).

Offering a sacrifice to other than Allāh is a major sin and act of *shirk*. Those who commit it would be liable to Allāh's wrath and curse. 'Alī (☺) reported that Allāh's Messenger (☺) said:

«لعن اللهُ من لعن والديه، ولعن اللهُ من ذبحَ لغير اللهِ، ولعنَ اللهُ من آوى مُحدِثاً، ولعن اللهُ من غيَّر منارَ الأرض.»

‹Allāh curses anyone who curses his parents; Allāh curses anyone who offers a slaughter to other than Allāh; Allāh curses anyone who gives abode to an innovator (in the *Dīn*); and Allāh curses anyone who changes land boundaries (thereby transgressing without right).› [1]

USING A SHARP KNIFE

Slaughtering the animals should be done quickly and skillfully, using a sharp knife. Shaddād Bin Aws (☺) reported that Allāh's Messenger (☺) said:

«إن اللهَ كتب الإحسانَ على كلِّ شيءٍ، فإذا قَتَلتُم فأحسِنوا القِتلَةَ، وإذا ذبحتُم فأحسِنوا الذَّبحَ، ولِيُحِدَّ أَحَدُكم شفرتَه، ولْيُرِحْ ذَبيحَتَه.»

‹Allāh requires that all deeds be well-performed. So when you kill, kill in a good manner, and when you slaughter, slaughter in a good manner. And let the one of you (who performs the slaughter) sharpen his blade and make it easy for his kill.› [2]

'Ā'ishah (☺) reported that once Allāh's Messenger (☺) sacrificed (for '*īd*) a large-horned ram with black legs, chest, belly, and eyes. When he was ready to slaughter it he said to her, «يا عائشةُ! هلمِّي المُدْيَةَ.» ‹O 'Ā'ishah, bring the knife.› Then he said, «اشحذيها بحجرٍ.» ‹Sharpen it on a stone.› Then he took the knife, laid down the ram, and

---

1   Recorded by Muslim, Aḥmad, and others.

2   Recorded by Muslim, Abū Dāwūd, and others.

slaughtered it while saying:

«بسم الله، اللّهم تقبّل من محمدٍ وآل محمد، ومن أمةِ محمد.»

‹With Allāh's Name (I slaughter). O Allāh, accept from Muḥammad and Muḥammad's family, and from Muḥammad's *Ummah*.› [1]

Furthermore, the knife may not be made from teeth (or tusks) or nails (or claws). Rāfi' Bin Khadīj (ﷺ) reported that he said to the Prophet (ﷺ), "O Allāh's Messenger, we will face the enemies tomorrow, but we do not have knives (to slaughter any injured animals)." The Prophet (ﷺ) replied:

«ما أنهر الدمَ وذُكِر اسمُ اللهِ عليه فكلوه، ليس السنَّ والظُّفرَ. وسأحدّثكم عن ذلك: أما السنُّ فعظمٌ، وأما الظُّفرُ فمُدى الحبشية.»

‹If the animal's blood is poured out (using any sharp tool), and if Allāh's Name is pronounced on it, then you may eat from it. But do not use teeth or nails (to kill it). I will tell you why: as for teeth, they are bones; and as for nails, they are the Abyssinians' knives.› [2]

The reason for the prohibition of using teeth, bones, and nails is that knives made from them cause pain and torture to the slaughtered animal, which contradicts the requirement of showing mercy to it, as is further explained below.

Mercy Toward the Animal

Out of Allāh's (ﷻ) great and boundless favors on us, He subjugated some animals for our sustenance. This does not give us permission to torture these animals to any degree beyond the minimum needed for killing them. Thus, the animals should be slaughtered with a sense of

1 Recorded by Muslim, Abū Dāwūd, and others.

2 Recorded by al-Bukhārī, Muslim, and others.

mercy and compassion. This includes hiding the knife from the animal's sight until the last minute, and avoiding killing the animals within each others' sight.

Qurrah Bin Iyās al-Muzanī (⌖) reported that a man told Allāh's Messenger (⌖), "O Allāh's Messenger! Indeed, even when I slaughter a goat, I show mercy to it." The Prophet (⌖) said:

« والشاةُ إن رحِمتَها رَحِمَكَ اللّهُ. »

‹Even for a sheep (or goat), if you show it mercy Allāh will show mercy to you.› [1]

Ibn 'Abbās (⌖) reported that the Prophet (⌖) saw a man preparing to slaughter a goat. He laid it down and stood over it, his foot on its side, sharpening his blade, while it watched him with alarm. The Prophet (⌖) said to him:

«أفلا قبل هذا؟ أتريدُ أن تميتَها موتتين؟»

‹Should you not have done it (the sharpening) before this (the slaughter)? Do you wish to give it death twice?› [2]

In another report, the Prophet (⌖) said:

«أتريد أن تميتها موتاتٍ؟ هلاّ حددتَ شفرتَك قبل أن تضجِعَها؟»

‹Do you want to give it death many times? Should you not have sharpened your blade before laying it down?› [3]

---

1   Recorded by Aḥmad, aṭ-Ṭabarānī, and others. Verified to be authentic by al-Albānī (aṣ-Ṣaḥīḥah no. 26).

2   Recorded by aṭ-Ṭabarānī and al-Bayhaqī. Verified to be authentic by al-Albānī (aṣ-Ṣaḥīḥah no. 24).

3   Recorded by al-Ḥākim. Verified to be authentic by al-Albānī (aṣ-Ṣaḥīḥah no. 24).

LAYING THE ANIMAL DOWN

It is recommended to lay the animal down before slaughtering it (except for camels). This is what the Prophet (ﷺ) did when he slaughtered the black-legged ram as in 'Ā'ishah's (﵂) earlier *ḥadīth*. Commenting on that *ḥadīth*, an-Nawawī (﵀) said:

> "This shows that it is recommended to lay the sheep down during slaughtering. They should not be slaughtered while standing or sitting, but while lying down. This is more merciful, and is supported by a number of *ḥadīth*s. Furthermore, there is a consensus among the Muslims, which conforms with the *'ulamā'*'s opinion and the Muslims' practice, that the animals should be laid on their left side, because it is easier for the slaughterer to hold the knife with his right hand and the animal's head with his left." [1]

Anas (﵁) also reported:

> ”ضحى رسول الله بكبشين أملحين أقرنين، ذبحُهما بيده، وسمّى وكبّر.
>
> رأيتُه واضعاً قدمه على صِفاحِهما ويقول: «بسم الله والله أكبر.»“

> "Allāh's Messenger sacrificed (for *'īd*) two wide-eyed and large-horned rams. He slaughtered them with his hand while pronouncing Allāh's name and declaring His greatness. I saw him place his foot on their flanks while saying, ⟨*Bismi 'llāhi wallāhu akbar* — **with Allāh's name; Allāh is the Greatest**).⟩" [2]

From this *ḥadīth*, we also see that it is recommended for the person conducting the slaughtering to place his foot on the animal's side near the neck. This would facilitate the slaughtering process.

In addition, we have seen from an-Nawawī's above statement that

---

1　*Sharḥu Muslim* 13:130.

2　Recorded by al-Bukhārī, Muslim, and others.

it has been the practice of the *salaf* to lay the animal down on its left side, so that the person slaughtering it would be able to cut its throat with his right hand while holding its head with the left.

It has also been the practice of the *salaf* to turn the animal so as to face the direction of *Qiblah* while being slaughtered. Nāfiʿ (ﷺ) reported that Ibn ʿUmar (ﷺ) used to dislike eating from an animal that was slaughtered facing away from the *Qiblah.* [1]

CUTTING THE THROAT

We have seen from Rāfiʿ's earlier *ḥadīth* (p. 78) that one of the requirements of correct slaughtering is that the blood should be poured out. This is done by cutting the throat. Ibn ʿAbbās (ﷺ) said:

"الذكاةُ في الحلقِ واللبَّةِ."

> "(Correct) slaughtering is applied to the throat and windpipe." [2]

The acceptable practice among the Muslims is to cut the food-passage (larynx), the windpipe, and the two jugular veins. An-Nawawī (ﷺ) said:

> "Ibn ul-Munthir said, 'There is a consensus among the *ʿulamāʾ* that when the windpipe, the larynx, and the two jugular veins are cut and the blood is poured, correct slaughtering is accomplished. However, the *ʿulamāʾ* differ in regard to cases where the four passages are not all cut ...'" [3]

---

1 Recorded by ʿAbd ur-Razzāq with an authentic *isnād* (as in *Aḥkām ul-Mawlūd*).

2 Recorded by Ibn Ḥibbān and others from Ibn ʿAbbās and other companions (ﷺ). Verified to be authentic by al-Albānī (*Irwāʾ ul-Ghalīl* no. 2542). A *ḥadīth* similar to this and attributed to the Prophet (ﷺ) is verified by al-Albānī to be extremely weak (*Irwāʾ ul-Ghalīl* no. 2541).

3 *Sharḥu Muslim* 13:133.

PRONOUNCING ALLĀH'S NAME

It is required to pronounce Allāh's name over an animal while slaughtering it. We have seen above that the Prophet (ﷺ) did this when he slaughtered the rams. He also commanded Rāfiʿ Bin Khadīj (p. 78) to pronounce Allāh's name over the slaughtered animals.

Pronouncing Allāh's name demonstrates that the animal is dedicated to Allāh and not to any false god. Allāh (ﷻ) says:

﴿فَكُلُوا۟ مِمَّا ذُكِرَ ٱسْمُ ٱللَّهِ عَلَيْهِ إِن كُنتُم بِـَٔايَـٰتِهِۦ مُؤْمِنِينَ ۝﴾ الأنعام ١١٨

«So eat of that (meat) upon which Allāh's Name has been pronounced (at the time of slaughter), if you have faith in His Signs.» [1]

And He (ﷻ) says:

﴿وَلَا تَأْكُلُوا۟ مِمَّا لَمْ يُذْكَرِ ٱسْمُ ٱللَّهِ عَلَيْهِ وَإِنَّهُۥ لَفِسْقٌ.﴾ الأنعام ١٢١

«And do not eat of that (meat) upon which Allāh's Name has not been pronounced; that would indeed be a grave disobedience.» [2]

These *āyāt*, as well as Rāfiʿ's *ḥadīth*, clearly require pronouncing Allāh's Name upon the meat at the time of slaughter.

In the first of the above two *āyāt* (6:118), Allāh (ﷻ) permits the believers to eat from animals that were purely dedicated to Him during slaughtering. In the second *āyah* (6:121), Allāh (ﷻ) prohibits eating from animals that were not purely dedicated to Him (but to other false gods), and considers eating their meat a grave disobedience. This is further clarified in the following two *āyāt*:

﴿قُل لَّآ أَجِدُ فِيمَآ أُوحِيَ إِلَيَّ مُحَرَّمًا عَلَىٰ طَاعِمٍ يَطْعَمُهُۥٓ إِلَّآ
أَن يَكُونَ مَيْتَةً أَوْ دَمًا مَّسْفُوحًا أَوْ لَحْمَ خِنزِيرٍ فَإِنَّهُۥ رِجْسٌ،

---

1 *Al-Anʿām* 6:118.

2 *Al-Anʿām* 6:121.

أَو فِسْقًا أُهِلَّ لِغَيْرِ ٱللهِ بِهِ.﴾ الأنعام ١٤٥

«Say (O Muḥammad), "I do not find among what was revealed to me anything forbidden to one who would eat it, unless it be a dead animal, or blood spilled out, or the flesh of swine — for indeed, these are impure. Also (forbidden) is a (slaughter of) disobedience dedicated to other than Allāh."» [1]

And:

﴿حُرِّمَتْ عَلَيْكُمُ ٱلْمَيْتَةُ وَٱلدَّمُ وَلَحْمُ ٱلْخِنزِيرِ، وَمَآ أُهِلَّ لِغَيْرِ ٱللهِ بِهِ، وَٱلْمُنْخَنِقَةُ وَٱلْمَوْقُوذَةُ وَٱلْمُتَرَدِّيَةُ وَٱلنَّطِيحَةُ، وَمَا أَكَلَ ٱلسَّبُعُ، إِلاَّ مَا ذَكَّيْتُمْ، وَمَا ذُبِحَ عَلَى ٱلنُّصُبِ، وَأَنْ تَسْتَقْسِمُوا بِالأَزْلاَمِ. ذَالِكُمْ فِسْقٌ.﴾ المائدة ٣

«Prohibited to you are dead animals, blood, swine flesh, what has been dedicated to other than Allāh, and what has been killed by strangling or by a violent blow or by head-long fall or by gorging, and that from which a wild animal ate — except what you are able to slaughter (before its death), and those which are sacrificed on stone alters, and (also prohibited is) that you seek decision through divining arrows. (All of) this is grave disobedience.» [2]

Thus, if Allāh's name is not pronounced at the time of slaughtering because of ignorance or forgetting, this does not make the animal prohibited — unless it is dedicated to other than Allāh.

SUMMARY

From the above, we conclude that correct slaughtering should be

---

1 *Al-Anʿām* 6:145.

2 *Al-Māʾidah* 5:3.

performed as follows:

1. The animal should be laid down on its left side facing the *Qiblah*.

2. A sharp tool should be used in order to spill the blood and minimize the animal's pain.

3. Nails, teeth, or bones (of humans or animals) may not be used for slaughtering.

4. The throat and windpipe should be cut, and the blood should be poured out.

5. Only Allāh's name may be pronounced over a slaughtered animal. Pronouncing other names makes the slaughtered animal a grave disobedience dedicated to other than Allāh.

Dispensing of the *ʿAqīqah*'s Meat

DIVIDING THE MEAT

Making analogy with the *uḍḥiyah* (*ʿīd* sacrifice), some scholars recommend dividing a *ʿaqīqah* into three parts, eating one part, feeding the second, and giving the rest as charity. This has no authentic proof in the Sunnah.

Thus, it is left open for those offering *ʿaqīqah* to dispense of it in a way suitable to their condition and finances. They may keep it all, give it away, cook it and feed the people, and so on.

FEEDING

Many scholars recommend cooking the *ʿaqīqah*'s meat and inviting others to feast on it. This has been practiced by the Muslims since early times. Muʿāwiyah (🏵️) Bin Qurrah (🏵️) [1] reported:

---

1 Qurrah al-Muzanī was a *ṣaḥābī*, and his son Muʿāwiyah was a *tābiʿī*. Muʿāwiyah's son, Iyās grew up to become a brilliant judge.

> "When my son Iyās was born, I invited a number of the Prophet's (ﷺ) companions and fed them. They supplicated (for the boy) and I said, 'May Allāh bless your supplication. And I will now supplicate, so say *āmīn* to what I say.' Then I made a long supplication for him." [1]

There is no specific text in the Sunnah prescribing a feast for the ʿ*aqīqah*. However, there are general texts encouraging the Muslims to feed others. Since the ʿ*aqīqah* is slaughtered as a display of gratitude to Allāh, and since at least some of the meat will normally be given away, it is best to give it away in a cooked form. Ibn ul-Qayyim (رحمه الله) said:

> "It is recommended to cook it rather than give it away as raw meat ... thereby relieving the poor people and the neighbors from the need to cook; this is an act of added benevolence and an expression of gratitude (to Allāh) for this favor." [2]

However, some people are under the wrong impression that the purpose of the ʿ*aqīqah* is to invite people to the feast. They direct more concern to this than to the sacrifice itself, sometimes buying the meat instead of slaughtering. This is wrong, as it misses the basic idea behind the ʿ*aqīqah*, which is the sacrifice.

As for those who are invited to a ʿ*aqīqah* feast, it is recommended for them to attend, unless there are violations to Islām practiced by the attendees [3]. Ibn ʿUmar (رضي الله عنه) reported that Allāh's Messenger (ﷺ) said:

«إذا دعا أحدُكم أخاه فليجب، عرساً كان أو نحوه.»

---

1 Recorded by al-Bukhārī in *al-Adab ul-Mufrad* no. 1255. Verified to be authentic by al-Albānī (*Ṣaḥīḥ ul-Adab il-Mufrad*).

2 *Tuḥfat ul-Mawdūd* 49-50.

3 For a detailed discussion of the ettiquettes required from the host and gusests in regard to a *walīmah* or other feasts, the reader is referred to the Authors, "The Quest for Love and Mercy".

> **‹When one of you invites his brother, he should respond to his invitation — whether it is for a wedding feast or something similar.›** [1]

Wisdom Behind the *ʿAqīqah*

CHILD'S MORTGAGE

Central to understanding the wisdom behind the *ʿaqīqah* is the interpretation of "mortgage" in Samurah's (ﷺ) earlier *ḥadīth*:

«كل غلام رهينة بعقيقته، تُذبح عنه يومَ سابعه ويُسمّى فيه ويُحلَقُ رأسُه.»

> **‹Every child is mortgaged by its *ʿaqīqah*. It should be slaughtered for it on its seventh day, its (the child's) hair should be shaved, and it should be named.›** [2]

The *ʿulamāʾ* differ in interpreting "mortgage" in this *ḥadīth*. Imām Aḥmad (ﷺ) said:

> "The meaning of 'mortgage' in the *ḥadīth* is that the child is confined from interceding for its parents (on Judgment Day)." [3]

Ibn ul-Qayyim (ﷺ) strongly challenged this view, proposing a better and more reasonable understanding. He said:

> "There is a difference (among the scholars) in regard to the meaning of this "mortgage".

---

1 Recorded by al-Bukhārī, Muslim, and others.

2 Recorded by an-Nasāʾī, Abū Dāwūd, and others. Verified to be authentic by al-Albānī (*Ṣaḥīḥ ul-Jāmiʿ* no. 4541, and *Irwāʾ ul-Ghalīl* no. 1165).

3 Reported by al-Khallāl in *al-Jāmiʿ*.

To some of them, it means that the child will be prevented from interceding for its parents (on Judgment Day). This was said by ʿAṭā' and followed by Imām Aḥmad.

This opinion is clearly debatable, because a child's intercession for its parent has no priority over the opposite (i.e., a parent's intercession for a child). Intercession is not the purpose of being a parent. The same is true about all other relationships and lineages. Allāh (ﷻ) says:

﴿يَٰٓأَيُّهَا ٱلنَّاسُ ٱتَّقُواْ رَبَّكُمْ وَٱخْشَوْاْ يَوْمًا لَّا يَجْزِي وَالِدٌ عَن وَلَدِهِۦ وَلَا مَوْلُودٌ هُوَ جَازٍ عَن وَالِدِهِۦ شَيْـًٔا﴾ لقمان ٣٣

«O people, revere your Lord, and fear a Day when no parent will avail his child, nor will a child avail his parent at all.» [1]

... Thus, no one will intercede for anyone on Judgment Day except after Allāh's permission and consent. And His (ﷻ) permission depends on (a) the deeds of the person who is interceded for — in terms of belief (in Allāh) and purity (from *shirk*), and (b) the intercessor's position and closeness to Allāh. This closeness is not earned by lineage or parenthood or ancestry. Even for the Master of intercessors (Muḥammad ﷺ), the one of highest status before Allāh (ﷻ), he told his uncle and aunt and daughter:

«لا أغني عنكم (لا أملك لكم) من الله شيئاً.»

‹I cannot suffice (or protect) you in any way from Allāh.› [2]

The Prophet (ﷺ) also said in regard to his major

1 *Luqmān* 31:33.

2 Recorded by al-Bukhārī, Muslim, and others from Abū Hurayrah (رضي الله عنه).

intercession (on Judgment Day), when he will prostrate before his Lord:

«فيَحُدُّ لي حداً، فأُخرجهم من النار وأدخلهم الجنة.»

‹He will permit me a specific number (of people) that I will take out from the Fire and admit into *Jannah*.› [1]

Thus, his intercession will be for a specific number of people that Allāh will specify for him, and his intercession will not go past them.

How then can one say that a child will intercede for its parent, and that if the parent did not offer *ʿaqīqah* for it, the child will be prevented from interceding?

Furthermore, you do not say for a person who does not intercede for others that he is mortgaged. There is nothing in this term (mortgage) supporting this usage. Allāh (ﷻ) only indicates that a person will be mortgaged by what he earned. Allāh (ﷻ) says:

﴿كُلُّ نَفْسٍ بِمَا كَسَبَتْ رَهِينَةٌ.﴾ المدثر ٣٨

«Every soul will be retained (or mortgaged) for what it had earned (in its first life).» [2]

And He (ﷻ) says:

﴿أُوْلَٰئِكَ ٱلَّذِينَ أُبْسِلُواْ بِمَا كَسَبُواْ.﴾ الأنعام ٧٠

«Those are the ones who are put into captivity (in the Fire) because of what they had earned.» [3]

A mortgaged person is imprisoned because of an act that he or someone else did …

---

1 Recorded by al-Bukhārī, Muslim, and others from Anas and Abū Hurayrah (ﷺ).

2 *Al-Muddath-thir* 74:38.

3 *Al-Anʿām* 6:70.

Allāh has made the child's sacrifice a means of releasing it from confinement with the devil that attaches himself to it from the moment that it enters into this world, stinging it in its side.

The *ʿaqīqah* then provides for a person ransom and redemption from Satan's confinement and imprisonment, and from hindering his pursuance of deeds that would benefit him in his final abode.

Thus, it is as if a person is confined because Satan had slain him with the knife that he uses on his allies and followers. Having made an oath to his Lord that he would destroy all but a few of Ādam's progeny, he closely watches for the emergence of a child into this life. As soon as it emerges, he rushes to it, embraces it, and ascertains that it remains in his fist and under his confinement, and from his allies and party. He is most keen to accomplish this, and thus, the majority of newborns are of his followers and belong to his party …

Allāh has thus legislated for the parents a means of releasing their child from Satan's confinement in the form of a redeeming slaughter. If this slaughter is not performed for the child, the child remains mortgaged by it. This is the meaning of the Prophet's (ﷺ) (above) *ḥadīth* in which he commanded that blood be poured on its behalf to save it from being mortgaged.

Had the mortgage been applicable to the parents, the Prophet (ﷺ) would have said, "Pour blood for YOURSELVES so that you would deserve your child's intercession."

The Prophet (ﷺ) commanded that the apparent harm be removed from the child, and that blood be poured to remove the hidden harm because of its mortgage. This indicates then that the intention is to cleanse the newborn from both forms of harm: the apparent and the hidden — and Allāh knows best." [1]

1 *Tuḥfat ul-Mawdūd* pp. 48-49.

INSIGHTS INTO THE 'AQĪQAH'S WISDOM

The scholars have given insights into the wisdom behind the legislation of 'aqīqah in Islām. In the following, we present the most important of those as proposed by Ibn ul-Qayyim (رحمه الله) [1], Waliyy Ullāh id-Dahlawī (رحمه الله) [2], and others:

1. The 'aqīqah is a considerate way of declaring the birth and lineage of the newborn. It is far better than announcing the birth in the marketplaces, newspapers, media, etc.

2. The 'aqīqah provides a way of feeding the needy Muslims. This makes it one of the important Islāmic means of promoting generosity, suppressing stinginess, and incurring multiple rewards.

3. The 'aqīqah is a declaration of happiness for the birth of a new Muslim, adding to the number of Muslims that will be displayed by the Prophet (ﷺ) on the Day of Resurrection.

4. The 'aqīqah strengthens the ties among the Muslims because they come together to feast and celebrate the birth of the newborn.

5. The 'aqīqah is an act that distinguishes the Muslims from the Jāhilī pagans who used to rub the child's head with animal blood, or the Christians who baptize their children with water.

6. The 'aqīqah is a sacrificial act that reminds of Ibrāhīm's (ﷺ) sacrifice and the ram that Allāh (ﷻ) sent down as a ransom for Ibrāhīm's son Ismā'īl (ﷺ). It strengthens the Muslims' attachment to their righteous ancestors and encourages them to be consistent in doing good like those ancestors did.

7. The 'aqīqah is an act of obedience and benevolence that, with Allāh's permission, benefits the child and helps protect it from harm and evil.

---

1   In Tuḥfat ul-Mawdūd.

2   In Ḥujjat Ullāh il-Bālighah.

8. The ʿ*aqīqah* ransoms the child and ends its mortgage. It is quite possible, within Allāh's wisdom and decree, that He (ﷻ) makes the ʿ*aqīqah* a cause for good health, security and upbringing of the child, and for protecting it from Satan throughout its life, making each part of the ʿ*aqīqah* a ransom for the corresponding part of the child.

Smearing Blood on a Newborn's Head?

An old *Jāhilī* practice, subsequently abolished by Islām, was to smear a newborn's head with the ʿ*aqīqah*'s blood. Buraydah (رضي الله عنه) reported:

"كنا في الجاهلية إذا ولد لأحدنا غلامٌ ذبح شاةً ولطخ رأسَه بدمها.
فلما جاء الله بالإسلام كنا نذبح شاةً ونحلق رأسه ونلطخه بزعفران."

"When a child was born to one of us during *Jāhiliyyah*, he would slaughter a goat and smear its blood over the child's head. After Allāh brought Islām, we (were commanded to) slaughter the goat, shave the baby's head, and cover it with saffron." [1]

ʿAbd al-Muzanī (رضي الله عنه) reported that the Prophet (ﷺ) said:

«يُعقُّ عن الغلام ولا يُمسُّ رأسُه بدم.»

‹A ʿ*aqīqah* is to be slaughtered for a newborn. But its head should not be touched with blood.› [2]

And ʿĀʾishah (رضي الله عنها) reported:

---

1 Recorded by Abū Dāwūd, al-Ḥākim, and others. Verified to be authentic by al-Albānī (*aṣ-Ṣaḥīḥah* no. 2452 and *Irwāʾ ul-Ghalīl* no. 1172).

2 Recorded by Ibn Mājah, aṭ-Ṭabarānī (in *al-Awsaṭ*), and aṭ-Ṭaḥāwī. Verified to be authentic by al-Albānī (*aṣ-Ṣaḥīḥah* no. 1996 & 2452, *Irwāʾ ul-Ghalīl* vol. 4, p.389, and *Ṣaḥīḥ ul-Jāmiʿ* no. 8108).

"كان أهلُ الجاهلية يجعلون قُطنةً في دم العقيقةِ ويُحيلونه على رأس الصبيِّ فأمر رسول اللّه أن يُجعل مكان الدم خلوقاً."

> "During *Jāhiliyyah*, the people would soak a piece of cotton in the *'aqīqah*'s blood and pass it over the newborn's head. (After Islām,) Allāh's Messenger (ﷺ) commanded that the blood be substituted with saffron perfume." [1]

Question and Answers

In this section, we cite answers to questions posed to prominent contemporary Muslim *'ulamā'*.

Delaying the *'Aqīqah* for Financial Reasons

Question: When a man got a child, he did not have money to offer *'aqīqah*. After one year or more, he had the money. Should he slaughter the *'aqīqah* then, or does the obligation cease for him?

Answer: It is recommended for him to offer the *'aqīqah* whenever it becomes possible for him to do so — even after one year or more.

Indeed, from Allāh is the facility. And prayers and peace be upon our Prophet Muḥammad (ﷺ) and his family and companions.

Signed by:
The Permanent Committee for Scholarly Research & Fatwā
Attendees:
'Abd ul-'Azīz Bin Bāz (President)
'Abd ur-Razzāq 'Afīfī (Deputy)
'Abdullāh Bin Ghadayān (Member)
'Abdullāh Bin Qa'ūd (Member)

1 Recorded by Ibn Ḥibbān, Abū Ya'lā, and al-Bayhaqī. Verified to be authentic by al-Albānī (*aṣ-Ṣaḥīḥah* no. 2452 and *Irwā' ul-Ghalīl* vol. 4, p. 389).

Buying Meat Instead of Slaughtering

Question: Is it permissible to buy a number of kilograms of meat instead of slaughtering a *ʿaqīqah*?

Answer: No, it is not permissible. A goat should be slaughtered for a female baby and two goats for a male baby.

Indeed, from Allāh is the facility. And prayers and peace be upon our Prophet Muḥammad (ﷺ) and his family and companions.

Signed by:
The Permanent Committee for Scholarly Research & Fatwā
Attendees:
ʿAbd ul-ʿAzīz Bin Bāz (President)
ʿAbd ur-Razzāq ʿAfīfī (Deputy)
ʿAbdullāh Bin Qaʿūd (Member)

ʿAqīqah for a Short-Lived Baby

Question: A baby was born alive after a six-month term, but died the same day. Is it required to offer *ʿaqīqah* for it?

Answer: It is recommended to slaughter *ʿaqīqah* for this baby even though it died right after birth. The *ʿaqīqah* should be slaughtered on the seventh day of birth, and the (dead) baby should be named. This is based on what is recorded by Aḥmad, al-Bukhārī, and the Compilers of the *Sunan* [1] from Salmān Bin ʿĀmir that the Prophet (ﷺ) said:

«معَ الغلامِ عقيقة، فأَهْرِيقوا عنهُ دماً، وأميطوا عنه الأذى.»

‹A *ʿaqīqah* is prescribed for every child. Thus shed blood on its behalf, and remove the harm off it.› [2]

This ruling is also based on what was reported by al-Ḥasan from Samurah (ؓ) that the Prophet (ﷺ) said:

---

1 This refers to Abū Dāwūd, an-Nasāʾī, at-Tirmithī, and Ibn Mājah.

2 Recorded by at-Tirmithī, an-Nasāʾī, and others. Verified to be authentic by al-Albānī (*Ṣaḥīḥ ul-Jāmiʿ* no. 4253 & 5877, and *Irwāʾ ul-Ghalīl* no. 1171).

«كل غلام رهينة بعقيقته، تُذبح عنه يومَ سابعه ويُسمّى ويُحلَق.»

‹Every child is mortgaged [1] by its ʿaqīqah. It should be slaughtered for it on the seventh day, its hair should be shaved, and it should be named.›

This is recorded by Aḥmad and the Compilers of the *Sunan*, and was verified by at-Tirmi<u>th</u>ī to be authentic.

The *ʿaqīqah* is two goats for a boy and one goat for a girl …

Indeed, from Allāh is the facility. And prayers and peace be upon our Prophet Muḥammad (ﷺ) and his family and companions.

Signed by:
The Permanent Committee for Scholarly Research & Fatwā
Attendees:
ʿAbd ul-ʿAzīz Bin Bāz (President)
ʿAbd ur-Razzāq ʿAfifī (Deputy)
ʿAbdullāh Bin Ghadayān (Member)
ʿAbdullāh Bin Qaʿūd (Member)

Question: Is it required to offer *ʿaqīqah* for a baby who dies before the seventh day?

Answer: If a baby dies before the seventh day, its *ʿaqīqah* should still be slaughtered on the seventh. The baby's death before the seventh does not prevent slaughtering it on the seventh. As for the *sharʿī* evidences specifying the time for slaughtering the *ʿaqīqah*, we do not find any of them indicating that it drops for a baby who dies before the seventh …

Indeed, from Allāh is the facility. And prayers and peace be upon our Prophet Muḥammad (ﷺ) and his family and companions.

Signed by:
The Permanent Committee for Scholarly Research & Fatwā
Attendees:
ʿAbd ur-Razzāq ʿAfifī (Deputy)

---

1 The meaning of this "mortgage" is discussed in depth near the end of this chapter.

'Abdullāh Bin Ghadayān (Member)
'Abdullāh Bin Manī' (Member)

'Aqīqah for a Miscarried Fetus?

Question: Is the *'aqīqah* required for a miscarried fetus whose gender is clear?

Answer: The *'aqīqah* is not required for a miscarried fetus, even if its gender is clear — if it is dropped before life is blown into it. The reason for this is that in this case it cannot be called a baby or a newborn …

Indeed, from Allāh is the facility. And prayers and peace be upon our Prophet Muḥammad (ﷺ) and his family and companions.

Signed by:
The Permanent Committee for Scholarly Research & Fatwā
Attendees:
'Abd ul-'Azīz Bin Bāz (President)
'Abd ur-Razzāq 'Afifī (Deputy)
'Abdullāh Bin Ghadayān (Member)

Question: Is the *'aqīqah* required for three miscarried male fetuses, the first dropped after four months less three days, the second dropped after three months and seventeen days, and the third dropped after two months?

Answer: The *'aqīqah* is recommended for a miscarried fetus if it is dropped after life has been blown into it, which occurs after four months of pregnancy. Therefore, in your case, the *'aqīqah* in not to be offered for any of the three fetuses.

Signed by:
The Permanent Committee for Scholarly Research & Fatwā

Storing the *'Aqīqah*'s Meat

Question: Is it permissible to store the *'aqīqah*'s meat in the freezer?

Answer: It is recommended to eat some of the *ʿaqīqah*'s meat, give away some, and feed some to the relatives and neighbors … And there is no specified time for distributing the meat, but it was left open …

Signed by:
ʿAbd ul-ʿAzīz Bin Bāz

CHAPTER 5

CIRCUMCISION

Overview

Origin of Circumcision

Circumcision is an act of cleanliness that was first ordained by Allāh (ﷻ) for His prophet Ibrāhīm (عليه السلام). Subsequently, it became a consistent practice among Ibrāhīm's descendants and followers, including the Jews and Muslims, until our time.

Abū Hurayrah (رضي الله عنه) reported that Allāh's Messenger (ﷺ) said:

«كان أولُ من ضيَّفَ الضَّيفَ إبراهيمَ، وهو أولُ من ٱختتنَ على رأسِ ثمانينَ سنةً، واختتنَ بالقَدُّوم.»

‹Ibrāhīm (عليه السلام) was the first man to host guests. He was also the first man to be circumcised — at the age of eighty. And he was circumcised with an axe.› [1]

Description of the Process

The male sexual organ is called "penis". The penis consists of a head called "glans", and a shaft. The shaft is covered with skin that ends at the base of the glans in a junction called the "frenar band". At birth, the glans is encased in a skin covering called the "foreskin", or "prepuce", which is a continuation of the shaft's skin. The "frenulum", or "frenum", is a connecting mucous membrane on the underside of the penis, similar to that beneath the tongue.

Circumcision is a minor surgery that removes the foreskin, resulting

---

1 Recorded by Ibn ʿAsākir. Verified to be authentic by al-Albānī (*aṣ-Ṣaḥīḥah* no. 725).

in complete exposure of the glans. This surgery includes:

1. Cutting around the frenar band and removing the foreskin.

2. Splitting the frenum and pushing it back until the crown of flesh is fully uncovered.

3. Drawing the blood out of the wound and surrounding areas.

4. Putting ointment, bandages, and gauze pads to help stop the bleeding and heal the wound properly.

The following diagram [1] shows a comparison between an uncircumcised and a circumcised penis.

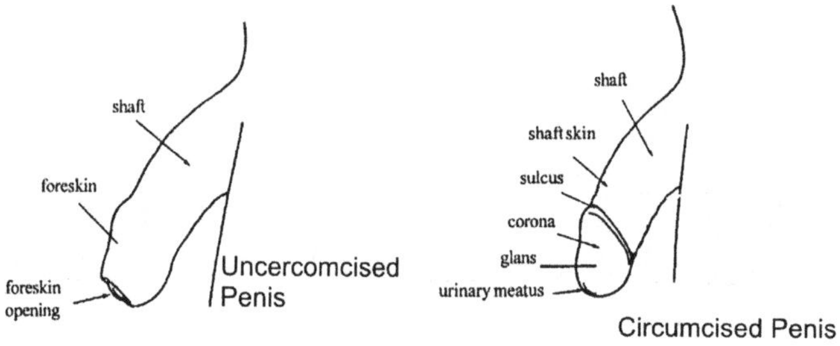

Circumcision in the Islāmic Texts

ONE OF THE CHARACTERISTICS OF *FIṬRAH*

There are a number of practices that are labeled as "Characteristics of *Fiṭrah*" because they conform with the true, pure, and unadulterated human nature. Allāh's Messenger (ﷺ) names circumcision as one of these characteristics.

Abū Hurayrah (رضي الله عنه) reported that Allāh's Messenger (ﷺ) said:

«الفطرة خمس: الختان، والاستحداد، وقص

1 Courtesy of www.cirp.org.

الشارب، وتقليم الأظافر، ونتف الإبط. »

‹There are five qualities of *fiṭrah*: circumcision, shaving the pubic hair, trimming the mustache, clipping the nails, and plucking the armpit hair.› [1]

Commenting on this *ḥadīth*, Abū Bakr Bin al-ʿArabī (رحمه الله) said:

"I view that all five qualities mentioned in this *ḥadīth* are mandatory, because anyone who neglects them would not appear like a human being — much less a Muslim." [2]

In another narration, the Prophet (ﷺ) named ten or eleven qualities of *fiṭrah*. ʿĀʾishah (رضي الله عنها) reported that Allāh's Messenger (ﷺ) said:

«عشر من الفطرة: قص الشارب، وإعفاء اللحية، والسِّواك،
والمضمضة واستنشاق الماء، وقص الأظافر وغسل البراجم،
ونتف الإبط، وحلق العانة، وانتقاص الماء، والاختتان. »

‹There are ten qualities of *fiṭrah*: trimming the mustache, sparing the beard, *siwāk* (brushing the teeth), inhaling water (to clean the nose) and rinsing the mouth, clipping the nails, washing the finger knuckles, plucking the armpit hair, shaving the pubic hair, washing the private parts with water, and circumcision.› [3]

---

1   Recorded by al-Bukhārī, Muslim, and others.

2   Reported by Ibn Ḥajar in *Fatḥ ul-Bārī* 10:417.

3   A combined report recorded by Muslim, Abū Dāwūd, Aḥmad, Ibn Abī Shaybah, and others (*Ṣaḥīḥ ul-Jāmiʿ* no. 2222). A similar *ḥadīth* is recorded by Aḥmad, Ibn Mājah, and Abū Dāwūd from ʿAmmār (رضي الله عنه), and is verified to be *ḥasan* by al-Albānī (*Ṣaḥīḥ ul-Jāmiʿ* no. 5906).

A Prophetic Command

Allāh's Messenger (ﷺ) commanded a new Muslim to get circumcised.

Kulayb al-Juhanī (ﷺ) reported that he came to the Prophet (ﷺ) and told him that he had embraced Islām. The Prophet (ﷺ) then commanded him:

«ألق عنك شعرَ الكُفرِ واْختَتِن.»

‹Shave off the hair of *kufr*, and get circumcised.› [1]

A Practice of the Father of Prophets

We have seen earlier that circumcision was first performed by Ibrāhīm (ﷺ) in fulfillment of a command by Allāh (ﷻ).

Similar to the earlier narration, Abū Hurayrah (ﷺ) reported that Allāh's Messenger (ﷺ) said:

«اختتن إبراهيمُ وهو ابنُ ثمانينَ سنةً بالقَدُّم.»

‹Ibrāhīm (ﷺ) was circumcized with an axe when he was eighty years old.› [2]

Al-Marwazī reported that Imām Aḥmad (ﷺ) was asked about this and he explained:

"He (Ibrāhīm) used the (sharp) edge of the axe." [3]

A Practice of the *Ṣaḥābah*

Circumcision was practiced by the *ṣaḥābah* — even though they often delayed it until the child was older. Ibn ʿAbbās (ﷺ) was asked, "How old were you when Allāh's Messenger (ﷺ) passed away?" He replied:

---

1 Recorded by Abū Dāwūd and Aḥmad. Verified to be *ḥasan* by al-Albānī (*Ṣaḥīḥ ul-Jāmiʿ* no. 1251 and *Irwāʾ ul-Ghalīl* no. 79).

2 Recorded by al-Bukhārī, Muslim, and others.

3 *Tuḥfat ul-Mawdūd* p. 95.

"أنا يومئذٍ مختون. وكانوا لا يختِنون الرجلَ حتى يُدرك."

"I was then circumcised. And they used not to circumcise a male until he reaches the age of discernment." [1]

Ruling

Ibn ul-Qayyim's Reasoning

In what follows, we summarize the most important reasons mentioned by Ibn ul-Qayyim (ﷺ) [2] as proof that circumcision is obligatory:

1. Allāh commanded the Prophet Muḥammad (ﷺ) to follow the pure creed of Ibrāhīm [3], and circumcision is a part of it.

2. Allāh's Messenger (ﷺ) commanded Kulayb al-Juhanī to get circumcised when he embraced Islām.

3. Circumcision is one of the clear and apparent practices that distinguish between Muslims and *kāfir*s.

4. Circumcision causes pain and may result in complications and serious repercussions. This would not be allowed for the sake of a noncompulsory act.

5. Islām prohibits exposing one's *'awrah*, or looking at someone else's *'awrah* or touching it without a necessity. Circumcision involves committing these three prohibitions (exposing the *'awrah*, looking at it, and touching it). This would not be possible unless circumcision is obligatory.

6. Islām prohibits cutting any part of a human body unless Allāh

---

1 Recorded by al-Bukhārī, Aḥmad, and others.

2 In *Tuḥfat ul-Mawdūd* pp. 100-110.

3 As in *an-Naḥl* 16:123.

commands and ordains it. Circumcision must then be obligatory to make it possible for the person performing it to cut the foreskin.

7. An uncircumcised person is liable to impurity and uncleanliness because of the remains of urine underneath his foreskin. This could nullify his prayer and other acts of worship.

Our Conclusion

We saw in the earlier texts that Ibrāhīm (ﷺ) started the *sunnah* of circumcision, that the Prophet (ﷺ) commanded a new Muslim to get circumcised, and that circumcision has been a consistent practice of Muslims from the time of the *ṣaḥābah*.

Based on this, in addition to Ibn ul-Qayyim's above reasoning, we accept the position that circumcision is obligatory. Al-Albānī (رحمه الله) said:

> "As for the ruling of circumcision, the correct opinion according to us is that it is obligatory. This is the opinion of the majority of *'ulamā'*, such as Mālik, Ash-Shāfi'ī, and Aḥmad. Ibn ul-Qayyim took this position as well and presented fifteen different reasons to support it. Even though those reasons cannot individually prove this position, there is no doubt that they can collectively do so." [1]

Date of Performing Circumcision

The Earlier the Better

Being obligatory, circumcision should be performed at the earliest possible date. Thus, it is permissible to circumcise a male baby during his first few days, especially since this has a number of benefits:

1. It would make it easier for the child to heal quickly.

---

1 *Tamām ul-Minnah* p. 69.

2. The child would not feel the effect of pain at this early age.

3. Circumcision requires exposing the private parts, which makes it more disliked to do so for an older child than a newborn.

Narrations Specifying the Seventh

Some people believe that circumcision should be performed on the seventh day. However, this is only based on weak narrations that cannot hold as acceptable evidence.

The first narration, from Jābir (ﷺ), says:

> "Allāh's Messenger (ﷺ) offered *ʿaqīqah* for al-Ḥasan and al-Ḥusayn and circumcised them on the seventh day (from birth)." [1]

Note that the first part of this narration is true as we have shown in the discussion of *ʿaqīqah*.

The second narration, from Ibn ʿAbbās (ﷺ), says:

> "There are seven practices that are part of the Sunnah for a male baby on the seventh day: he should be named … and circumcised … " [2]

Some *ʿulamāʾ*, such as Imām Mālik (ﷺ), dislike performing the circumcision on the seventh day because this resembles the Jews' practice. [3]

Imām Aḥmad (ﷺ) said:

> "Performing circumcision on the seventh day is permissible. Al-Ḥasan (al-Baṣrī) disliked it only for fear of resembling the Jews. But this is not apparent …

1 Recorded by aṭ-Ṭabarānī (in *aṣ-Ṣaghīr*), Ibn ʿAdiyy, and others. Verified to be weak by al-Albānī (*Tamām ul-Minnah* p. 68).

2 Recorded by aṭ-Ṭabarānī (in *al-Awsaṭ*) and verified to be weak by al-Albānī (*Tamām ul-Minnah* p. 68).

3 Ibn Taymiyyah's *Majmūʿ ul-Fatāwī* 21:113.

> Wahab Bin Munabbih was asked about this, and he said, 'It is recommended to do it on the seventh day because it is easier for the baby. A baby is born with numbness in all of its body, and cannot feel pain for seven days. If it is not circumcised by then (the seventh), let him grow stronger before you do it.'" [1]

We conclude from the above that the seventh day has no special significance in this case. Circumcision may be performed on, before, or after the seventh, based on the parents' convenience and the child's health.

DELAYING CIRCUMCISION UNTIL THE AGE OF DISCERNMENT

We have seen in Ibn 'Abbās's (﷛) earlier report that often the *ṣaḥābah* would not circumcise their children until they reached the age of discernment, which is normally past seven years.

This practice did not necessarily rely on a command from the Prophet (ﷺ). It is very likely that they delayed the circumcision until the child was stronger and healthier, rather than make him liable to dangerous or fatal infections in his first days, especially with the limited hygienic and medical conditions in those days.

Al-Māwardī (﷛) said:

> "Circumcision has two dates: a date of obligation and a date of recommendation. The date of obligation is the attainment of puberty. And the date of recommendation is on the seventh day after birth. One is urged not to postpone it beyond the recommended date without an excuse." [2]

NEW MUSLIMS

When an uncircumcised man embraces Islām, he should get circumcised as early as possible. This was the case with Kulayb al-

---

1 *Tuḥfat ul-Mawdūd* p. 112.

2 Reported by Ibn Ḥajar in *Fatḥ ul-Bārī* 10:342.

Juhanī in the *ḥadīth* cited earlier.

Benefits and Wisdom

Circumcision is a means of completing and perfecting the *fiṭrah* upon which Allāh (ﷻ) created the people. It is done by command from Allāh and guidance from His messengers. Thus, it establishes a way of conforming with Allāh's legislations, even in the private genital area, which is the most personal part of a human's body. It shows submission to Allāh's command and willingness to live by His laws apparently and secretly.

Ibn ul-Qayyim said:

> "Circumcision is one of the beauties of the legislations that Allāh ordained for His servants. It completes the *fiṭrah* upon which He created them … Circumcision was initially ordained to complete the Pure Religion. Allāh made a covenant with Ibrāhīm, promising to make him a leader for the people and a father of many nations. He promised to raise the prophets and kings from his seed and to multiply his progeny. He told him that the sign to this covenant is that they will circumcise every newborn among them … Circumcision is then a sign of entering into the religion of Ibrāhīm … For those with the Pure religion, circumcision is similar to baptism and dyeing for the worshipers of the cross …
>
> Allāh's "dye" is the Pure Religion because it dyes the hearts with knowing Him, loving Him, sincerity to Him, and worshiping Him alone without partners. It also dyes the bodies with the qualities of *fiṭrah*, such as circumcision, shaving the pubic hair, trimming the mustache, clipping the nails, plucking the armpit hair, rinsing the mouth, inhaling water (to clean the nose), *siwāk* (brushing the teeth), and washing the private parts. Allāh's *fiṭrah* then appears in the hearts and

bodies of the followers of the Pure Religion." [1]

Circumcision is an important hygienic method of maintaining the cleanliness of male genitals by eliminating an important hideout for filth and germs. Ibn ul-Qayyim (ﷺ) said:

> "What adornment is better than removing excessive foreskin, pubic hair, armpit hair, mustache hair, and nails? Indeed, Satan likes to hide, habituate, and dwell in these things … The uncircumcised foreskin is uglier than excessively long nails, mustaches, or pubic hair …" [2]

Circumcision of Females

Description

Female circumcision is largely similar to male circumcision, but is applied to the clitoris instead of the penis. Just like the foreskin surrounding the glans, the clitoris is surrounded by a small hood connected to two flaps of skin called the "labia minora".

Female circumcision involves removing part or all of the clitoral hood and the labia minora.

Excessive Circumcision

Pharaonic circumcision in the Nile Valley is as old as recorded history, and continues to be practiced in Sudan, Egypt, and other African countries. Because of its clearly brutal and destructive nature, it is often called "female genital mutilation".

Pharaonic circumcision involves excision of the clitoris, the labia minora and the inner, fleshy layers of the labia majora. The remaining outer edges of the labia majora are then brought together so that when the wound has healed they are fused so as to leave only a pinhole-

---

1 *Tuḥfat ul-Mawdūd* pp. 113-114.

2 *Tuḥfat ul-Mawdūd* p. 115.

sized opening. Urination and menstruation must thereafter be accomplished through this remaining pinhole-sized aperture.

FEMALE CIRCUMCISION IN ISLĀMIC TEXTS

There is a popular assumption that female circumcision has no place in Islām. This is not true, because female circumcision was practiced during the Prophet's (صلى الله عليه وسلم) time and he approved it. It continued to be practiced by the *ṣaḥābah* and *salaf* after him.

Anas (رضي الله عنه) reported that Allāh's Messenger (صلى الله عليه وسلم) said to a woman in al-Madīnah who circumcised women:

$$\text{«إِذَا خَفَضْتِ فَأَشِمِّي وَلَا تُنْهِكِي، فَإِنَّهُ أَنْضَرُ (أَسْرَى) لِلْوَجْهِ وَأَحْظَى (أَحَبُّ) لِلزَّوْجِ.»}$$

‹When you trim (the skin surrounding the clitoris), do it slightly and not excessively. This would bring beauty to the woman's face and please her husband.› [1]

'Ā'ishah (رضي الله عنها) reported that Allāh's Messenger (صلى الله عليه وسلم) said:

$$\text{«إِذَا ٱلْتَقَى ٱلْخِتَانَانِ وَجَبَ ٱلْغُسْلُ.»}$$

‹When the two locations of circumcision (of man and woman) meet, *ghusl* [2] becomes obligatory.› [3]

Similarly, 'Ā'ishah (رضي الله عنها) reported that Allāh's Messenger (صلى الله عليه وسلم) said:

$$\text{«إِذَا جَلَسَ بَيْنَ شُعَبِهَا ٱلْأَرْبَعِ، وَمَسَّ ٱلْخِتَانُ ٱلْخِتَانَ، فَقَدْ وَجَبَ ٱلْغُسْلُ.»}$$

‹Once he (the man) sits between her (the woman's)

---

1 Recorded by al-Ḥākim, aṭ-Ṭabarānī (in *al-Awsaṭ*) and others from Anas and others. Verified to be authentic by al-Albānī (*aṣ-Ṣaḥīḥah* no. 722).

2 *Ghusl* is a ritual bath that is required after intercourse. For a full discussion of *ghusl*, the reader is referred to the Author's, "Closer than a Garment".

3 Recorded by Muslim, Aḥmad, and others.

> **four limbs and the (man's) location of circumcision touches the (woman's) location of circumcision, the *ghusl* becomes compulsory.›** [1]

And in a third narration, 'Ā'ishah (ﷺ) reported that Allāh's Messenger (ﷺ) said:

«إذا جاوز الختانُ الختانَ وجبَ الغسل.»

> **‹When the (man's) location of circumcision enters past the (woman's) location of circumcision, *ghusl* becomes obligatory.›** [2]

In the above narrations, the Prophet (ﷺ) describes both the male and female sex organs as "*khitān*", which means, "location of circumcision". This again indicates that female circumcision was a known and acceptable practice. Commenting on this, Imām Aḥmad (ﷺ) said:

> "This provides evidence that women used to be circumcised." [3]

RULING

From the above, we see that female circumcision is voluntary. It is recommended for women with excessive labia growth, which is more common among women in warm climates.

Violations and Innovations

There are many violations and innovations relating to circumcision. In what follows we list a few of them:

---

1 Recorded by al-Bukhārī, Muslim, and others.

2 Recorded by at-Tirmiḏhī, Ibn Mājah, and Aḥmad. Verified to be authentic by al-Albānī (*al-Mishkāt* no. 442 & *Irwā'ul-Ghalīl* no. 80).

3 *Tuḥfat ul-Mawdūd* p. 117.

1. For males: Removing, in addition to the foreskin, some of the shaft's skin, leading to great pain and serious harm to the child.

2. For females: Excessive removal of the labia or other genital parts, as in the case of Pharaonic circumcision.

3. Establishing a celebration for the occasion of circumcision in which animals are slaughtered, food is served, congratulations are conferred, money and gifts are given, and so on.

CHAPTER 6

OTHER NEWBORN *SUNNAHS*

There are some other *sunnahs* relevant to a newborn during its first few days of life. In this chapter, we discuss the most common of them.

Taḥnīk

DEFINITION

Taḥnīk is to chew some food and then insert it into a baby's mouth [1]. Usually, the food is dates, and is rubbed against the baby's *ḥanak* (upper jaw or palate) so that the baby would suck on it or eat it. Some of the wisdom behind this practice is discussed below.

AUTHENTIC REPORTS

There are several authentic reports of the Prophet (ﷺ) performing *taḥnīk* for newborns. For example, Anas (ﷺ) and Sahl Bin Saʻd (ﷺ) reported:

"كان النبيُّ يُؤتى بالصِبيانِ فيُبرِّك عليهم ويُحنِّكُهم."

> "Newborns were occasionally brought to Allāh's Messenger (ﷺ). He would invoke Allāh's blessings over them and perform *taḥnīk* for them." [2]

Anas (ﷺ) also reported that when his mother, Umm Sulaym, gave birth to his younger brother, ʻAbdullāh, she told him to take him to the Prophet (ﷺ) with some dates. The Prophet (ﷺ) took some of the

---

1 *Lisān ul-ʻArab.*

2 Recorded by al-Bukhārī and Muslim.

dates, chewed on them, mixing them with his saliva, opened the baby's mouth, and rubbed the chewed dates inside his mouth. The baby started hungrily sucking the sweetness of the dates together with Allāh's Messenger's (ﷺ) saliva. Thus the first thing to enter the baby's stomach was the saliva of Allāh's Messenger (ﷺ). The Prophet (ﷺ) then said:

«انظروا إلى حب الأنصار التمر.» أو «أبت الأنصارُ إلاّ حبَّ التمر.»

‹Watch how the *Anṣār* love dates!› or **‹The *anṣār* refuse but to like dates.›** [1]

Abū Mūsā al-Ashʿarī (رضي الله عنه) reported:

"وُلد لي غلام، فأتيتُ به النبي، فسماه إبراهيم،
فحنّكه بتمرةٍ، ودعا له بالبركة، ودفعه إلي."

"A baby-boy was born for me. I took him to the Prophet (ﷺ) who named him Ibrāhīm, chewed on a date and made him suck it, invoked blessings for him, and then gave him back to me." [2]

And Asmā' Bint Abī Bakr (رضي الله عنها) reported:

"I conceived ʿAbdullāh Bin az-Zubayr (رضي الله عنه) in Makkah. I migrated to al-Madīnah near the end of my pregnancy and gave birth to ʿAbdullāḥ in Qubā' [3]. After the delivery, I took my baby to Allāh's Messenger (ﷺ) who put him on his lap, called for a date, chewed it, spit into the baby's mouth, rubbed the date inside his mouth, and supplicated and invoked blessings for him. Thus the first thing to enter ʿAbdullāḥ's body was the saliva of Allāh's Messenger (ﷺ). He was the first child born for the *muhājirūn* in al-Madīnah. And the Muslims were

1 Recorded by al-Bukhārī, Muslim, and others.

2 Recorded by al-Bukhārī, Muslim, and others.

3 A suburb of al-Madīnah.

extremely pleased with his birth because they were previously told the Jews had cast a spell on them so that they would not have any children." [1]

DISCUSSION AND RULING

Based on the above reports, an-Nawawī (⸪) concludes:

"Among the benefits in these narrations are the following:
1. The recommendation of performing *taḥnīk* for a newborn at birth. There is a consensus (among the *'ulamā'*) in this regard.
2. A righteous man or woman should perform the *taḥnīk* for the baby.
3. It is preferable to perform *taḥnīk* with dates, even though other foods will work." [2]

And al-'Aynī (⸪) said:

"The wisdom behind *taḥnīk* is the expectation that the baby would then attain *īmān* and its sweetness, because dates are the fruits of the tree that the Prophet (⸪) likened to a believer — especially if the person who performs *taḥnīk* is one of the virtuous people or righteous *'ulamā'*, so that his saliva will enter the child's stomach. Don't you see that when Allāh's Messenger (⸪) performed *taḥnīk* for 'Abdullāh Bin az-Zubayr, he ('Abdullāh) attained virtues and qualities of perfection beyond description? He was a reciter of the Qur'ān and a virtuous man in Islam and in sublime goodness — all by virtue of his (the Prophet's) blessed saliva." [3]

---

1   Recorded by al-Bukhārī, Muslim, and others.

2   *Sharḥ Muslim* 14:372.

3   *'Umdat ul-Qārī* 21:84.

However, al-Albānī (🙐) disapproved of performing *tahnīk* with any person's saliva after the Prophet (🙐). The Prophet's (🙐) saliva was absolutely blessed. Because of this, his companions used to compete over his spit, catching it with their hands, and rubbing it over their bodies. This merit does not apply to the saliva of any human after him. We never heard that the people brought their children for *tahnīk* to Abū Bakr or 'Umar, the best two men after the Prophet (🙐). How then can we recommend performing *tahnīk* with the saliva of lesser Muslims, regardless of how righteous they might be? [1]

Based on the above, we conclude the following:

1. It is recommended to perform *tahnīk* for a newborn soon after its birth.

2. *Tahnīk* should be performed with a date. The date may be softened with water or saliva so that the baby would be able to suck on it.

3. Introducing saliva into a baby's mouth with the belief that such an act imparts blessings to the baby has no evidence (except what was in the case of the Prophet 🙐) and should therefore be avoided.

Shaving the Head and Giving Charity

It is required to shave a newborn's head on the seventh day and give *ṣadaqah* equal to its hair's weight in silver. Allāh's Messenger (🙐) commanded his daughter Fāṭimah (🙐) to do this for her children al-Ḥasan and al-Ḥusayn (🙐).

AUTHENTIC NARRATIONS

Abū Rāfi' and 'Alī (🙐) reported that when Fāṭimah (🙐) gave birth to al-Ḥasan and, later on, al-Ḥusayn, Allāh's Messenger (🙐) told her:

---

1   Paraphrased from a discussion by al-Albānī in one of the tapes of *Silsilat ul-Hudā wan-Nūr*.

«يا فاطمةُ، ٱحلِقي رأسَه، وتصدقي بزنةِ شعره فضةً.»

‹O Fāṭimah, shave his head, and give charity equal to his hair's weight in silver.› [1]

Salmān Bin ʿĀmir aḍ-Ḍabbī reported that Allāh's Messenger (ﷺ) said:

«معَ الغلامِ عقيقة، فأَهْريقوا عنهُ دماً، وأميطوا عنه الأذى.»

‹A *ʿaqīqah* is prescribed for every child. So, shed blood on its behalf and remove the filth off it.› [2]

Commenting on this *ḥadīth*, al-Albānī (رحمه الله) said:

"Ibn Sīrīn said that **‹... Remove the harm off it›** refers to shaving the head. He indicated that this was his own understanding, not having an authentic report in this regard. Also, Abū Dāwūd narrated (no. 2840) with an authentic *isnād* that al-Ḥasan (al-Baṣrī) used to say that 'removing the filth' means 'shaving the head'. It possibly has another meaning, as mentioned by Abū Jaʿfar aṭ-Ṭaḥāwī, which is to refrain from smearing the newborn's head with blood, as was done during *Jāhiliyyah* times." [3]

Similarly, ʿAbdullāh Bin ʿAmr (رضي الله عنه) reported:

"أمر النبيُّ بتسميةِ المولودِ يومَ سابعِه،
ووضعِ الأذى عنهُ، والعقِّ."

"The Prophet (ﷺ) commanded us to name a newborn

---

1 Recorded by Aḥmad, al-Bayhaqī, and others. Verified to be *ḥasan* (good) by al-Albānī (*Irwāʾ ul-Ghalīl* no. 1175.

2 Recorded by at-Tirmi<u>th</u>ī, an-Nasāʾī, and others. Verified to be authentic by al-Albānī (*Ṣaḥīḥ ul-Jāmiʿ* no. 4253 & 5877, and *Irwāʾ ul-Ghalīl* no. 1171).

3 *Irwāʾul-Ghalīl* vol. 4, p. 400.

on its seventh day, as well as to remove the filth off it
and slaughter its *ʿaqīqah*." [1]

BOTH BOYS AND GIRLS SHOULD BE SHAVED

The obligation of shaving a newborn's head applies to both boys and
girls. There is no evidence for those who restrict the shaving to the
boys. Rather, the reasoning given in Salmān's *ḥadīth* (removing the
filthy hair) should hold for both genders. In addition, the Prophet (ﷺ)
gave a general rule, as is reported by 'Ā'ishah (﵂):

«إنّما النساء شقائقُ الرجال.»

‹Indeed, women are nothing but full sisters of
men.› [2]

DATE OF SHAVING

The above *ḥadīth*s indicate that, similar to the *ʿaqīqah*, shaving the
head should be done on the seventh day of birth.

THE WHOLE HEAD SHOULD BE SHAVED

When shaving a newborn's head, one should avoid *qazʿ*, which is to
shave part of the head and leave the rest unshaved.

Ibn 'Umar (﵂) reported that the Prophet (ﷺ) saw a boy with part
of his head shaved and the other part unshaved. He (ﷺ) prohibited
doing this and said:

«احلقوه كلَّه أو اتركوهُ كُلَّه.»

‹Shave it all or spare it all.› [3]

---

1   Recorded by at-Tirmithī and Ibn Abī Shaybah. Verified to be *ḥasan* by al-Albānī
    (*Ṣaḥīḥ at-Tirmithī* no. 2269).

2   Recorded by Abū Dāwūd, ad-Dārimī, and others. Verified to be authentic by al-
    Albānī (*aṣ-Ṣaḥīḥah* vol. 1 p. 347).

3   Recorded by Abū Dāwūd, an-Nasā'ī, and others. Verified to be authentic by al-

Ibn ʿUmar (ﷺ) similarly reported:

"نهى رسول الله عن القزع: أن يُحلَقَ من رأس الصبي مكانٌ ويُترك مكان."

"Allāh's Messenger (ﷺ) prohibited *qazʿ*, which is shaving part of a boy's head and sparing the rest part." [1]

Ibn Ḥajar (ﷺ) commented on this issue saying:

"Some scholars hold the opinion that *qazʿ* is prohibited because it disfigures one's appearance, others say that it is the look of Shayṭān, and others that it is the look of the Jews... *Qazʿ* is limited to the hair on the head, not that of the sideburns or the back of the neck." [2]

Ibn ul-Qayyim (ﷺ) reported that Ibn Taymiyyah (ﷺ) said:

"This indicates Allāh's and His Messenger's absolute love of fairness. Allāh requires fairness in all matters — even between a human being and himself. (For example,) it is prohibited to partially shave the head because this would be unfair to the head, keeping some of it covered and baring the rest. Similarly, the Prophet (ﷺ) prohibited sitting partially in the shade [3] because it constitutes unfairness to part of the body. He also prohibited walking with one shoe and required wearing shoes in both feet or walking barefoot. [4]

As for *qazʿ*, it is four types:

1. Shaving separate streaks here-and-there from the

Albānī (*Ṣaḥīḥ ul-Jāmiʿ* no. 212 and *aṣ-Ṣaḥīḥah* no. 1123).

1 Recorded by al-Bukhārī, Muslim, and others.

2 *Fatḥ ul-Bārī*.

3 Recorded by Aḥmad, Abū Dāwūd, and others from Abū Hurayrah (ﷺ). Verified to be authentic by al-Albānī (*aṣ-Ṣaḥīḥah* no. 837, 838).

4 Recorded by al-Bukhārī, Abū Dāwūd, and others from Abū Hurayrah (ﷺ).

head, making it appear like broken clouds.

2. Shaving the center and leaving the sides, as the Christian monks do.

3. Shaving the sides and leaving the center, as is done by many of the vile and lowly people.

4. Shaving the front and leaving the back." [1]

This clearly indicates the prohibition of some hair styles whereby parts of the head's hair are completely shaved, as is done with the mohawk, or as is more common now where parts or creases of the head are shaved.

Shaving the Head upon Embracing Islām

As soon as a newborn impinges on its new life, its prior hair should be shaved. Similarly, as soon as a man impinges on his new life as a Muslim, he should shave his prior hair.

The Prophet (ﷺ) commanded a new Muslim to do so. Kulayb al-Juhanī (ﷺ) reported that he came to the Prophet (ﷺ) and told him that he has embraced Islām. The Prophet (ﷺ) then commanded him:

«ألق عنك شعر الكفر واختَتِن.»

‹Shave off the hair of *kufr*, and get circumcised.› [2]

Note that circumcision is also required in both cases. Note also that shaving the head of new Muslims applies only to men. We have no authentic reports that the Prophet (ﷺ) commanded any woman who embraced Islām to shave her head.

---

1 *Tuḥfat ul-Mawdūd* 64.

2 Recorded by Abū Dāwūd and Aḥmad. Verified to be *ḥasan* by al-Albānī (*Ṣaḥīḥ ul-Jāmiʿ* no. 1251 and *Irwāʾ ul-Ghalīl* no. 79).

GIVING CHARITY

We have seen that the Prophet (ﷺ) commanded his daughter Fāṭimah to weigh her baby's shaved hair and give a charity equal to its weight in silver. In his earlier report (p. 115), ʿAlī (رضي الله عنه) added:

> "We weighed the hair and found its weight to be a *dirham* or less."

Thus, the value of this charity would be quite small, and is more symbolic than real. Still, those who cannot afford paying that little are exempt from giving this charity.

It should be noted that, since the Prophet (ﷺ) specified silver, it is not permissible to pay a charity in this case equal to the hair's weight in gold. Ibn Ḥajar (رحمه الله) said:

> "All reports agree that the charity is given in silver, and none of them mentions gold." [1]

As for the date of this charity, it is also the seventh day of birth, because it is linked to shaving the hair.

Calling *Athān* and *Iqāmah*?

Many scholars recommend calling *athān* in a newborn's right ear and *iqāmah* in its left ear. This is based on three reports recorded in the books of *Ḥadīth*. However, all of them are weak, and the second and third of them are fabricated, as is indicated in the footnotes.

1. Abū Rāfiʿ reported:

> "I saw Allāh's Messenger (ﷺ) call the *athān* in the ear of al-Ḥasan Bin ʿAlī when his mother Fāṭimah gave birth to him." [2]

---

1 *Fatḥ ul-Bārī* 4:148.

2 Recorded by Abū Dāwūd, at-Tirmithī, and others. Verified to be weak by al-Albānī

2. Al-Ḥasan Bin ʿAlī (🙵) reported that Allāh's Messenger (🙵) said:

"Whoever gets a new baby and calls *athān* in its right ear and *iqāmah* in its left ear, it will never be harmed by *Umm uṣ-Ṣibyān* [1]." [2]

3. Ibn ʿAbbās (🙵) reported:

"The Prophet (🙵) called *athān* in the ear of al-Ḥasan Bin ʿAlī on the day that he was born, and he called *iqāmah* in his left ear." [3]

Therefore, there is no reliable evidence for calling *athān* or *iqāmah* for a newborn. Both acts should thus be avoided as being *bidʿah*s.

(*ad-Daʿīfah* vol. 1, p. 493). Note that al-Albānī (🙵) at first considered this *hadīth* authentic (in *Irwāʾ ul-Ghalīl*, *aṣ-Ṣaḥīḥ Abī Dāwūd*, and *Ṣaḥīḥ ut-Tirmithī*) but later found, as noted above, based on further evidence, that it is not.

1   *Umm uṣ-Ṣibyān* literally means, "the Mother of Kids". It refers to a harmful wind that afflicts the babies and causes them to fall sick (al-ʿAynī in *al-ʿAlam ul-Hayyib*).

2   Recorded by Abū Yaʿlā, Ibn us-Sunnī, and others. Verified to be fabricated by al-Albānī (*ad-Daʿīfah* no. 321 and *Irwāʾ ul-Ghalīl* no. 1174).

3   Recorded by al-Bayhaqī in *Shuʿab ul-Īmān*. Verified to be fabricated by al-Albānī (*ad-Daʿīfah* vol. 1, pp. 493-494).

CHAPTER 7

PROTECTING THE BABY FROM EVIL

Ruqyah

DEFINITION AND RULING

Ruqyah consists of words said or written in the form of *du'ā'* or <u>*th*</u>*ikr* for the purpose of protection or cure. It is sometimes accompanied with other actions, such as blowing or wiping over the thing to which it is applied. [1]

People from most cultures and religions use various forms of *ruqyahs*. Most of those *ruqyahs* contain magic, *shirk*, senseless words, lies, etc. In English, a *ruqyah* is called spell, charm, incantation, and so on.

The Prophet (ﷺ) warned against using *ruqyahs* that contain *shirk*. 'Awf Bin Mālik al-Ashja'ī (ﷺ) narrated that he said to the Prophet (ﷺ), "O Allāh's Messenger! We used to apply *ruqyahs* during *Jāhiliyyah*. What do you think of this?" The Prophet (ﷺ) replied:

«اعرِضوا عليَّ رُقاكم. لا بأسَ بالرُّقى ما لم يكن فيه شِرك.»

‹Present your *ruqyahs* to me. There is nothing wrong with them as long as they do not involve *shirk*.› [2]

There are some important conditions that must be satisfied in a *ruqyah* to be permissible. They were summarized by Ibn Ḥajar (ﷺ):

> "There is a consensus among the *'ulamā'* that a *ruqyah* is permissible when it satisfies three conditions:

---

1 A more detailed discussion of *ruqyah* is presented in the Author's, "Sickness, Regulations and Exhortations".

2 Recorded by Muslim.

1. It should be with Allāh's words (Qur'ān) or using His names and attributes.
2. It should be in Arabic or of an intelligible meaning.
3. One must believe that it does not have an independent power by itself, but by Allāh (ﷻ)." [1]

Best *Ruqyahs*

It is best to apply *ruqyahs* that have been reported in the *Sunnah*. This includes specific portions of the *Qur'ān*, such as *al-Fātiḥah* (1:1-7), *āyat ul-Kursī* (2:255), and the last three *sūrahs* (112, 113, 114). It also includes other authentic supplications seeking Allāh's help and protection. [2]

Abū Sa'īd al-Khudrī (رضي الله عنه) reported that Jibrīl visited the Prophet (ﷺ) while sick [3] and said to him, "O Muḥammad, are you suffering (from the pain)?" He replied, **‹Yes!›** Jibrīl then said:

«بسم الله أرقيك، من كل شيء يؤذيك، من شر كل نفسٍ
أو عين حاسد، الله يشفيك، بسم الله أرقيك.»

***‹Bismillāhi arqīk, min kulli shay'in yu'thīk, min sharri kulli nafsin aw 'ayni ḥāsid*" — With Allāh's Name I shelter you, from all that ails you, from the evil of any soul, and that of the envious eye. May Allāh cure you; with Allāh's Name I shelter you.›** [4]

'Uthmān Bin 'Affān (رضي الله عنه) reported that Allāh's Messenger (ﷺ) said:

«ما من عبد يقول في صباحِ كُلِ يومٍ ومساءِ كلِّ ليلةٍ:

---

1 *Fatḥ ul-Bārī* 10:240.

2 The reader is again referred to the Author's, "Sickness, Regulations and Exhortations" for additional details.

3 Obviously, the *ṣaḥābah* could not see Jibrīl (عليه السلام). Thus, in this *ḥadīth*, Abū Sa'īd (رضي الله عنه) is reporting something that the Prophet (ﷺ) had told him.

4 Recorded by Muslim and others.

"بسم اللهِ الذي لا يضرُّ معَ ٱسْمِهِ شيءٌ في الأرضِ ولا في السّماءِ، وهو ٱلسّميعُ العليم." ثلاثَ مراتٍ فيضرُّه شيءٌ.»

‹Nothing would harm a *ʿabd* who says three times every morning and evening:
"*Bism illāh il-la<u>th</u>ī lā yaḍurru maʿ asmihī shayʾun fil arḍi walā fis-samāʾi wahuw as-samīʿ ul-ʿalīm* — (I shelter myself) with the name of Allāh, the One with whose name nothing can cause harm on earth or in the heaven. He is the Hearer, the Knower."› [1]

The *muʿawwi<u>th</u>āt* (the protecting ones), presented below, are the last three *sūrahs* of the *Qurʾān*. The last two of them, called the two *muʿawwi<u>th</u>āt* (the protecting two), carry a clear meaning of *ruqyah*. *Sūrat ul-Ikhlāṣ* (112) does not explicitly carry such meaning, but contains concise and strong words of praise for Allāh (ﷻ), making it an important introduction to the succeeding two *sūrahs*.

﴿قُلْ هُوَ ٱللَّهُ أَحَدٌ ۝ ٱللَّهُ ٱلصَّمَدُ ۝ لَمْ يَلِدْ وَلَمْ يُولَدْ ۝ وَلَمْ يَكُن لَّهُۥ كُفُوًا أَحَدٌۢ ۝﴾ الإخلاص ١-٤

«Say, "He is Allāh, the One and Unique. Allāh, the Eternal Refuge. He neither begets nor was he born. There is no equal to Him."» [2]

﴿قُلْ أَعُوذُ بِرَبِّ ٱلْفَلَقِ ۝ مِن شَرِّ مَا خَلَقَ ۝ وَمِن شَرِّ غَاسِقٍ إِذَا وَقَبَ ۝ وَمِن شَرِّ ٱلنَّفَّٰثَٰتِ فِي ٱلْعُقَدِ ۝ وَمِن شَرِّ حَاسِدٍ إِذَا حَسَدَ ۝﴾ الفلق ١-٥

«Say, "I seek refuge with the Lord of daybreak, from the evil of what he created, and from the evil

1 Recorded by Abū Dāwūd, at-Tirmi<u>th</u>ī, and others. Verified to be authentic by al-Albānī (*Ṣaḥīḥ ut-Targhīb* no. 655).

2 *Al-Ikhlāṣ* 112:1-4.

of darkness when it settles, and from the evil of the blowers in knots, and from the evil of an envier when he envies."» [1]

﴿قُلْ أَعُوذُ بِرَبِّ ٱلنَّاسِ ۝ مَلِكِ ٱلنَّاسِ ۝ إِلَٰهِ ٱلنَّاسِ ۝ مِن شَرِّ ٱلْوَسْوَاسِ ٱلْخَنَّاسِ ۝ ٱلَّذِي يُوَسْوِسُ فِي صُدُورِ ٱلنَّاسِ ۝ مِنَ ٱلْجِنَّةِ وَٱلنَّاسِ ۝﴾ الناس ١-٦

«Say, "I seek refuge with the Lord of the people, the King of the people, the God of the people, from the evil of a retreating whisperer, who whispers (evil) in the breasts of the people, (whether he is) from among *jinns* or the people."» [2]

Khubayb (ﷺ) reported that he went with other men on a dark night seeking the Prophet (ﷺ) to lead them in prayer. When they found him, the Prophet (ﷺ) said to Khubayb, «قُلْ.» ‹**Say!**› Not knowing what to say, Khubayb remained silent. The Prophet (ﷺ) made a second demand, «قُلْ.» ‹**Say!**› Again, Khubayb remained silent. On the third time, Khubayb said, "O Allāh's Messenger, what should I say?" The Prophet (ﷺ) replied:

«قل: (قل هو اللّٰهُ أحد) والمعوِّذَتين، حين تمسي وحين تُصبحُ ثلاثَ مراتٍ، تكفيك كلَّ شيءٍ.»

«Say "*Qul huwa 'Llāhu ahad*" and the two *muʿawwithāt* three times in the evening and in the morning. This would protect you from all (harmful) things.» [3]

ʿĀ'ishah (ﷺ) reported:

---

1 *Al-Falaq* 113:1-5.

2 *An-Nās* 114:1-6.

3 Recorded by Abū Dāwūd, at-Tirmithī, and others. Verified to be authentic by al-Albānī (*Ṣaḥīḥ ut-Targhīb wat-Tarhīb* no. 649).

"When Allāh's Messenger (ﷺ) went to bed, he would bring the palms of both hands together, and blow into them while reciting "*Qul huwa 'Llāhu aḥad*" [1], "*Qul aʿūthu bi rabb il-falaq*" [2], "*Qul aʿūthu bi rabb in-Nās*" [3]. He would then rub with them whatever he could reach of his body, starting with his head, face, and the front part of his body. He would do this three times. When he was too ill, he asked me to do this for him." [4]

Abū Saʿīd al-Khudrī (رضي الله عنه) reported:

"كان رسول الله يتعوذ من الجان وعين الإنسان، حتى نزلت المعوّذتان، فلما نزلت أخذ بهما وترك ما سواهما."

"Allāh's Messenger (ﷺ) used to seek (Allāh's) protection from *jinns* and the human eye (with various supplications) — until the two *muʿawwithāt* were revealed. After that, he adhered to them and left all else." [5]

Protecting the Baby

The Evil Eye

Envy is one of the greatest evils among Allāh's creation. It is what caused Satan to rebel against Allāh's (ﷻ) command. And it is what causes people to make plots and inflict wars against each other.

One of envy's ugly manifestations is the evil eye. When an envious person looks at something that he (or she) admires, his look causes an

1 *Sūrah* 112.

2 *Sūrah* 113 (cited above).

3 *Sūrah* 114 (cited above).

4 Recorded by al-Bukhārī and Muslim.

5 Recorded by at-Tirmithī and Ibn Mājah. Verified to be authentic by al-Albānī (*al-Mishkāt* no. 4563).

immediate harm or damage to that thing.

Asmā' Bint 'Umays (🕮) narrated that she said to the Prophet (🕮), "O Allāh's Messenger, the children of Ja'far are easily afflicted with the evil eye. Should I seek *ruqyah* for them?" He replied:

«نعم، فإنه لو كان شيءٌ سابقٌ القدرَ لسبقته العينُ.»

‹Yes! If anything were to race the *qadar* (Allāh's decree), it would be the evil eye.› [1]

'Ā'ishah (🕮) reported:

"أمر النبيُّ أن نسترقيَ (أسترقي) من العين."

"the Prophet (🕮) commanded me (or us) to seek *ruqyah* from the eye." [2]

Umm Salamah (🕮) reported that Allāh's Messenger (🕮) saw in her house a young girl whose face appeared yellowish. He said:

«استرقوا لها، فإن بها النظرةَ.»

‹Seek *ruqyah* for her, because she is struck with an evil eye.› [3]

RUQYAHS FOR CHILDREN

Children are especially vulnerable to evil eyes, harmful insects, and devils. Because of this, the Prophet (🕮) applied *ruqyah* to children and urged others to do the same, as we saw above in the case of Ja'far's children and in Umm Salamah's *ḥadīth*, and as in the following reports.

'Ā'ishah (🕮) reported that the Prophet (🕮) heard a little child crying. So he said:

---

1 Recorded by Aḥmad and others. Verified to be authentic by al-Albānī (*Mishkāt ul-Maṣābīḥ* no. 4560).

2 Recorded by al-Bukhārī, Muslim, and others.

3 Recorded by al-Bukhārī.

«ما لصبيِّكم هذا يبكي؟ فهلاّ استرقيتُم له من العين؟»

‹Why is this child crying? Wouldn't you seek to treat him with *ruqyah* from the evil eye?› [1]

Allāh's complete words are His commands and decree that never err, and that are most truthful, just, wise, and overwhelming. There is a number of *ḥadīth*s relating that the Prophet (ﷺ) performed *ruqyah* with Allāh's complete words.

ʿAbdullāh Bin ʿAbbās (رضي الله عنه) reported that the Prophet (ﷺ) sought Allāh's protection for his grandchildren, al-Ḥasan and al-Ḥusayn, with the same supplication that Ibrāhīm (عليه السلام) said for his children Ismāʿīl and Isḥāq:

«أعيذكما بكلمات الله التامة من كل شيطان وهامّة،

ومن كل عين لامّة»

***‹Uʿīthukumā bikalimāt illāh it-tāmmah, min kulli shayṭānin wa-hāmmah, wa min kulli ʿaynin lāmmah* — I shelter both of you with Allāh's complete words from every devil and harmful creature, and from every envious eye.›** [2]

And Allāh (ﷻ) tells us that upon delivering Maryam, her mother sought Allāh's protection for her and her descendents from Satan:

﴿فَلَمَّا وَضَعَتْهَا قَالَتْ: "رَبِّ إِنِّي وَضَعْتُهَآ أُنثَىٰ - وَٱللَّهُ أَعْلَمُ بِمَا وَضَعَتْ - وَلَيْسَ ٱلذَّكَرُ كَٱلْأُنثَىٰ، وَإِنِّي سَمَّيْتُهَا مَرْيَمَ، وَإِنِّي أُعِيذُهَا بِكَ وَذُرِّيَّتَهَا مِنَ ٱلشَّيْطَٰنِ ٱلرَّجِيمِ." ۝﴾ آل عمران ٣٦

«When she (Maryam's mother) delivered her, she said, "My Lord, I have delivered a female — And Allāh was most Knowing of what she delivered —

1 Recorded by Aḥmad; verified to be authentic by al-Albānī (*aṣ-Ṣaḥīḥah* no. 1048).

2 Recorded by al-Bukhārī.

and the male is not like the female. And I have named her Maryam. And I seek Your protection for her and her progeny from Satan, the outcast."» [1]

ELIMINATING THE "DETERRENTS" OF GOOD

There are many "deterrents" that divert or reduce the effect of *ruqyah*s and supplications. Such deterrents should be removed from the presence of children at all times, especially during their sleep. "Deterrents of good" include music, images, and all other acts of disobedience that may be committed in a child's presence. Some of those deterrents will be discussed in the next chapter.

PROTECTION WITH AMULETS AND TALISMANS?

The supplications mentioned above should be soberly and sincerely uttered by the appropriate individuals.

Some people write their *ruqhah*s on paper or engrave them on gold and silver, thereby forming amulets that they hang on babies' chests or around their necks. This brings a number of harms, such as the following:

1. This would not produce the desired protection, because it is not done as instructed in the Sunnah.

2. This is a loathsome *bid'ah* because it was not taught or practiced by the Prophet (ﷺ) or his companions (ﷺ).

3. This may constitute *shirk* because the people who use these amulets tend to believe that they have an independent protective power.

4. This ultimately leads the ignorant to using amulets containing magical terms and senseless words made up by devils and soothsayers. This is indeed an extremely shameful level of deviation and *shirk*.

---

1 *Āl 'Imrān* 3:36.

Shaykh Ṣāliḥ al-Fawzān said:

> "It is not permissible to hang protective charms or (Qur'ānic) writings on adults or children. All of this is classified under the *tamīmah*ṣ (amulets) that the Prophet (ﷺ) prohibited. If those amulets contain nonsense, obscurities, words of unknown meaning, names of *jinn*s or devils, and so on, then they are unanimously prohibited because they contradict true faith and surely lead to *shirk.*
>
> If those amulets contain Qur'ān and authentic supplications (only), they are still prohibited according to the most correct opinion of the *'ulamā'*. The reason for this prohibition is that hanging them would open the door to hanging the other prohibited (*shirkī*) amulets. Additionally, hanging some of the Qur'ān on a baby shows disrespect of the Qur'ān ..." [1]

Blue Beads, Horseshoe, and Other Charms

It is prohibited to use for protection blue beads, horseshoes, or other symbols and charms that the ignorant use, thinking that they have protective powers. Using them is a serious act of *shirk* that the Prophet (ﷺ) prohibited as we saw earlier.

Ibn Mas'ūd (رضي الله عنه) reported that he saw on his wife's neck a tied string (for *ruqyah*). He cut it off her neck and said, "Indeed, the family of Ibn Mas'ūd are in no need of joining with Allāh that which He did not permit. Truly, I heard Allāh's Messenger (ﷺ) say:

«إن الرُّقى والتمائمَ والتِوَلَة شرك.»

> **‹Indeed, (incorrect) *ruqyahs*, amulets, and *tiwalahs* [2], all manifest *shirk*.›**" [3]

---

1 *Al-Muntaqā Min Fatāwā Ṣāliḥ al-Fawzān* 1:166-168.

2 Charms that women use for maintaining their husbands' love.

3 Recorded by Abū Dāwūd. Verified to be authentic by al-Albānī (*aṣ-Ṣaḥīḥah* no. 2972, *Ṣaḥīḥ ut-Targhīb wat-Tarhīb* no. 3457).

ʿĪsā Bin ʿAbd ir-Raḥmān Bin Abī Laylā reported that he went to visit Abū Maʿbid ʿAbdullāh Bin ʿUkaym al-Juhanī (ﷺ) when the latter was afflicted with redness [1]. ʿĪsā suggested to him, "Why don't you hang an amulet (for cure)?" Abū Maʿbid responded, "Death would be easier than this. I heard Allāh's Messenger (ﷺ) say:

«من تعلَّق شيئاً وُكِل إليه.»

‹Anyone who hangs something (for protection) will be yielded to that thing.›" [2]

This means that such a person will not get the desired protection because Allāh (ﷻ) will yield him to that thing from which he sought help without right.

MAKING *DUʿĀ'* AND *THIKR* ON BEHALF OF THE BABY?

Some parents reason that, since their baby is still incapable of saying *duʿā'* and *thikr* on its own, it would be good that they say them for it. Thus when they finish feeding it, they say, "*Al-ḥamdu lillāh.*" They say the same when the baby sneezes. They say the supplications of going to sleep and rising from sleep on behalf of the baby, and so on.

This practice shows excessive concern and may classify as *bidʿah* for two reasons. First, we have no knowledge that the *ṣaḥābah* or their true followers did this. Second, the supplications and *ruqyah*s that we cited earlier were recommended by the Prophet (ﷺ) himself, and they should provide the necessary protection for the baby.

---

1 This is a disease that produces swelling and redness in the face and other afflicted parts of the body.

2 Recorded by Abū Dāwūd and at-Tirmithī. Verified to be *ḥasan* by al-Albānī (*Ṣaḥīḥ ut-Targhīb wat-Tarhīb* no. 3456).

CHAPTER 8

DETERRENTS OF GOOD

Why It Does Not Work?

We often hear an outcry from concerned parents that they did all that is possible to protect their child from harm and evil. They said all the authentic supplications and applied all the authentic *ruqyah*s, but nothing worked! The child keeps falling sick. It appears to be under a magical spell or possessed by a *jinn*.

When we inquire from those parents about the environment they have established for their child, we often find that it contains a number of wrongs that constitute strong deterrents for the acceptance of *ruqyah*s, thereby aiding harm and evil in attacking their child.

Among those deterrents are images, music, bells, television, and any other act of disobedience that is committed or maintained in the child's proximity. In this section, we discuss a few of the deterrents.

Dolls and Other Images

MODERN CHILDREN'S "TOYDOM"

It has become universally acceptable, or even recommended, to have images of all forms, colors, and sizes on children's clothes, beds, walls, and so on.

A large part of the children's toys are personified after animals and fictitious creatures. We see Micky Mouse, Goofy, Donald Duck, Bugs Bunny, and the newer Little Mermaid, Lion King, and other cartoon characters decorating and populating our children's world.

Our babies' rooms, shelves, and beds are filled with dolls and stuffed animals. Teddy bears are accepted as legitimate longtime companions for our children, with their companionship often extending into adolescence and beyond.

Our children spend long hours dressing, tending, and talking to human-like dolls and stuffed animals.

PROHIBITION OF IMAGES IN ISLĀM

In this section, "image" or "picture" means a two-dimensional painting or photograph, or a three-dimensional statue or figure, made to resemble humans, animals, or fictitious living creatures. The relevant part of the image is the head, because it is the part that reflects the actual resemblance. Allāh's Messenger (ﷺ) said:

«الصورة الرأس، فإذا قُطع الرأس فلا صورة.»

‹The (prohibited) image is the head. When the head is removed, it is not an image anymore.› [1]

Making images is a major sin in Islām. A Muslim should not make an image or help in making it unless it fulfills a legitimate need that cannot be fulfilled otherwise.

'Ā'ishah (﵂) reported that once Allāh's Messenger (ﷺ) came into her room and found that she had a curtain covering an alcove in the room. The curtain had some images drawn on it. When the Prophet (ﷺ) saw it, his face showed anger and he said:

«إن الذين يصنعون هذه الصور يُعذَّبون يوم القيامة،

ويُقال لهم أحيوا ما خلقتم.»

‹Indeed, those who make these images will be tortured on the Day of Resurrection and will be told, "Give life to what you have created."›

So she removed the curtain, cut it, and made pillows with it. [2]

Ibn Mas'ūd (﵁) reported that Allāh's Messenger (ﷺ) said:

---

1   Recorded by al-Ismā'īlī from Ibn 'Abbās (﵂). Verified to be authentic by al-Albānī (aṣ-Ṣaḥīḥah no. 1921 and Ṣaḥīḥ ul-Jāmi' no. 3864).

2   Recorded by al-Bukhārī, Muslim, and others.

«إن أشد الناس عذاباً يوم القيامة المصوِّرون.»

‹Indeed, the people who will receive the most punishment on Resurrection Day are those who make images.› [1]

IMAGES DRIVE THE ANGELS AWAY

We have seen above the great punishment promised for those who make images. In addition, there is an immediate punishment for those who display images: They lose the company of the angels of mercy who would otherwise engulf the believers with help and protection. These angels do not like the proximity of the images that represent disobedience to Allāh (ﷻ).

Abū Ṭalḥah, ʿAlī, and others (ﷺ) reported that Allāh's Messenger (ﷺ) said:

«إن الملائكة لا تدخل بيتاً فيه كلبٌ أو صورة.»

‹Indeed, the angels do not enter a house in which there is a dog or an image.› [2]

Images that are on display in a certain room drive the angels of mercy away from that room. This gives the devils better access to the houses, bodies, and lives of people. Subsequently, this allows Satan to cause more damage and harm.

PERMISSION OF DOLLS AND TOY ANIMALS

Excluded from the prohibition of making images are toys that are hand-made by children. ʿĀʾishah (ﷺ) had such toys during the early years of her marriage, and the Prophet (ﷺ) did not show any disapproval of them. ʿĀʾishah (ﷺ) reported:

"I used to play with dolls, and some of my young

1 Recorded by Muslim, Aḥmad, and others.

2 Recorded by al-Bukhārī, Muslim, and others.

> female friends used to come play with me. When Allāh's Messenger (ﷺ) came home, my friends would hide away, returning after he left. (Sometimes) he himself would tell them to come play with me." [1]

She also narrated that when Allāh's Messenger (ﷺ) came back from the battle of Tabūk or Khaybar, she had an alcove covered with a curtain. The wind blew away the curtain exposing some dolls. He asked, «ما هذا يا عائشة؟» **‹What is this, O ʿĀ'ishah?›** She replied, "These are my dolls." He saw in their midst a horse with leather wings and asked, «ما هذا الذي أرى وسطهن؟» **‹What is this that I see in their midst?›** She said, "A horse." He asked, «وما هذا الذي عليه؟» **‹And what is that thing on it?›** She replied, "Two wings." He exclaimed, «فرس له جناحان؟» **‹A horse with two wings?›** She said, "Didn't you know that Sulaymān's horses had wings?" So he laughed until she could see his canine teeth. [2]

Conclusion

From the above, we conclude the following:

1. **It is prohibited to make images.** Photographs and video pictures are no exception. Thus, it is not allowed to take pictures of babies to display them or put them in a wallet or in a family album.

2. **It is prohibited to display images.** It is very sad to see many Muslims hanging family pictures on their walls or displaying them on desks and dressers. We should be careful to hide away all pictures, even those of newspapers, when they are not being used.

3. As an exception to (1) and (2) above, **it is permissible to make children's toys and dolls** that resemble images. However, those toys should be **crudely hand-made** so as to serve the purpose of teaching sewing, decoration, and other house-keeping activities.

---

1 Recorded by al-Bukhārī, Muslim, and others.

2 Recorded by Abū Dāwūd, an-Nasā'ī, and others. Verified to be authentic by al-Albānī (*Ṣaḥīḥ Abī Dāwūd* no. 4123).

This exception should not be widened to encompass today's images and toys that are made to closely match Allāh's creation. By Islāmic standards, many of today's toys are classified as idols that should be eliminated from a Muslim's house.

4. In analogy to (3) above, **it is permissible to make images that are needed for a legitimate purpose** that cannot be otherwise fulfilled. This includes passport and identity pictures, images absolutely needed for instructional purposes, and so on.

5. The **prohibition** is more emphasized in the case **of images that make anti-Islāmic propaganda or call to corruption**. We see that modern toys and dolls, being mostly made by non-Muslims, project and emphasize cultures and ideologies alien to Islām. And among the worst types of dolls populating the Muslim houses are barbies, which are female dolls shaped after the lewd Western taste for sensual women.

We would never want to deprive our children from the company and care of the angels of mercy. Yet, this is exactly what happens when we fill their rooms and our houses with images and idols.

Fatwās Concerning Images on Clothes

Shaykh Ṣāliḥ Bin ʿUthaymīn (ﷺ) said:

> "The *ʿulamāʾ* say that it is prohibited to dress a baby with anything that is prohibited for adults to wear. Garments with images are prohibited for adults to wear; so, it is prohibited for babies to wear them as well. The Muslims should boycott those clothes and shoes (with images) so that the people of evil and corruption would not attack us (Muslims) from this direction." [1]

Shaykh Ṣāliḥ al-Fawzān said:

1 *Majmūʿ Fatāwā wa-Rasāʾil Ṣāliḥ al-ʿUthaymīn* 2:275.

> "It is not permissible to buy clothes that have images of beings with souls, such as humans, animals, and birds. Making and using images are prohibited because of the numerous *ḥadīths* prohibiting this and strongly warning against it. The Prophet (ﷺ) cursed those who make images and indicated that they will be severely punished on the Day of Resurrection. Thus it is not allowed to wear a garment with images or make a baby wear it. One should buy clothes that do not have images, which are available in plenty — all praise is due to Allāh." [1]

Fatwās Concerning Dolls

Shaykh Ṣāliḥ Bin ʿUthaymīn (رحمه الله) said:

> "It is surely permissible for little girls to play with dolls that have no clear features. This would be similar to the dolls with which ʿĀʾishah (رضي الله عنها) played. However, if a doll has clearly distinctive features making it resemble a human being — especially if it also has motion or voice — I would have a reservation in my heart against it, because it would then be clearly competing with Allāh's creation …
>
> I believe that it is prohibited to make dolls in a way resembling Allāh's creation. This would be considered of the *taṣwīr* (making of images) that is, without a doubt, prohibited. And if they (the dolls) come to us from the Christians and others non-Muslims, the ruling would then be as stated above.
>
> As for purchasing such dolls, I urge that we should instead buy toys that have no images, such as bicycles, toy cars, winches, and so on." [2]

Shaykh Ṣāliḥ al-Fawzān said:

---

1 *Al-Muntaqā Min Fatāwā Ṣāliḥ al-Fawzān* 3:339-340.

2 *Majmūʿ Fatāwā wa-Rasāʾil Ṣāliḥ al-ʿUthaymīn* 2:277-278.

"It is not permissible to hold possession of images of beings with souls, except for the necessary ones such as photographs of identity card, driving license, and so on. All other images are not permissible to possess — not even children's toys or images used for teaching them. The reason for this is the general texts prohibiting making images or using them.

There are many children's toys with no images. The opinion of those who permit using images for children's toys is weak. They rely on the *ḥadīth* of 'Ā'ishah's (عظيم) toys when she was young. However, some scholars say that this *ḥadīth* is abrogated by the later prohibition of making images. Others say that the images described in this *ḥadīth* are not like the images known today. They were made of rags and sticks and did not resemble an animal the way today's images do. This is the more correct opinion, and Allāh knows best. As for today's images, they precisely resemble animals — some of them even moving like animals." [1]

Music

Some people believe that "classical" and soft music has a soothing effect on babies. Based on this non-Islāmic concept, music competes with images in filling the child's world. Music is played constantly in children's amusement parks, movies, and restaurants. Many of the babies' toys play music when touched, pressed, or hugged. Even infant toys such as rattles and swings play musical segments.

Unfortunately, many Muslims view music as an innocent practice. Thus, they make it an essential part of their children's life. This is an error that conflicts with authentic texts. Furthermore, there is a consensus among the early scholars of *Islām*, including the Four *Imām*s, that music is prohibited.

Anas, 'Imrān, Abū Umāmah, 'Alī, and Abū Hurayrah (رضي الله عنهم) reported that Allāh's Messenger (ﷺ) said:

---

1   *Al-Muntaqā Min Fatāwā Ṣāliḥ al-Fawzān* 3:338-339.

«ليكوننّ في هذه الأمةِ خسفٌ وقذفٌ ومسخ، وذلك إذا شربوا الخمور، واتّخذوا القيناتِ، وضربوا بالمعازف.»

‹There will be among (the people of) this *Ummah* earth-collapse, stoning, and metamorphosis. That will be when they drink alcoholic beverages, keep female singers, and play on musical instruments.› [1]

Anas (رضي الله عنه) reported that Allāh's Messenger (ﷺ) said:

«صوتان ملعونان في الدنيا والآخرة: مزمارٌ عند نِعمةٍ، ورنّةٌ عند مصيبة.»

‹Two sounds are cursed (by Allāh) in this life and the hereafter: flute (music) for a good fortune, and wailing for a misfortune.› [2]

Bells and Ringing

Similar to music, many of the babies' toys have bells or produce a ringing sound. This applies more to infants' toys, such as rattles.

Abū Hurayrah (رضي الله عنه) reported that Allāh's Messenger (ﷺ) said:

«لا تصحَبُ الملائكةُ رُفقةً فيها كلب أو جرس.»

‹The angels do not join (in travel) a company who have with them a dog or a bell.› [3]

Abū Hurayrah (رضي الله عنه) reported that Allāh's Messenger (ﷺ) said:

---

1 Recorded by Aḥmad, at-Tirmithī, and others. Verified to be authentic by al-Albānī (*Ṣaḥīḥ ul-Jāmiʿ* no. 5467 & *aṣ-Ṣaḥīḥah* no. 2203).

2 Recorded by al-Bazzār, aḍ-Ḍiyā' ul-Maqdisī, and others. Verified to be *ḥasan* by al-Albānī (*Ṣaḥīḥ ut-Targhīb wat-Tarhīb* no. 3527 and *aṣ-Ṣaḥīḥah* no. 427).

3 Recorded by Muslim, Abū Dāwūd, and others. There are similar reports from other *ṣaḥābah* including ʿĀ'ishah, Umm Ḥabībah, Anan, and Ibn ʿUmar (رضي الله عنهم).

«الجرسُ مزامير الشيطان.»

⟨The bell is (one of) Satan's flutes.⟩ [1]

Bunānah reported that she was with 'Ā'ishah (radiallahu anha) when a young girl was brought in wearing an anklet with ringing bells. 'Ā'ishah asked for the girl to be taken away unless her bells were removed. She then explained that she heard Allāh's Messenger (sallallahu alayhi wa sallam) say:

«لا تدخل ا لملائكة بيتاً فيه جرس.»

⟨The angels do not enter into a house in which there is a bell.⟩ [2]

Television

Television encompasses all of the evils that we covered earlier in this chapter, plus many others. From the moment that a baby can discern what it sees, the TV starts playing a major role, mostly destructive, in forming the child's personality and establishing the child's principles. It is not surprising then that we include it among the repellents of good and even consider it one of their worst.

Shaykh 'Abd ul-'Azīz Bin Bāz (rahimahullah) said:

> "With regard to television, it is a dangerous device. Its harmful effects are great — like those of the cinema, or even worse. From the research that has been written about it, and from the words of experts in Arab countries and elsewhere, we know enough to conclude that it is dangerous and very harmful to Islāmic beliefs, morals and the society's condition. The reason for this is that it includes presentations of bad morals, tempting scenes, immoral pictures, semi-nakedness, destructive

---

1   Recorded by Muslim, Abū Dāwūd, and others.

2   Recorded by Abū Dāwūd. Verified to be *ḥasan* by al-Albānī (*Ṣaḥīḥ ut-Targhīb wat-Tarhīb* no. 3120).

> speech, and disbelief. It encourages imitation of the disbelievers in conduct, way of dressing, honoring their (non-Muslim) leaders. (At the same time, it encourages) neglect of the Islamic conduct and ways of dressing, and belittling the Islāmic scholars and heroes. It damages their image by portraying them in a disdainful manner that makes the people despise and disregard them. It teaches cheating, stealing, plotting, and committing acts of violence. Without doubt, anything that produces so much evil should be stopped and shunned ..." [1]

Celebrating Birthdays

Celebrating birthdays is one of the clearest acts in which the Muslims imitate non-Muslims without reason [2]. Birthdays have reached such a high degree of importance in some Muslims' lives that, to them, neglecting them is as bad as neglecting one of Islām's two annual *ʿīd*s!

By introducing innovations and wrong practices like birthdays into our children's lives, from their early childhood, we would be imparting to them life-long misconceptions and deviation.

Shaykh Ṣāliḥ Bin ʿUthaymīn (ﷺ) said:

> "Celebrating a child's birthday is either an act of worship or a normal habitual practice.
>
> 1. If it is an act of worship then it is an innovation (*bidʿah*) in Allāh's religion. It is confirmed from the Prophet (ﷺ) that he warned against *bidʿah*s and indicated that they are acts of misguidance. He said:
>
> «وإياكم وَمُحْدَثَاتِ الأُمُورِ،

---

1 *Al-Fatāwā* 3:227.

2 For a detailed discussion of this subject, the reader is referred to the Author's, "Celebrations in Islām".

فإن كلَّ بِدْعَةٍ ضَلالَةٌ، وكلَّ ضَلالَةٍ في ٱلنَّار.»

‹Beware of the (religious) matters that are innovated (by the people), for every innovated matter is an act of misguidance that (whoever initiated it) will reside in the Fire.› [1]

2. If it is a habitual practice then it carries two violations:

   a) It constitutes considering *ʿīd* a day that is not so. This exhibits impoliteness before Allāh and His Messenger (ﷺ) by instituting a day of celebration without Allāh's permission. When Allāh's Messenger (ﷺ) arrived at al-Madīnah, he found that *al-Anṣār* had two (annual) celebration days. So he said:

«قدمت عليكم ولكم يومان تلعبون فيهما في الجاهلية.
وقد أبدلكم الله بهما خيراً منهما: يومَ النحر ويومَ الفطر.»

‹When I came to al-Madīnah, you had two days that you celebrated from *Jāhiliyyah*. Indeed, Allāh has substituted them for you with two better days: The day of *al-Fiṭr* (Breaking the Fast) and the day of *an-Naḥr* (Sacrifice).› [2]

   b) It constitutes imitating Allāh's enemies, because this practice is not from the Muslims' practices but came to them from other nations. The Prophet (ﷺ) said:

---

1 Recorded by Aḥmad, Abū Dāwūd, and others from al-ʿIrbāḍ Bin Sāriyah (ﷺ). Verified to be authentic by al-Albānī (*Ṣaḥīḥ ul-Jāmiʿ* no. 2549 and *Irwāʾ ul-Ghalīl* no. 2455).

2 Recorded by Aḥmad, Abū Dāwūd, and others, from Anas (ﷺ). Verified to be authentic by al-Albānī (*Ṣaḥīḥ ul-Jāmiʿ* no. 4381).

«من تشبه بقوم فهو منهم.»

‹Whoever imitates a people is one of them.› [1]" [2]

---

1 Recorded by Abū Dāwūd from Ibn ʿUmar (ﷺ) and aṭ-Ṭabarānī (in *al-Awsaṭ*) from Ḥuthayfah (ﷺ). Verified to be authentic by al-Albānī (*Ṣaḥīḥ ul-Jāmiʿ* no. 6149 and *Irwāʾ ul-Ghalīl* no. 1269).

2 *Fatāwā Manār ul-Islām* 1:43-45.

CHAPTER 9

OTHER BABY ISSUES

Ṭahārah (Cleanliness and Purity) Issues

BABIES' URINE

The human urine is *najis* (impure or filthy). Its traces should be completely washed off if it falls on a garment, sheet, carpet, etc. There is one exception to this: the urine of a male baby whose main source of nourishment is breast-feeding. In this latter case, the location of urine may be merely sprayed with water without thorough washing.

Umm Qays Bint Miḥṣan (🌸) reported that she handed to the Prophet (🌸) a young male baby of hers that had not eaten food (i.e., he was still breast-feeding). The baby urinated over the Prophet's (🌸) clothes. The Prophet (🌸) asked for some water, and sprayed it over the spot without washing it. [1]

Similarly, 'Ā'ishah (🌸) reported that a male baby was brought to Allāh's Messenger (🌸) to make *taḥnīk* for him. The boy urinated over the Prophet's (🌸) garment. The Prophet (🌸) sprayed water over his garment without fully washing it. [2]

'Alī Bin Abī Ṭālib (🌸) reported that Allāh's Messenger (🌸) said:

«بولُ الغلام الرضيع يُنضَحُ، وبولُ الجاريةِ يُغسَل.»

**‹The urine of a breast-fed male baby is sprayed, and
the urine of a breast-fed female baby is washed.›** [3]

There are several other authentic reports to the same meaning by

---

1   Recorded by al-Bukhārī, Muslim, and others.

2   Recorded by al-Bukhārī, Muslim, and others.

3   Recorded by Aḥmad, Abū Dāwūd, and others. Verified to be authentic by al-Albānī (*Irwā'ul-Ghalīl* no. 166).

Umm Kurz, Umm al-Faḍl, and Abū as-Samḥ (⁣⁣).

Since spraying a baby's urine with water does not remove the urine, the above narrations indicate that the urine of a breast-fed male baby is *ṭāhir* (clean).

Note that a male baby's urine is *ṭāhir* only while his main nourishment comes from breast-feeding — even though he may be eating other supportive foods. Only when breast-feeding becomes a minor portion of his diet would his urine become *najis*.

The *'ulamā'* have various speculations regarding this distinction between male and female babies. Having not found any of their opinions strong enough to present here, we only submit that this is Allāh's and His Messenger's (⁣⁣) judgment — whether or not we fully understand its underlying wisdom.

CARRYING BABIES DURING THE PRAYER

Abū Qatādah (⁣⁣) reported that Allāh's Messenger (⁣⁣) once led the people in prayer while carrying upon his shoulder his granddaughter Umāmah Bint Zaynab (from Abū al-'Aṣ Bin ar-Rabī'). When he stood, he held her. And when he prostrated, he set her down. [1]

Commenting on this, Ibn ul-Qayyim (⁣⁣) said:

> "(This indicates) the permission of carrying children even when the condition of their clothes is not known (whether *ṭāhir* or *najis*) …
>
> This was clearly during an obligatory prayer. It provides a refutation of those who have paranoia (in regard to moving during the prayer). It indicates that infrequent movement during the prayer does not invalidate it — if there is need for it. It also reflects mercy toward the children, teaches humbleness and good manners, and indicates that touching little children

---

1　Recorded by al-Bukhārī, Muslim, and others. A more detailed report of this *ḥadīth*, recorded by Abū Dāwūd, says that the Prophet (⁣⁣) led the *ṣaḥābah* in the *ẓuhr* or *'aṣr* prayer while he carried Umāmah. However, this report has been verfied to be weak by al-Albānī (*Ḍa'īfu Abī Dāwūd* no. 920).

does not invalidate *wuḍū'*." [1]

And an-Nawawī (ﷺ) said:

> "Some of the Mālikīs claim that this *ḥadīth* is abrogated, others claim that it is an exclusive act of the Prophet's (ﷺ), and others claim that there was a necessity (for carrying Umāmah). However, all of these are invalid and rejected claims, because they have no evidence. The *ḥadīth* does not indicate anything that violates the rules of *Shar'*. A human being is (initially) *ṭāhir*, and what is within the belly is immaterial. As for the children's clothes and bodies, they are considered *ṭāhir* until there is proof to the contrary. Also, movement during the prayer does not invalidate it — if it is slight and discontinuous. The proofs for this are overwhelming." [2]

Bringing Babies into the *Masjid*

The above *ḥadīth* of Abū Qatādah clearly indicates that, contrary to some claims, it is permissible to bring young children into the *masjid*. This is further supported by another *ḥadīth* from Abū Qatādah.

Abū Qatādah (ﷺ) reported that Allāh's Messenger (ﷺ) said:

«إني لأدخلُ في الصلاة، فأريد إطالَتَها، فأسمع بكاء الصبيِّ،
فأتجوّزُ في صلاتي مما أعلمُ من وَجْدِ أمِّه من بُكائه.»

‹Indeed, I start the prayer intending to extend it. Then I hear a baby's cry, and I shorten my prayer because I know its mother's concern for its crying.› [3]

1 *Tuḥfat ul-Mawdūd* p. 134.

2 *Sharḥu Ṣaḥīḥi Muslim* as reported by Ibn Ḥajar in *Fatḥ ul-Bārī* 1:778.

3 Recorded by al-Bukhārī and Muslim.

TOUCHING A BABY'S PRIVATE PARTS

The mother or other adults would often need to touch a baby's private area for cleaning, changing, checking temperature, and so on. An often-raised concern is whether this touching invalidates *wuḍū'*. The simple answer is that it does not, because there is no evidence that it does.

Many scholars reason that since touching one's private area invalidates *wuḍū'*, touching a baby's private area invalidates *wuḍū'* as well. However, this analogy is not correct because of the difference between the two cases. In addition, the *ḥadīths* of the Prophet (ﷺ) clearly indicate that touching one's private area does not necessarily invalidate *wuḍū'* — unless it is done with lust.

Busrah Bint Ṣafwān (ﷺ) reported that the Prophet (ﷺ) said:

«إذا مسَّ أحدُكم ذكَرَه فليتوضّأ.»

> **‹When one of you touches his penis, he should perform *wuḍū'*.›** [1]

Abū Hurayrah (ﷺ) reported that Allāh's Messenger (ﷺ) said:

«إذا أفضى أحدُكم بيده إلى فرجه، وليس بينهما ستر ولا حجاب، فليتوضأ.»

> **‹When one of you reaches with his hand to his genitalia, without a separation, he should perform *wuḍū'*.›** [2]

Talq Bin ʿAlī (ﷺ) reported that he went with other men to Allāh's Prophet (ﷺ). While they were there, a man who appeared to be a bedouin came and asked, "O Prophet of Allāh! What do you say in regard to a man who touches his penis (during the prayer) after having performed *wuḍū'*?" The Prophet (ﷺ) replied:

---

1 Recorded by Aḥmad, Abū Dāwūd, and others. Verified to be authentic by al-Albānī (*Irwā'ul-Ghalīl* no. 116 and *Ṣaḥīḥu Abī Dāwūd* no. 181).

2 Recorded by Ibn Ḥibbān, al-Bayhaqī, and others. Verified to be authentic by al-Albānī (*aṣ-Ṣaḥīḥah* no. 1235).

«وهل هو إلا بَضْعَةٌ (أو مُضغةٌ) منه؟»

‹Is it anything but a piece of flesh from his body?› [1]

Commenting on this *ḥadīth*, al-Albānī (ﷺ) said:

> "This contains a subtle indication that the touching not requiring *wuḍū'* is only that which is not associated with lust, because in this case it is possible to liken touching that part to touching any other part of the body. Contrary to this is the touching with lust, which is not then similar to touching other parts of the body where the touching is not associated with desire. This should be quite obvious. Thus, this *ḥadīth* does not serve as evidence for the Ḥanafīs who say that touching never invalidates *wuḍū'*. It can only serve as evidence for those who say that touching without lust does not invalidate *wuḍū'*, whereas touching with lust does because of Busrah's *ḥadīth*. This reconciles between the two *ḥadīth*, and is the opinion that *Shaykh ul-Islām* Ibn Taymiyyah chose in some of his books, as I remember." [2]

Piercing the Ears

Piercing involves two acts that are normally prohibited in Islām: changing Allāh's (ﷻ) original creation, and causing unnecessary harm and pain.

Changing Allāh's Creation

Cutting animals' ears and changing the way Allāh created them constitute a sinful act of disobedience. Changing Allāh's creation

1 Recorded by Abū Dāwūd, at-Tirmiḏẖī, and others. Verified to be authentic by al-Albānī (*Ṣaḥīḥu Abī Dāwūd* no. 182, 183).

2 *Tamām ul-Minnah* p. 103.

without permission demonstrates obedience of the Devil, as Allāh (ﷻ) says:

﴿وَإِن يَدْعُونَ إِلَّا شَيْطَٰنًا مَرِيدًا ۝ لَعَنَهُ ٱللَّهُ. وَقَالَ لَأَتَّخِذَنَّ مِنْ عِبَادِكَ نَصِيبًا مَفْرُوضًا ۝ وَلَأُضِلَّنَّهُمْ وَلَأُمَنِّيَنَّهُمْ وَلَءَامُرَنَّهُمْ فَلَيُبَتِّكُنَّ ءَاذَانَ ٱلْأَنْعَٰمِ، وَلَءَامُرَنَّهُمْ فَلَيُغَيِّرُنَّ خَلْقَ ٱللَّهِ. وَمَن يَتَّخِذِ ٱلشَّيْطَٰنَ وَلِيًّا مِّن دُونِ ٱللَّهِ فَقَدْ خَسِرَ خُسْرَانًا مُّبِينًا ۝﴾ النساء ١١٧-١١٩

«They call (instead of Allāh) upon none but rebellious Satan, whom Allāh has cursed. And he had said (to Allāh), "I will surely take from among Your servants a specific portion. I will mislead them, give them false promises, command them so they will slit the ears of cattle, and command them so they will change the creation of Allāh." Certainly, whoever takes Satan as an ally instead of Allāh is in tremendous loss.» [1]

This prohibition of slitting the ears applies even more to human beings. Allāh (ﷻ) has honored human beings and fashioned them in the best form:

﴿لَقَدْ خَلَقْنَا ٱلْإِنسَٰنَ فِي أَحْسَنِ تَقْوِيمٍ ۝﴾ التين ٤

«Verily, We have created the human being in the best of stature.» [2]

Changing this stature without permission is indeed an act of atrocity and deviation that deserves punishment.

For the same reason, the Messenger (ﷺ) has declared that the women who change what Allāh (ﷻ) has created (such as removing their facial hair, wearing wigs, filing their teeth, or tattooing their bodies) seeking by that to improve their appearance, are accursed by

1 *An-Nisā'* 4:117-119.

2 *At-Tīn* 95:4.

Allāh (ﷻ). Ibn Masʿūd (رضي الله عنه) reported that Allāh's Messenger (ﷺ) said:

«لعن الله الواشمات والمستوشمات، والنامصات والمتنمصات،
والواصلات، والمتفلّجات للحُسن، المغيرات خلق الله.»

‹Allāh curses those (women) who tattoo (for others) and those who get tattoos, those who pluck the facial hair (for others) and those who have their facial hair plucked, those who connect their hair with other (fake) hair, and those who file their teeth for beauty — they all change Allāh's creation.› [1]

Inflicting Harm and Pain

Harming a human being without reason is strongly prohibited as well. Allāh (ﷻ) says:

﴿وَٱلَّذِينَ يُؤْذُونَ ٱلْمُؤْمِنِينَ وَٱلْمُؤْمِنَٰتِ بِغَيْرِ مَا ٱكْتَسَبُوا۟ فَقَدِ ٱحْتَمَلُوا۟
بُهْتَٰنًا وَإِثْمًا مُّبِينًا ۝﴾ الأحزاب ٥٨

«And those who harm believing men and women for what they do not deserve have certainly born upon themselves a slander and manifest sin.» [2]

ʿAbdullāh Bin ʿAbbās and ʿUbādah Bin aṣ-Ṣāmit (رضي الله عنهما) reported that Allāh's Messenger (ﷺ) said:

«لا ضرر ولا ضرار.»

‹No harm may be inflicted on oneself or others.› [3]

1 Recorded by al-Bukhārī and Muslim.

2 *Al-Aḥzāb* 33:58.

3 Recorded by Aḥmad and Ibn Mājah. Verified to be authentic by al-Albānī and others (*aṣ-Ṣaḥīḥah* no. 250).

EARRINGS DURING THE PROPHET'S TIME

There are a few reports in the Sunnah indicating that the Muslim women during the Prophet's (ﷺ) time wore earrings, and the Prophet (ﷺ) did not condemn or prohibit this.

Ibn ʿAbbās (ﷺ) reported that he saw the Prophet (ﷺ) pray the two *rakʿāt* on the day of *ʿĪd* then walk with Bilaal (ﷺ) to where the women sat. He (ﷺ) admonished them and urged them to give *ṣadaqah.* They responded by giving their rings, earrings, and other jewelry items. [1]

If it was prohibited to wear earrings, the Prophet (ﷺ) would have declared it when he saw the jewelry that the women gave.

In the long *ḥadīth* known as the *ḥadīth* of Umm Zarʿ [2], ʿĀʾishah (ﷺ) reported that the Prophet (ﷺ) told her that Umm Zarʿ said the following about her husband:

«"زَوْجِي أبو زَرْعٍ، وما أبو زرْعٍ؟ أَنَاسَ مِنْ حُلِيٍّ أُذُنَيَّ..."»

‹"My husband was Abū Zarʿ. And what would you know about Abū Zarʿ! He made my ears heavy with jewelry ..."›

In the conclusion of this *ḥadīth*, the Prophet (ﷺ) said to ʿĀʾishah:

«يا عائشةُ، كُنتُ لكِ كأبي زرعٍ لأمِّ زرعٍ.»

‹O ʿĀʾishah! I am to you like Abū Zarʿ was to Umm Zarʿ.› [3]

This indicates the Prophet's (ﷺ) approval, among other things, of Abū Zarʿ's giving earrings to Umm Zarʿ to wear.

Zaynab Bint Nabīṭ (ﷺ), who was Anas Bin Mālik's (ﷺ) wife, reported:

---

1 Recorded by al-Bukhārī, Muslim, and others.

2 The full *ḥadīth* is cited in the Author's, "The Fragile Vessels".

3 Recorded by al-Bukhārī, Muslim, and others.

"Abū Umāmah (⚬) requested from the Prophet (⚬) to give some jewelry (when he wins it from wars, etc.) to my mother and aunt. Later on, some jewelry was brought before the Prophet (⚬) including earrings made of gold and pearls. The Prophet (⚬) gave them some of the earrings. When I grew up, I found some of that jewelry in my family's house." [1]

CONCLUSION

We have seen that it is prohibited to pierce any part of the body, because it involves changing Allāh's creation and inflicting harm and pain. This general rule holds all the time, with only one exception that derives from the *hadīths* presented in the previous subsection.

Most of the *'ulamā'* conclude that it is permissible for women to have their earlobes pierced in order to wear earrings on them. They argue that had it been prohibited, the Prophet (⚬) would have taken the occasion to explain this to the people and warn them against it. Ibn ul-Qayyim (⚬) said:

"As for piercing a girl's ear, it is permissible for the purpose of wearing jewelry. This was stated by Imām Aḥmad. He also stated that it is disapproved to do it for a boy. The difference between the two is that a female needs to wear jewelry, making piercing her ears of benefit — contrary to a boy." [2]

However, because of the earlier discussed prohibition of inflicting pain and piercing, as well as other numerous warnings in the *Sunnah* against imitating the *kuffār* or the other gender, the conclusion should be qualified as follows:

1. It is permissible to pierce a female's earlobes in order to place earrings on them.

---

1   Recorded by Ibn Sa'd, al-Bayhaqī, and others. Verified to be *ḥasan* by Mustafā al-'Adwī (*Jāmi'u Aḥkām in-Nisā'* 4:442).

2   *Tuḥfat ul-Mawdūd* p. 126.

2. Only one hole is permitted in each ear.

3. No other parts of the body (nose, navel, tongue, etc.) may be pierced, because this involves imitation of the *kuffār*.

4. Males may not pierce their ears or wear earrings, because this is a strictly feminine adornment in Islām. In addition, this is done nowadays by singers and other corrupt individuals that a Muslim should avoid imitating.

Kissing Children and Showing Mercy to Them

It is recommended to show mercy to children in various ways. This was often done by the Prophet (ﷺ), as we have shown throughout this book. For instance, he rubbed over children's heads, gave them gifts, called them with nick names and *kunyahs*, performed *taḥnīk* and supplicated for them, taught them simple instructions, carried them during and outside the prayer, and kissed them.

Abū Hurayrah (رضي الله عنه) reported that Allāh's Messenger (ﷺ) kissed al-Ḥasan Bin ʿAlī (رضي الله عنهما) in the presence of al-Aqraʿ Bin Ḥābis at-Tamīmī. Al-Aqraʿ commented, "Indeed, I have ten children and have never kissed any of them." Allāh's Messenger (ﷺ) looked at him and said:

«مَن لا يَرحمُ لا يُرحَم.»

‹He who does not show mercy, no mercy will be shown to him (by Allāh).› [1]

ʿĀ'ishah (رضي الله عنها) reported that some bedouins who visited Allāh's Messenger (ﷺ) asked his companions, "Do you kiss your children?" The companions replied, "Yes!" The bedouins said, "By Allāh, we never kiss them." So the Prophet (ﷺ) said:

«أوَأَملِكُ لكم إن نزعَ اللهُ من قلوبكم الرحمةَ؟»

---

1 Recorded by al-Bukhārī, Muslim, and others.

‹What can I do for you if Allāh has removed mercy from your hearts?› [1]

Abū Hurayrah (⁕) reported:

"Indeed, Allāh's Messenger (⁕) used to stick his tongue out for al-Ḥasan Bin 'Alī. When the baby saw the redness of the Prophet's (⁕) tongue, he rushed to him." [2]

Breast-Feeding

DEFINITION AND DURATION

Allāh (⁕) ordained breast-feeding for humans and animals. It is a period during which the babies grow and build strength while enjoying the closeness and attention of the mother. At the end of the breast-feeding term, the child is "weaned" from the mother in preparation for becoming an independent being.

The normal duration of breast-feeding for humans is about two years. Allāh (⁕) says:

$$﴿وَوَصَّيْنَا ٱلْإِنسَٰنَ بِوَٰلِدَيْهِ، حَمَلَتْهُ أُمُّهُ وَهْنًا عَلَىٰ وَهْنٍ، وَفِصَٰلُهُ فِي عَامَيْنِ.﴾ لقمان ١٤$$

«We have enjoyed upon the human being to treat his parents kindly. His mother bore him with weakness upon weakness; and his weaning is in two years.» [3]

And Allāh (⁕) says:

---

1 Recorded by al-Bukhārī, Muslim, and others.

2 Recorded by Abū ash-Shaykh (in *Akhlāq un-Nabī*) and al-Baghawī (in *Sharḥ us-Sunnah*). Verified to be authentic by al-Albānī (*aṣ-Ṣaḥīḥah* no. 70).

3 *Luqmān* 31:14.

﴿وَوَصَّيْنَا ٱلْإِنْسَـٰنَ بِوَالِدَيْهِ، حَمَلَتْهُ أُمُّهُ كُرْهًا وَوَضَعَتْهُ كُرْهًا،
وَحَمْلُهُ وَفِصَـٰلُهُ ثَلَاثُونَ شَهْرًا.﴾ الأحقاف ١٥

«We have enjoyed upon the human being to treat his parents kindly. His mother bore him with hardship and delivered him with hardship. And his gestation and weaning (period) is thirty months.» [1]

According to Ibn ʿAbbās (رضي الله عنهما) and many other *ʿulamāʾ*, the difference between the two *āyāt* (30 versus 33 months) reflects the difference between a short-term (6-month) and a full-term (9-month) pregnancy.

Historical Background

Breast-feeding has been the practice of humans from earliest times. Never was artificial baby-nursing widely practiced prior to this modern time.

Allāh's messengers were no exception — they too were breast-fed. When Mūsā (عليه السلام) was a baby, Allāh (ﷻ) revealed to his mother to throw him into the river. Down the river, Mūsā was discovered by Pharaoh's family who decided to adopt the unidentified baby. However, there was a serious problem: the baby would not suckle from any woman's breast. Allāh (ﷻ) says:

﴿وَحَرَّمْنَا عَلَيْهِ ٱلْمَرَاضِعَ مِن قَبْلُ.﴾ القصص ١٢

«And We have previously made it prohibited for him (to suckle from) all wet-nurses (other than his mother).» [2]

In his childhood, the Prophet Muḥammad (ﷺ) suckled from his mother Āminah, Thuwaybah — a slave girl of his uncle Abū Lahab [3], Umm Ayman (Usāmah Bin Zayd's mother), and Ḥalīmah as-

1 *Al-Aḥqāf* 46:15.

2 *Al-Qaṣas* 28:12.

3 Recorded by al-Bukhārī and Muslim from Umm Ḥabībah (رضي الله عنها).

Saʿdiyyah [1].

In recent times, the woman has left her home to work in careers inferior and less fulfilling than that for which she has been created [2]. This has forced her to drop many of her natural practices. Pregnancies are now mostly avoided or reduced to three or less in a lifetime. Breast-feeding is almost completely abolished, giving way to formula milk and processed baby-food. This denies babies a great amount of psychological, emotional, and physical benefits.

IMPORTANCE OF BREAST-FEEDING IN ISLĀM

Islām emphasizes the importance of breast-feeding in various ways. In what follows, we highlight a few of them.

1. In Islām, breast-feeding is clearly an obligation upon both parents. The mother provides the milk, and the father provides the material support. This is discussed further in the next subsections.

2. Islām partially gives to the relationships resulting from breast-feeding a status similar to that of blood relationships [3]. ʿĀ'ishah, Ibn ʿAbbās, and ʿAlī (ﷺ) reported that Allāh's Messenger (ﷺ) said:

«إن اللّهَ حرّمَ من الرضاعِ ما حرّمَ من الولادةِ (النسبِ).»

‹Indeed, Allāh has prohibited (marriage) among suckling relatives, as He has prohibited it among birth (or blood) relatives.› [4]

3. A married man or women who commits adultery deserves the capital

1 Recorded by Ibn Ḥibbān, Abū Dāwūd, and others from ʿAbdullāh Bin Jaʿfar (ﷺ). Verified to be *ḥasan* by a<u>th</u>-<u>Th</u>ahabī and others.

2 A detailed discussion of the woman's responsibilities is presented in the Author's, "The Fragile Vessels".

3 A detailed discussion of this is presented in the Author's, "The Quest for Love and Mercy".

4 Recorded by al-Bukhārī, Muslim, and others. Review *Irwā'ul-Ghalīl* no. 1876 for the various narrations of this *ḥadīth*.

punishment of stoning to death [1]. For a married woman, however, she is allowed time to breast-feed her baby or find someone to breast-feed it before she is stoned.

A woman came to the Prophet (ﷺ) and confessed that she was pregnant from *zinā*. The Prophet (ﷺ) asked a man from the *Anṣār* to take her into his custody until she delivered her baby. After delivery, the Prophet (ﷺ) said:

«إذن لا نرجُمُها وندعُ ولدَها صغيراً ليس له من يُرضِعُه.»

‹We cannot stone her and leave her young baby with no one to breast-feed it.›

A man from the *Anṣār* pledged to provide a wet-nurse for the baby. The Prophet (ﷺ) then had her stoned and said:

«لقد تابت توبةً لو قُسِمت بين سبعينَ من أهل المدينةِ لوَسِعتهم.
وهل وجدتَ توبةً أفضلَ من أن جادت بنفسِها للّهِ تعالى؟»

‹Indeed, she has repented such a repentance that, were it to be divided among seventy of al-Madīnah's residents it would encompass them. Have you seen a better repentance than giving herself for Allāh (ﷻ)?› [2]

LEGISLATIVE TEXTS

The following texts from the Qur'ān cover most of the regulations pertaining to breast-feeding.

Allāh (ﷻ) says:

﴿وَٱلْوَالِدَاتُ يُرْضِعْنَ أَوْلَادَهُنَّ حَوْلَيْنِ كَامِلَيْنِ لِمَنْ أَرَادَ أَن يُتِمَّ

---

1 A detailed discussion of this is presented in the Author's, "Closer than a Garment".

2 A combined report recorded by Muslim, Abū Dāwūd, and others. Its various parts were verified to be authentic by al-Albānī (*Irwā'ul-Ghalīl* no. 2322, 2333).

ٱلرَّضَاعَةَ. وَعَلَى ٱلْمَوْلُودِ لَهُ رِزْقُهُنَّ وَكِسْوَتُهُنَّ بِٱلْمَعْرُوفِ. لاَ
تُكَلَّفُ نَفْسٌ إِلاَّ وُسْعَهَا. لاَ تُضَآرَّ وَالِدَةٌ بِوَلَدِهَا، وَلاَ مَوْلُودٌ لَهُ
بِوَلَدِهِ. وَعَلَى ٱلْوَارِثِ مِثْلُ ذَٰلِكَ. فَإِنْ أَرَادَا فِصَالاً عَن تَرَاضٍ
مِنْهُمَا وَتَشَاوُرٍ فَلاَ جُنَاحَ عَلَيْهِمَا، وَإِنْ أَرَدتُّمْ أَن تَسْتَرْضِعُوٓاْ
أَوْلاَدَكُمْ، فَلاَ جُنَاحَ عَلَيْكُمْ إِذَا سَلَّمْتُم مَّآ ءَاتَيْتُم بِٱلْمَعْرُوفِ.
وَٱتَّقُواْ ٱللَّهَ، وَٱعْلَمُوٓاْ أَنَّ ٱللَّهَ بِمَا تَعْمَلُونَ بَصِيرٌ ۝﴾ البقرة ٢٣٣

«Mothers may breast-feed their children two complete years for whoever wants to complete the nursing period. Upon the father is their (the mothers') provision and clothing according to what is reasonable. No person is charged with more than his capacity. No mother should be harmed through her child, nor should a father be. And upon the heir (of the father) is a similar obligation (if the father dies). And if they both (parents) desire weaning through mutual consent and consultation, there is no blame upon either of them. And if you wish to have your children breast-fed by a substitute, there is no blame upon you as long as you give payment according to what is reasonable. And revere Allāh and know that Allāh is Seeing of what you do.» [1]

And Allāh (ﷻ) says in regard to the divorced wives' *ʿiddah* (waiting period):

﴿أَسْكِنُوهُنَّ مِنْ حَيْثُ سَكَنتُم مِّن وُجْدِكُمْ، وَلاَ تُضَآرُّوهُنَّ لِتُضَيِّقُواْ
عَلَيْهِنَّ. وَإِن كُنَّ أُوْلَٰتِ حَمْلٍ فَأَنفِقُواْ عَلَيْهِنَّ حَتَّىٰ يَضَعْنَ حَمْلَهُنَّ.
فَإِنْ أَرْضَعْنَ لَكُمْ فَـَٔاتُوهُنَّ أُجُورَهُنَّ، وَأْتَمِرُواْ بَيْنَكُم بِمَعْرُوفٍ، وَإِن

1 *Al-Baqarah* 2:233.

تَعَاسَرْتُمْ فَسَتُرْضِعُ لَهُ أُخْرَىٰ ۝ لِيُنفِقْ ذُو سَعَةٍ مِّن سَعَتِهِۦ، وَمَن قُدِرَ
عَلَيْهِ رِزْقُهُۥ فَلْيُنفِقْ مِمَّآ ءَاتَىٰهُ ٱللَّهُ. لَا يُكَلِّفُ ٱللَّهُ نَفْسًا إِلَّا مَآ ءَاتَىٰهَا،
سَيَجْعَلُ ٱللَّهُ بَعْدَ عُسْرٍ يُسْرًا ۝﴾ الطلاق ٦-٧

«(During their ʿ*iddah*,) lodge them (your divorced wives) of where you dwell out of your means, and do not harm them in order to oppress them. And if they should be pregnant then spend on them until they give birth. And if they breast-feed for you, give them their payment and negotiate among yourselves in the acceptable way. But if you are in dispute, then another woman may breast-feed for him (the father).

Let a man of wealth spend from his wealth. And he whose provision is restricted, let him spend from what Allāh has given him. Allāh does not require from a soul except according to what He has given it. Allāh will bring about after hardship ease.» [1]

Regulations

From the above, we derive the following regulations concerning breast-feeding:

1. Unless she has a legitimate excuse, a mother is required to breast-feed her baby for two full years.

2. In case of the father's death, his heirs are responsible for the father's obligations.

3. During the breast-feeding term, the baby's father is required to support the mother, even if she was divorced from him.

4. The father should support the mother appropriately in accordance with his means.

---

1 *Aṭ-Ṭalāq* 65:6-7.

5. It is impermissible for the father to prevent the mother from breast-feeding her baby in order to cause her harm and aggravation. Similarly, it is impermissible for the mother to refuse to breast-feed her baby in order to harm or aggravate the father.

6. If one of the baby's parents thinks that there is need to wean the baby prior to the end of the two-year term, he (or she) should consult with the other parent. Weaning would then be allowed after the consultation and a joint agreement.

7. With the parent's joint agreement, it is permissible to hire another woman to breast-feed the baby.

ADVANTAGES OF BREAST-FEEDING

Breast-feeding has many advantages over artificial feeding. In what follows we present a selected list of them as proposed by some physicians [1]:

1. The mother's milk is assured to be clean and sterilized.

2. The mother's milk always has the right temperature for the baby.

3. The mother's milk is available whenever the baby needs it.

4. The mother's milk remains fresh and does not go bad in storage.

5. The mother's milk is suitable to the baby's digestive system.

6. The mother's milk contains all the necessary nutrients for the baby.

7. The mother's milk provides the baby with immunity against various infections.

8. Breast-feeding suppresses obesity in mothers and babies.

---

1 Adapted from an article by Dr. Fārūq Musāhil published in al-Ummah journal (50:1405), Qatar.

9. Breast-feeding strengthens affection and emotional ties between the mother and her baby.

10. Breast-feeding may be performed as an act of worship seeking through it Allāh's pleasure and acceptance.

PREGNANCY OF A NURSING MOTHER

If a breast-feeding mother gets pregnant, the quality of her milk is usually degraded. Some scholars recommend avoiding intercourse with a breast-feeding woman or taking measures to avoid impregnating her.

The Prophet (ﷺ) permitted having intercourse with a pregnant woman. Furthermore, he did not consider it necessary or useful to practice early withdrawal (as a measure of birth-control) with her. Juthāmah Bint Wahb (﵂) reported that the Prophet (ﷺ) said:

«لقد هممتُ أن أنهى عن الغِيلة، حتى ذكرت أن الرومَ

وفارسَ يصنعون ذٰلك فلا يضرُّ أولادَهم. »

‹I was about to prohibit having intercourse with a nursing women, but then realized that the Romans and Persians do it and it does not harm their children.›

He (ﷺ) was then asked about early withdrawal and he replied, «ذلك الوأد الخفي. » ‹That is the secret killing of children.› [1]

Saʿd Bin Abī Waqqāṣ (﵁) reported that a man came to Allāh's Messenger (ﷺ) and said, "I perform early withdrawal with my wife." The Prophet (ﷺ) asked him, «لِمَ تفعل ذلك؟» ‹Why do you do that?› He replied, "I pity her child (that she nurses)." Allāh's Messenger (ﷺ) said:

«لو كان ذٰلك (الغَيْلُ) ضارّاً ضرَّ فارسَ والرومَ. »

‹If it is harmful for a woman to continue breast-

---

1   Recorded by Muslim and others.

feeding after conception, it would have harmed the Persians and Romans.› [1]

We conclude from this the following:

1. It is permissible for a man to have intercourse with his breast-feeding wife.

2. It is permissible, but not recommended, to practice early withdrawal with the breast-feeding woman.

3. If the nursing woman gets pregnant, she does not have to stop breast-feed her baby. However, if her physical condition is such that her pregnancy clearly degrades her milk, she may need to terminate her breast-feeding and find an alternative wet-nurse (not easy in our times) or milk substitute for her baby.

Concluding Remarks from Ibn ul-Qayyim

We concude this section by a number of selected advices from Ibn ul-Qayyim concerning breast-feeding:

> "Babies should only be fed the (mother's) milk until their teeth appear. Their stomach and digestive system (in the early months) are incapable of handling (solid) food. When the baby's teeth come out, its stomach becomes strong and ready for food. Indeed, Allāh (ﷻ) delays the growth of teeth until the baby needs the food. This is from His wisdom and kindness, and out of mercy toward the mother and her breast's nipples, so that the baby would not bite them with its teeth.
>
> The babies should be given solid food in a gradual manner, starting with soft foods, such as wet bread, (animal) milk, yogurt, meat broth, …
>
> The parents should not be too disturbed by the baby's crying and screaming, especially when it is

1 Recorded by Muslim.

hungry for milk. That crying benefits the baby tremendously, training its limbs, widening its intestines, broadening its chest, …

The complete breast-feeding term is two years. This is a right for the baby — if it needs it and cannot do without it. Allāh confirmed this with the word "complete", saying ﴿حَوْلَيْنِ كَامِلَيْنِ﴾ **«Two complete years,»** so that no one would assume it to be less than this …

When the breast-feeding mother wants to wean the baby, she should do so gradually … she should train it because of the harm involved in a sudden change of habits …

And care should be taken not to force the baby to walk before it is ready, because that would cause its legs to become bent and twisted …

When a nursing woman is approached (with intercourse) by a man, she may get pregnant, which is one of the worst things for the baby who is nourished by her milk. The good blood would then be redirected to nourish the fetus in her womb … This would cause the milk in her breasts to become scarce and bad … Thus, when a nursing women gets pregnant, it is best to prevent her from breast-feeding her baby and seek another wet-nurse for it … "[1]

---

1 *Tuḥfat ul-Mawdūd* 140-145.

APPENDIX I: LIST OF NAMES

Introduction

In what follows, we present a selection of proposed names for boys and girls. Most of these are names of prophets, *ṣaḥābah*, and other individuals from among the righteous *salaf*.

General Guidelines

The following guidelines should be taken into consideration in regard to the forthcoming list:

1. **Sorting:** The names are sorted according to the English alphabetical order, with marks "ʾ" and "ʿ", standing for Arabic letters *hamzah* and *ʿayn,* given lowest priority. Letters with a dot or dash are given equal priority to the same letters without these marks.

2. **Meanings:** We have not included the meanings of the listed names because of space limitations. If one is interested in using a specific name, we recommend first finding its meaning in an Arabic lexicon or from knowledgeable individuals.

3. **Pronunciation:** In addition to carrying a good meaning, we further recommend selecting a name that is easy to pronounce.

4. **Names of Servitude:** Many boys' and girls' names may be constructed by prefixing one of Allāh's excellent names with the terms *ʿabd* (servant, slave, or worshiper), *ʿubayd* (a reduced form of *ʿabd*), or *amah* (feminine of *ʿabd*).

   Examples: Abd ul-Lāh (or ʿAbdullāh), ʿUbayd ul-Lāh, and Amat ul-Lāh (or Amatullāh).

   More details of this, in addition to a full list of Allāh's authentic names, are presented in the Appendix II.

5. **Disliked Names:** In the following list, some names are followed by an asterisk (*). These names were disliked by the Prophet (ﷺ). As we explained earlier in this book, the reason for the dislike was that they could cause confusion to some people when they hear them put in certain contexts.

   There probably are other names in the following lists of boys' and girls' names that have similar meanings to the disliked names. However, we did not take the time to mark them, leaving such a task to the interested readers.

Names of Boys

Name	الاسم
Abān	أبان
Ādam	آدم
Aflaḥ *	أفلح
Agharr	أغَرّ
Aḥmad	أحمد
Aḥnaf	أحنف
Anas	أنس
Arqam	أرقم
Asad	أسد
Asbāṭ	أسباط
Ash'ath	أشعث
Asīd	أَسِيد
Aslam	أسلم
Asqa'	أسقع
Aswad	أسود
As'ad	أسعد
Awfā	أوفى
Aws	أوس
Ayman	أيمن
Ayyūb	أيّوب
Azhar	أزهر
Badr	بدر
Bakkār	بكّار
Bakr	بكر
Barā'	براء
Bashīr	بشير
Bash-shār	بشّار
Baṣīr	بصير
Bassām	بسّام

Name	**الاسم**
Bayān	بيان
Bilāl	بلال
Bishr	بِشْر
Bukayr	بُكَيْر
Burayd	بُرَيْد
Buraydah	بُريدة
Burd	بُرْد
Bushayr	بُشَيْر
Busr	بُسْر
Ḍaḥḥāk	ضحّاك
Ḍamrah	ضَمْرة
Dāwūd	داود
Daylam	دَيلَم
Diḥyah	دِحية
Ḍimām	ضِمام
Dīnār	دينار
Ḍurayb	ضُرَيب
Fāḍil	فاضل
Faḍl	فضل
Fahd	فهد
Fākih	فاكِه
Falāḥ	فَلاح

Fāris	فارس
Farqad	فرقد
Fārūq	فاروق
Fātiḥ	فاتح
Fawwāz	فوّاز
Fayyāḍ	فيّاض
Fayṣal	فيصل
Fā'id	فائد
Fā'iz	فائز
Fihr	فِهر
Firās	فِراس
Fudayk	فُدَيك
Fuḍayl	فُضيل
Furāt	فُرات
Fu'ād	فؤاد
Ghazwān	غَزوان
Ghālib	غالب
Ghānim	غانم
Ghassān	غسّان
Ghayth	غيث
Ghāzī	غازي
Ghiyāth	غِياث

Name	**الاسم**
Ḥabbān	حَبّان
Ḥabīb	حبيب
Ḥābis	حابس
Hādī	هادي
Hadiyyah	هدية
Ḥāfiẓ	حافظ
Ḥafṣ	حفص
Ḥājib	حاجب
Ḥakīm	حكيم
Ḥamad	حَمَد
Ḥamdān	حمدان
Ḥamīd	حميد
Ḥāmid	حامد
Ḥammād	حَمّاد
Hammām	هَمّام
Ḥamzah	حمزة
Ḥanīf	حنيف
Hāni'	هانئ
Hannād	هنّاد
Ḥanẓalah	حنظلة
Ḥārith	حارث
Ḥārithah	حارثة
Ḥarīz	حَرِيز
Hārūn	هارون
Ḥasan	حسن
Hāshim	هاشم
Ḥasīb	حسيب
Ḥassān	حسّان
Ḥātim	حاتِم
Ḥawshab	حوشب
Ḥaydar	حيدر
Haytham	هيثم
Ḥayyān	حيّان
Ḥāzim	حازم
Ḥazm	حِزْم
Ḥibbān	حِبّان
Hilāl	هلال
Hishām	هشام
Ḥizām	حِزَام
Ḥubaysh	حُبيش
Hūd	هود
Ḥuḍayn	حُضَين
Hudbah	هُدْبة
Ḥujr	حُجْر

Name	**الاسم**
Ḥukaym	حُكَيْم
Humām	هُمام
Ḥumayd	حُمَيد
Ḥunayf	حُنَيف
Ḥunayn	حُنَين
Hunayy	هُنَيّ
Ḥurayth	حُرَيث
Ḥusām	حسام
Ḥusayn	حسين
Ḥuṣayn	حُصَين
Hushaym	هُشَيم
Ḥu<u>th</u>ayfah	حذيفة
Hu<u>th</u>ayl	هُذَيل
Ḥuyayy	حُيَيّ
Ibrāhīm	إبراهيم
Idrīs	إدريس
Ilyās	إلياس
Ilyasaʿ	إليسع
Isḥāq	إسحاق
Ismāʿīl	إسماعيل
Iyād	إياد
Iyās	إياس

Jabalah	جَبَلة
Jābir	جابر
Jabr	جبر
Jahm	جَهْم
Jamīl	جميل
Jarīr	جَرير
Jarrāḥ	جرّاح
Jāsir	جاسِر
Jasr	جَسْر
Jaʿfar	جعفر
Jubārah	جُبارة
Jubayr	جُبير
Jumayʿ	جُمَيع
Junādah	جُنادة
Junayd	جُنيد
Jundub	جُندُب
Jurayy	جُرَيّ
Kāmil	كامل
Kathīr	كثير
Kaysān	كَيْسان
Kaʿb	كعب
Khabbāb	خبّاب

Name	الاسم
Khadīj	خَدِيج
Khaḍir	خَضِر
Khalaf	خلف
Khālid	خالد
Khalīfah	خليفة
Khalīl	خليل
Khallād	خَلّاد
Khārijah	خارجة
Khaṣīf	خَصِيف
Khaṭīb	خطيب
Khaṭ ṭāb	خطّاب
Khayr	خير
Khubayb	خُبيب
Khufāf	خُفاف
Khulayd	خُلَيد
Khuṣayf	خُصَيف
Khuwaylid	خويلد
Khuzaym	خُزَيْم
Khuzaymah	خزيمة
Kinānah	كِنانة
Kumayl	كُمَيل
Kurayb	كُريب

Kuthayr	كُثَير
Labīb	لبيب
Labīd	لبيد
Layth	ليث
Luqmān	لقمان
Lu'ayy	لُؤَي
Maḥbūb	محبوب
Mahdī	مَهدي
Maḥfūẓ	مَحْفوظ
Māhir	ماهر
Maḥmūd	محمود
Mājid	ماجد
Makhlad	مَخْلَد
Mālik	مالك
Mamdūḥ	ممدوح
Manṣūr	منصور
Marthad	مَرْثَد
Marwān	مروان
Marzūq	مرزوق
Masarrah	مَسَرّة
Maslamah	مَسْلَمَة
Mas'ūd	مسعود

Name	الاسم
Maṭar	مَطَر
Maymūn	ميمون
Maysarah	ميسرة
Maʿbad	مَعْبَد
Maʾmūn	مأمون
Maʿmar	مَعْمَر
Maʿn	معن
Maʿqil	معقِل
Maʿrūf	معروف
Miḥjan	مِحْجَن
Miqdād	مِقداد
Miqdām	مِقدام
Miswar	مِسْوَر
Mubārak	مُبارَك
Mubash-shir	مُبَشِّر
Muḍar	مُضر
Mudrik	مُدْرِك
Mufliḥ	مُفلِح
Mughīrah	مغيرة
Mughīth	مغيث
Muhājir	مُهاجر
Muḥammad	محمد

Muhannā	مُهنّا
Muhannad	مهنّد
Muḥarrar	مُحَرَّر
Muḥriz	مُحْرِز
Muḥsin	محسِن
Muḥṣin	مُحْصِن
Mujāhid	مجاهد
Mujammiʿ	مُجَمِّع
Mukhtār	مُختار
Munīb	منيب
Munīr	منير
Munjid	مُنجِد
Munqith	مُنقذ
Munṣif	مُنصِف
Munthir	منذر
Muqaddam	مقدَّم
Muqarrin	مُقَرِّن
Muqātil	مقاتل
Murajjā	مُرَجّى
Murrah	مُرّة
Mūsā	موسى
Musaddad	مُسَدَّد

Name	الاسم
Musayyib	مُسَيِّب
Musā'id	مساعد
Mushrif	مُشرف
Muslim	مُسلِم
Musṭafā	مصطفى
Muṣ'ab	مصعب
Muṭahhar	مُطَهَّر
Muṭarrif	مُطَرِّف
Muṭayr	مُطَيْر
Muthannā	مُثَنّى
Muṭī'	مُطيع
Muṭṭalib	مُطَّلِب
Muṭ'im	مُطعِم
Muwaffaq	مُوفّق
Muẓaffar	مظفَّر
Mu'āfā	مُعافى
Mu'allā	مُعَلّى
Mu'ammal	مُؤَمَّل
Mu'ān	مُعَان
Mu'āth	معاذ
Mu'āwiyah	مُعاوية
Mu'awwath	مُعوّذ

Mu'taṣim	معتصم
Nabhān	نَبْهان
Nabīh	نبيه
Nabīl	نبيل
Nadīm	نديم
Naḍr	نَضْر
Nāfi' *	نافع
Nahār	نهار
Nājī	ناجي
Najīb	نجيب
Najīḥ *	نَجيح
Namir	نَمِر
Nasīb	نسيب
Nāṣiḥ	ناصح
Nāṣir	ناصر
Naṣr	نصر
Naṣṣār	نصّار
Nawf	نَوْف
Nawfal	نَوفل
Nawwāf	نوّاف
Nawwās	نوّاس
Nāyif	نايف

Name	الاسم
Nazīh	نزيه
Naẓīr	نظير
Nā'il	نائل
Na'īm	نعيم
Nizār	نزار
Nubayh	نُبَيْه
Nufayl	نُفيل
Nufay'	نُفَيع
Nūḥ	نوح
Nujayd	نُجَيْد
Nujayy	نُجَيّ
Numayr	نُمير
Nusayr	نُسَيْر
Nuṣayr	نُصَيْر
Nu'aym	نُعَيم
Nu'mān	نُعمان
Qaḥṭān	قحطان
Qāsim	قاسم
Qatādah	قتادة
Qays	قيس
Qa'qā'	قعقاع
Qudāmah	قُدامة

Qurrah	قُرّة
Quṣayy	قُصيّ
Qutaybah	قُتَيبة
Rabāḥ *	رباح
Rabī'	ربيع
Rabī'ah	ربيعة
Rafīq	رفيق
Rāfi' *	رافع
Rāghib	راغب
Rajā'	رجاء
Rājiḥ	راجح
Rashād	رشاد
Rashīd	رشيد
Rāshid	راشد
Rāsim	راسم
Rawḥ	رَوْح
Rawwād	رَوّاد
Rayḥān	ريحان
Razīn	رَزين
Rib'iyy	رِبعِيّ
Rifā'ah	رِفاعة
Riyāḥ	رِياح

Name	الاسم
Rubayḥ	رُبَيح
Rufayʿ	رُفَيْع
Ruḥayl	رُحَيْل
Rukānah	رُكانة
Ruwayfiʿ	رُوَيْفع
Ruzayq	رُزَيْق
Sābiq	سابق
Ṣābir	صابر
Saburah	سبُرة
Ṣadaqah	صدقة
Ṣādiq	صادق
Ṣafiyy	صفيّ
Ṣafwān	صفوان
Sahl	سهل
Sahm	سهم
Sakan	سَكَن
Ṣākhr	صخر
Ṣalāḥ	صلاح
Salām	سلام
Salamah	سَلَمة
Salāmah	سلامة
Salimah	سَلِمَة

Sallām	سلّام
Salm	سَلْم
Ṣāliḥ	صالح
Salīm	سَليم
Sālim	سالم
Salmān	سلمان
Ṣalt	صَلْت
Sāmī	سامي
Samīr	سمير
Samurah	سمُرة
Samʿān	سمعان
Sariyy	سَرِيّ
Sayf	سيف
Sayyār	سيّار
Saʿd	سعد
Sāʿī	ساعي
Sāʾib	سائب
Saʿīd	سعيد
Shabīb	شَبيب
Shaddād	شدّاد
Shafīq	شفيق
Shāfiʿ	شافع

Name	الاسم
Shāhīn	شاهين
Shahr	شهر
Shakal	شَكَل
Shākir	شاكر
Shaqīq	شقيق
Sharīf	شريف
Sharīk	شريك
Shaybah	شَيْبَة
Shaybān	شيبان
Shibl	شِبل
Shubayl	شُبَيْل
Shujāʿ	شُجَاع
Shurayḥ	شُريح
Shuʿayb	شعيب
Shuʿbah	شعبة
Ṣiddīq	صِدّيق
Ṣilah	صِلة
Simāk	سِماك
Sinān	سِنان
Sirāj	سراج
Ṣubayḥ	صُبَيح
Subayʿ	سُبيع
Ṣudayy	صُدَيّ
Sufyān	سُفيان
Ṣuhayb	صُهيب
Suhayl	سُهيل
Sukayn	سُكَيْن
Sulaym	سُليم
Sulaymān	سليمان
Sul ṭān	سلطان
Sumayr	سُمَير
Sumayy	سُمَيّ
Sunayn	سُنَين
Surayj	سُريج
Suwayd	سُويد
Suʿūd	سُعود
Ṭāhir	طاهر
Ṭalāl	طلال
Ṭalḥah	طلحة
Ṭālib	طالب
Talīd	تَليد
Ṭalīq	طليق
Ṭalq	طلْق
Tamīm	تَميم

Name	الاسم
Tammām	تَمّام
Ṭarafah	طَرَفَة
Ṭarīf	طريف
Ṭāriq	طارق
Ṭawd	طود
Ṭayyib	طيب
Thābit	ثابت
<u>Th</u>akwān	ذكوان
<u>Th</u>arr	ذَرّ
Thawbān	ثوبان
<u>Th</u>uhayl	ذُهَيل
Thumāmah	ثُمامة
<u>Th</u>uwayd	ذُوَيد
Tubayʿ	تُبَيْع
Ṭufayl	طُفيل
Ṭuhayr	طُهَير
Ṭuʿmah	طُعْمَة
Ubayy	أُبَيّ
Uhbān	أُهْبان
Umayy	أُمَيّ
Umayyah	أُميّة
Unays	أُنَيس

Usāmah	أسامة
Usayd	أسيد
Uways	أُويس
Wābil	وابل
Wābiṣah	وابصة
Waḍḍāḥ	وضاح
Wadīʿ	وديع
Wafāʾ	وفاء
Wafīq	وفيق
Wahb	وَهْب
Wajīh	وجيه
Wakīʿ	وكيع
Walīd	وليد
Wāqid	واقد
Wāṣil	واصل
Wasīm	وسيم
Wāsim	واسم
Wāsiʿ	واسع
Wāthiq	واثق
Wāʾil	وائل
Wuhayb	وُهَيب
Yaḥyā	يحيى

Name	الاسم
Yamān	يَمان
Yasār *	يسار
Yāsir	ياسر
Yazīd	يزيد
Ya'lā *	يعلى
Ya'qūb	يعقوب
Ya'rub	يعرُب
Yūnus	يونس
Yusayr	يُسَير
Yūsuf	يوسف
Ẓāfir	ظافر
Zāhir	زاهر
Ẓahīr	ظهير
Zakariyyā	زكريا
Zakī	زكي
Zayd	زيد
Zāyid	زايد
Zā'idah	زائدة
Zirr	زِرّ
Ziyād	زياد
Zubayd	زُبيد
Zubayr	زبير
Zufar	زُفَر
Zuhayr	زهير
Zur'ah	زُرْعة
'Abbād	عبَّاد
'Abbās	عباس
'Abdullāh	عبد اللّه
'Ābid	عابد
'Adiyy	عَدِي
'Adnān	عدنان
'Affān	عفّان
'Afīf	عفيف
'Ajlān	عجلان
'Alā'	علاء
'Aliyy ('Alī)	علي
'Alqamah	عَلقمة
'Āmir	عامر
'Ammār	عمّار
'Amr	عمرو
'Aqīl	عقيل
'Arfajah	عرفجة
'Arīb	عَرِيب
'Āṣim	عاصم

Name	الاسم
ʻAssāf	عسّاف
ʻAṭā'	عطاء
ʻĀṭif	عاطف
ʻAṭiyyah	عطية
ʻAwf	عوف
ʻAwn	عون
ʻAyyāsh	عيّاش
ʻĀ'id	عائد
ʻĀ'ish	عائش
ʻĀ'ith	عائذ
ʻĪd	عيد
ʻIkrimah	عِكرمة
ʻImād	عماد
ʻImrān	عمران
ʻIrbāḍ	عرباض
ʻĪsā	عيسى
ʻIsām	عصام

ʻIyāḍ	عِياض
ʻUbādah	عبادة
ʻUbayd	عُبيد
ʻUbaydullāh	عبيد اللّه
ʻUbaydah	عبيدة
ʻUfayr	عُفَير
ʻUmar	عمر
ʻUmārah	عُمارة
ʻUmayr	عمير
ʻUqayl	عُقَيْل
ʻUqbah	عُقبة
ʻUrwah	عُروة
ʻUtbah	عُتبة
ʻUthmān	عثمان
ʻUwaymir	عُويْمِر
ʻUyaynah	عُيَيْنَة

Names of Girls

Name	الاسم
Ālā'	آلاء

Amān	أمان
Amatullāh	أمة اللّه

Name	**الاسم**
Amīnah	أمينة
Āminah	آمنة
Anīsah	أَنيسة
Arwā	أروى
Aṣīlah	أصيلة
Āsiyah	آسية
Asmā'	أسماء
Athīlah	أَثيلة
Āyah	آية
Bādiyah	بادية
Bahiyyah	بهية
Banān	بَنان
Barīrah	بَريرة
Batūl	بتول
Buraydah	بُريدة
Bushrā	بُشْرى
Busrah	بُسْرة
Buthaynah	بُثينة
Dīmah	ديمة
Durrah	دُرّة
Faḍīlah	فضيلة
Fāḍilah	فاضلة
Fākhitah	فاخِتة
Fāṭimah	فاطمة
Fā'izah	فائزة
Fukayhah	فُكَيْهة
Ghufayrah	غُفَيْرة
Ghunayyah	غُنَيَّة
Ghuzaylah	غُزَيْلة
Ḥabāb	حَبَاب
Ḥabābah	حَبَابة
Ḥabībah	حبيبة
Ḥafīẓah	حفيظة
Ḥafṣah	حفصة
Ḥājar	هاجر
Ḥakīmah	حكيمة
Hālah	هالة
Ḥalīmah	حليمة
Ḥamīdah	حميدة
Ḥamnah	حَمْنة
Hanā'	هناء
Ḥanīfah	حنيفة
Ḥaṣān	حَصَان
Ḥasanah	حَسَنَة

Name	الاسم
Ḥasībah	حسيبة
Ḥassānah	حسّانة
Ḥawwā᾿	حواء
Ḥayāh	حياة
Hayā᾿	هياء
Hibat ul-Lāh	هبة اللّه
Hind	هِند
Ḥiṣṣah	حِصَّة
Hudā	هدى
Hujaynah	هُجَيْنة
Ḥumaydah	حُمَيْدة
Hunaydah	هُنَيْدة
Jamīlah	جميلة
Jumānah	جمانة
Juwayriyah	جويرية
Kaḥīlah	كَحِيلة
Karīmah	كريمة
Kathīrah	كثيرة
Khadījah	خديجة
Khālidah	خالدة
Khāliṣah	خالصة
Khawlah	خولة
Khayyirah	خَيِّرة
Khulaydah	خُلَيدة
Khulūd	خلود
Khuzaymah	خُزيمة
Kuḥaylah	كُحَيْلة
Labībah	لبيبة
Lamā	لمى
Lamīs	لَميس
Lamyā᾿	لمياء
Laṭīfah	لطيفة
Laylā	ليلى
Lubābah	لُبابة
Lubnā	لُبنى
Luhayyah	لُهَيَّة
Mājidah	ماجدة
Malikah	مَلِكة
Manāl	منال
Maryam	مريم
Maṣūn	مصون
Maymūnah	ميمونة
Mayyah	مَيَّة
Ma᾿mūnah	مأمونة

Name	الاسم
Mubārakah	مباركة
Mufīdah	مفيدة
Mulaykah	مُلَيْكة
Munā	منى
Munayyah	مُنْيَة
Munībah	منيبة
Munīfah	منيفة
Munīrah	منيرة
Musaykah	مُسَيْكة
Muznah	مُزنة
Muʿā<u>th</u>ah	مُعاذة
Nabīhah	نبيهة
Nabīlah	نبيلة
Nadā	ندى
Nādiyah	نادية
Nafīsah	نَفيسة
Najāh	نجاة
Najāḥ	نجاح
Nājiyah	ناجية
Najiyyah	نَجية
Najlāʾ	نجلاء
Nasīkah	نَسِيكة
Nawār	نَوَار
Nawf	نَوْف
Nazīhah	نزيهة
Nāʾilah	نائلة
Naʿīmah	نعيمة
Niʾam	نِعَم
Niʿmah	نِعمة
Nufaysah	نُفَيْسة
Nuhā	نُهى
Nuhayyah	نُهَيَّة
Nūrah	نُورة
Nusaybah	نُسيبة
Nuwaylah	نُوَيْلة
Nuʿmā	نُعْمى
Qurrah	قُرّة
Qarībah	قُرَيْبة
Rabāb	رَباب
Rābiyah	رابية
Rabīʿah	ربيعة
Rābiʿah	رابعة
Rāḍiyah	راضية
Raḍiyyah	رضيّة

Name	الاسم
Raḍwā	رَضْوى
Raḥmah	رحمة
Ramlah	رَمْلة
Randah	رندة
Rashīdah	رشيدة
Rāshidah	راشدة
Rāsimah	راسمة
Rawā᾽	رَواء
Rawḍah	روضة
Rāwiyah	راوية
Rayḥānah	ريحانة
Rayyā	ريّا
Razān	رزان
Razīnah	رَزينة
Rā᾽idah	رائدة
Rubā	رُبى
Rubayʿ	رُبَيْع
Rufaydah	رُفَيْدة
Rumayṣā᾽	رُمَيْصَاء
Rumaythah	رُمَيْثَة
Rumaythā᾽	رُمَيْثاء
Ruqayyah	رُقية
Ru᾽ā	رُؤى
Ṣabāḥ	صباح
Sābiqah	سابقة
Ṣābirah	صابرة
Sabīʿah	سَبيعة
Sadīdah	سديدة
Ṣafiyyah	صفية
Ṣahbā᾽	صهباء
Sahlah	سهلة
Sakīnah	سَكينة
Salāmah	سلامة
Ṣālihah	صالحة
Sālimah	سالمة
Sallāmah	سلّامة
Salmā	سلمى
Samḥah	سمحة
Sāmiyah	سامية
Sanā᾽	سناء
Saniyyah	سَنِية
Sārah	سارة
Sārrah	سارّة
Sarrā᾽	سَرّاء

Name	الاسم
Sawdah	سودة
Saʿīdah	سعيدة
Shafīqah	شفيقة
Shākirah	شاكرة
Shaqīqah	شقيقة
Sharaf	شرف
Sharīfah	شريفة
Shaymāʾ	شيماء
Shifāʾ	شفاء
Subayʿah	سُبَيعة
Sudaysah	سُدَيْسة
Suhaylah	سهيلة
Sukaynah	سُكَيْنة
Sukhaylah	سُخَيْلة
Sulāfah	سُلافة
Ṣulayḥah	صُلَيحة
Sulṭānah	سلطانة
Sumayyah	سمية
Suʿād	سعاد
Suʿdā	سُعْدى
Ṭāhirah	طاهرة
Tamīmah	تَمِيمة
Ṭarfah	طَرْفَة
Ṭaybah	طَيْبة
Taymāʾ	تيماء
Thāmirah	ثامرة
Thanāʾ	ثناء
Thurayyā	ثريا
Ṭulayḥah	طُلَيْحة
Tumāḍir	تُماضِر
Ulf	أُلْف
Umāmah	أُمامة
Umaymah	أُمَيمة
Umayyah	أُمَيّة
Unaysah	أُنَيْسة
Uns	أُنْس
Waḍḥāʾ	وضحاء
Wafāʾ	وفاء
Wājidah	واجدة
Wajīhah	وجيهة
Wāṣilah	واصلة
Wāʾilah	وائلة
Widād	وداد
Wiʾām	وِئام

Name	الاسم
Wuhaybah	وُهَيْبَة
Yumn	يُمن
Yumnā	يُمنى
Yusrā	يُسرى
Zāhidah	زاهدة
Zahrāʾ	زهراء
Zakiyyah	زكية
Zaynab	زينب
Zubaydah	زبيدة
‘Ābidah	عابدة
‘Ablah	عبلة
‘Adīlah	عديلة
‘Afāf	عفاف
‘Afīfah	عفيفة
‘Āliyah	عالية
‘Alyāʾ	علياء
‘Āmilah	عاملة
‘Āmirah	عامرة
‘Amrah	عَمْرَة
‘Aqīlah	عقيلة
‘Āṣimah	عاصمة
‘Aṣmāʾ	عصماء
‘Ātikah	عاتكة
‘Azīzah	عزيزة
‘Azzah	عَزَّة
‘Āʾidah	عائدة
‘Āʾishah	عائشة
‘Uhūd	عُهود
‘Ulā	عُلا
‘Ulayyah	عُلَيّة
‘Umārah	عُمَارة
‘Umayrah	عُمَيْرة
‘Uqaylah	عُقَيْلة

APPENDIX II: ALLĀH'S EXCELLENT NAMES

Introduction

In this appendix, we present an authentic list of Allāh's excellent names. These excellent names are needed for forming combined Islāmic names.

Prefixing Allāh's excellent names with ʿAbd, ʿUbayd, or Amah, results in boys' and girls' names, as is demonstrated in the following table:

Prefix	Name	Meaning	Gender
ʿAbd	ʿAbd ud-Dayyān	Servant of ad-Dayyān	Boy's
ʿUbayd	ʿUbayd ud-Dayyān	Small Servant of ad-Dayyān	Boy's
Amah	Amat ud-Dayyān	Female Servant of ad-Dayyān	Girl's

Rules Concerning Allāh's Names

There is a number of important rules that should be considered when dealing with Allāh's names:

1. All of Allāh's Names Are Excellent

Allāh's names are the most excellent and supreme of names. They reflect qualities of perfection that have no weakness or flaw in them.

2. Allāh's Names Have Distinctive Meanings

Allāh's various names are synonymous in that they all refer to Him alone. On the other hand, each name has a distinctive REAL meaning and describes a distinctive attribute or act of perfection.

3. ALLĀH'S NAMES REQUIRE EVIDENCE

Allāh's names are restricted to those authentically mentioned by Him. There is no room for the human intellect to construct and ascribe names to Him without evidence. We may not attribute to Allāh any name that He did not explicitly attribute to Himself in His Book or His Messenger's Sunnah.

4. ALLĀH'S NAMES ARE COUNTLESS

There is no limit to the number of Allāh's names. He (ﷻ) has mentioned many of them in His Book or His Messenger's (ﷺ) Sunnah. At the same time, he has kept many of them to Himself.

Based on Abū Hurayrah's following *hadīth*, some people think that Allāh's names are limited to ninety-nine.

Abū Hurayrah (ؓ) reported that Allāh's Messenger (ﷺ) said:

«إن لله تسعةً وتسعين إسماً، مائةً إلا واحداً،

من أحصاها دخل الجنة. وهو وترٌ يحب الوتر.»

‹Indeed, Allāh has ninety-nine names — one hundred minus one, whoever encompasses them (with knowledge and belief) will enter *Jannah*. And He (Allāh) is *Witr* (Unique) and loves *witr* (odd numbers).› [1]

However, this *hadīth* merely indicates that 99 of Allāh's names have special merit: whoever encompasses them will be sure to enter *Jannah*.

We will show below that, according to our research, 124 of Allāh's excellent names appear in the Qur'ān or Sunnah.

---

1   Recorded by al-Bukhārī, Muslim, and others.

List of Allāh's Authentic Excellent Names

SINGLE NAMES

The following list includes all of Allāh's authentic single-word names for which we were able to find evidence. Most of them are mentioned in the Qur'ān. A few of them, however, are only mentioned in authentic *ḥadīths* of the Prophet (ﷺ). The names that are only mentioned in *ḥadīths* are marked with an asterisk (*).

#	Allāh's Name	Short Meaning	الاسم
1	Ad-Dayyān*	The Supreme Judge & Ruler	الدّيّان
2	Al-Aḥad	The One & Unique	الأحد
3	Al-Ākhir	The Last	الآخر
4	Al-Akram	The Most Noble & Generous	الأكرم
5	Al-Awwal	The First	الأول
6	Al-A'lā	The Most High	الأعلى
7	Al-Badī'	The Incomparable & Originator	البديع
8	Al-Bāri'	The Originator	البارئ
9	Al-Barr	The Benevolent	البر
10	Al-Baṣīr	The All-Seeing	البصير
11	Al-Bāsiṭ*	The Giver to the Worthy	الباسط
12	Al-Bāṭin	The Intimate & Close	الباطن
13	Al-Fāṭir	The Creator & Originator	الفاطر
14	Al-Fattāḥ	The Establisher of Mercy & Justice	الفتاح
15	Al-Ghaffār	The Perpetual Forgiver	الغفار
16	Al-Ghāfir	The Forgiving	الغافر

#	Allāh's Name	Short Meaning	الاسم
17	Al-Ghafūr	The Forgiver in Plenty	الغفور
18	Al-Ghālib	The Predominant	الغالب
19	Al-Ghaniyy	The Self Sufficient	الغني
20	Al-Hādī	The Guide	الهادي
21	Al-Ḥafīẓ	The Guardian	الحفيظ
22	Al-Ḥāfiẓ	The Preserver	الحافظ
23	Al-Ḥakam	The Judge	الحَكَم
24	Al-Ḥakīm	The Wise	الحكيم
25	Al-Ḥākim	The Commander & Judge	الحاكم
26	Al-Ḥalīm	The Forbearing & Tolerant	الحليم
27	Al-Ḥamīd	The Praiseworthy	الحميد
28	Al-Ḥannān*	The Caring & Compassionate	الحنّان
29	Al-Ḥaqq	The Truth	الحق
30	Al-Ḥasīb	The Reckoner & Sufficer	الحسيب
31	Al-Ḥāsib	The Reckoner	الحاسب
32	Al-Ḥayiyy*	The Modest Who Loves Modesty	الحيِيّ
33	Al-Ḥayy	The Ever-Living	الحي
34	Al-Ilāh	The God	الإلٰه
35	Al-Jabbār	The Formidable & Restorer	الجبار
36	Al-Jamīl*	The One of Excellent Qualities	الجميل
37	Al-Jāmiʿ	The Gatherer	الجامع
38	Al-Jawād*	The Bountiful	الجواد

#	Allāh's Name	Short Meaning	الاسم
39	Al-Kabīr	The Magnificent & Grand	الكبير
40	Al-Kāfī	The Sufficient	الكافي
41	Al-Kafīl	The Guarantor	الكفيل
42	Al-Karīm	The Generous & Noble	الكريم
43	Al-Khabīr	The Well-Acquainted & All-Aware	الخبير
44	Al-Khāliq	The Creator	الخالق
45	Al-Khallāq	The Creator, Time-and-Again	الخلّاق
46	Al-Lāh	The Greatest Name	اللّه
47	Al-Laṭīf	The Subtle & Kind	اللطيف
48	Al-Majīd	The Glorious	المجيد
49	Al-Malik	The Sovereign	الملِك
50	Al-Malīk	The Sovereign	المليك
51	Al-Mālik	The Owner	المالك
52	Al-Mannān*	The Giver in Plenty	المنّان
53	Al-Matīn	The Powerful	المتين
54	Al-Mawlā	The Protector	المولى
55	Al-Mubīn	The Manifest & Manifesting	المبين
56	Al-Muhaymin	The Guard & Witness	المهيمن
57	Al-Muḥīṭ	The Acquainted & Embracing	المُحيط
58	Al-Muḥsin*	The Benevolent and Kind	المُحسِن
59	Al-Muḥyī	The Giver of Life	المُحْيي
60	Al-Mujīb	The Responsive	المجيب

#	Allāh's Name	Short Meaning	الاسم
61	Al-Muqaddim*	The Promoter of the Worthy	المُقَدِّم
62	Al-Muqtadir	The All-Capable	المقتدر
63	Al-Muqīt	The Custodian	المُقيت
64	Al-Muṣawwir	The Fashioner	المصور
65	Al-Musa"ir*	The One Who Fixes the Prices	المُسَعِّر
66	Al-Musta'ān	The One Whose Help Is Sought	المُستعان
67	Al-Mutakabbir	The Majestic	المُتكبّر
68	Al-Muta'āl	The Most Exalted	المتعال
69	Al-Mu'akh-khir*	The Repressor of the Unworthy	المُؤَخِّر
70	Al-Mu'min	The Grantor of Security	المؤمن
71	Al-Qābiḍ*	The Withholder from the Unworthy	القابض
72	Al-Qadīr	The Capable	القدير
73	Al-Qādir	The Capable & Competent	القادر
74	Al-Qahhār	The Prevailing	القهار
75	Al-Qāhir	The Subjugator	القاهر
76	Al-Qarīb	The Near	القريب
77	Al-Qawiyy	The Strong	القوي
78	Al-Qayyūm	The Sustainer of All	القيوم
79	Al-Quddūs	The Pure & Holy	القُدّوس
80	Al-Wadūd	The Loving	الودود
81	Al-Wahhāb	The Grantor	الوهاب
82	Al-Wāḥid	The One	الواحد

#	Allāh's Name	Short Meaning	الاسم
83	Al-Wakīl	The Trustee	الوكيل
84	Al-Waliyy	The Ally	الولي
85	Al-Wārith	The Inheritor	الوارث
86	Al-Wāsiʿ	The Encompassing	الواسع
87	Al-Witr*	The One & Unique	الوِتر
88	Al-ʿAfuww	The Pardoner	العفوّ
89	Al-ʿAlīm	The All-Knowing	العليم
90	Al-ʿĀlim	The Knowledgeable	العالِم
91	Al-ʿAliyy	The Sublime	العلي
92	Al-ʿAllām	The Most Knowledgeable	العلاّم
93	Al-ʿAẓīm	The Great	العظيم
94	Al-ʿAzīz	The Honorable & Mighty	العزيز
95	An-Naṣīr	The Helper	الناصر
96	An-Nāṣir	The Helper to Victory	النصير
97	An-Nūr	The Giver of Light & Guidance	النور
98	Ar-Rabb	The Lord	الرب
99	Ar-Rafīq*	The Gentle	الرفيق
100	Ar-Raḥīm	The Dispenser of Mercy	الرحيم
101	Ar-Rāḥim	The Merciful	الراحم
102	Ar-Raḥmān	The Most Merciful	الرحمٰن
103	Ar-Raqīb	The Watchful	الرقيب
104	Ar-Rāziq	The Sustainer	الرازق

#	Allāh's Name	Short Meaning	الاسم
105	Ar-Razzāq	The Ever-Sustainer	الرزاق
106	Ar-Ra'ūf	The Compassionate	الرؤوف
107	As-Salām	The One Who Is Clear from Ills	السلام
108	Aṣ-Ṣamad	The Eternal Refuge	الصمد
109	As-Samī'	The All-Hearing	السميع
110	As-Sayyid*	The Master	السيد
111	As-Sittīr*	The One Who Covers Sins & Ills	السِتّير
112	As-Subbūḥ*	The Exalted	السبّوح
113	Ash-Shāfī*	The Curer	الشافي
114	Ash-Shahīd	The Witness	الشهيد
115	Ash-Shākir	The Appreciative	الشاكر
116	Ash-Shakūr	The Ever-Appreciative	الشكور
117	At-Tawwāb	Repentance Facilitator & Acceptor	التواب
118	Aṭ-Ṭayyib*	The Good & Pure	الطيّب
119	Aẓ-Ẓāhir	The Apparent & Sublime	الظاهر

Combined Excellent Names

In the above list, we excluded Allāh's authentic names that are combined of two words. The reason for this is that such names cannot be used for forming human names. However, we list below, for convenience, Allāh's most commonly accepted combined names. All of these names appear in the Qur'ān.

#	Allāh's Name	Short Meaning	الاسم
1	Mālik ul-Mulk	The Dominion's Owner	مالك الملك

2	Muqallib ul-Qulūb*	The Turner of Hearts	مقلب القلوب
3	Thul-Faḍl	The One of Favors	ذو الفضل
4	Thul-Ikrām	The One of Honor	ذو الإكرام
5	Thul-Jalāl	The One of Greatness	ذو الجلال
6	Thul-Maʿārij	The One of Highness	ذو المعارج
7	Thuṭ-Ṭawl	The One of Bounties	ذو الطَّوْل

Names without Evidence

Many names are considered by some people as being excellent names of Allāh even though there is no evidence for them in Allāh's Book or His Messenger's Sunnah.

Most of the commonly cited unauthentic names appear in a weak *ḥadīth* recorded by at-Tirmithī and Ibn Mājah from Abū Hurayrah (﵁). The beginning of this *ḥadīth* is identical to the earlier *ḥadīth* of Abū Hurayrah (p. 184), but it goes on to list 99 names, among which there are 31 unauthentic names.

The commonly distributed list or poster of Allāh's 99 names includes 23 or 24 unauthentic names as well, most of which coming from the weak *ḥadīth* that we just mentioned.

In what follows, we list the most common unauthentc names, including those found in the above-mentioned *ḥadīth* and posters.

Wrong Name	**الاسم**
Aḍ-Ḍārr	الضار
Ad-Dā'im	الدائم
Al-Abad	الأبد
Al-Bāqī	الباقي
Al-Bārr	البار
Al-Bāʿith	الباعث
Al-Burhān	البرهان
Al-Huwah	الهُوَه
Al-Jalīl	الجليل

Wrong Name	الاسم
Al-Khāfiḍ	الخافض
Al-Mājid	الماجد
Al-Māniʿ	المانع
Al-Maqṣūd	المقصود
Al-Maʿbūd	المعبود
Al-Mubdiʾ	المبدئ
Al-Mughīth	المغيث
Al-Mughnī	المغني
Al-Muḥṣī	المحصي
Al-Mumīt	المميت
Al-Munīr	المنير
Al-Muntaqim	المنتقم
Al-Munʿim	المنعم
Al-Muqsiṭ	المقسط
Al-Mursil	المُرسِل
Al-Muthill	المذل
Al-Muʿīd	المعيد
Al-Muʿizz	المعز
Al-Muʿṭī	المعطي
Al-Qadīm	القديم
Al-Qāʾim	القائم
Al-Waḥīd	الوحيد
Al-Wājid	الواجد
Al-Wālī	الوالي
Al-Wāqī	الواقي
Al-ʿAdl	العدل
An-Nāfiʿ	النافع
Ar-Rāfiʿ	الرافع
Ar-Rashīd	الرشيد
Ar-Rāshid	الراشد
Aṣ-Ṣabūr	الصبور
Aṣ-Ṣādiq	الصادق
As-Sāmiʾ	السامع
As-Sātir	الساتر
As-Sattār	الستّار
Ash-Shadīd	الشديد
Aṭ-Ṭālib	الطالب
At-Tāmm	التام

REFERENCES

General "Newborn" and "Baby" References

Aḥkām ul-Mawlūd fis-Sunnat il-Muṭahharah (Regulations for the Newborn in the Purified Sunnah), Sālim ash-Shiblī and Muḥammad ar-Rabāḥ, al-Maktab ul-Islāmī, Beirut, 1415 (1994).

Aḥkām uṭ-Ṭifl (Rulings Pertaining to the Child), Aḥmad al-ʿĪsawī, Dār ul-Hijrah, Riyadh, 1412 (1992).

Al-Islām waṭ-Ṭifl (Islam's View of Children), Abd ur-Razzāq Ḥusayn, Institute of Islamic & Arabic Studies in America (IIASA), Virginia, 1411 (1990).

Fatāwā wa-Aḥkām Khāṣah biṭ-Ṭifl (Verdicts and Rulings Pertinent to the Child), Yūsuf al-ʿAtīq (compiler), Dār uṣ-Ṣumayʿī, Riyādh, 1419 (1998).

Manhaj ut-Tarbiyat in-Nabawiyyati liṭ-Ṭifl (the Prophetic Guidance in Educating the Child), Muḥammad Nūr Suwayd, ar-Rayyān Publishing Institute, Beirut, (1414) 1994.

Manners of Welcoming the New Born Child in Islām, Yūsuf al-ʿArīfī, Tr. Dāwūd Burbank, Maktaba Dar-us-Salam, Birmingham, UK, 1996.

Masʾūliyyat ul-Ab il-Muslim (the Muslim Parent's Responsibility), ʿAdnān Bā Ḥārith, Dār ul-Mujtamaʿ, Jeddah, 1413 (1992).

Tarbiyat ul-Awlād fil-Islām (Raising Children in Islām), ʿAbdullāh Nāṣiḥ ʿAlwān, Dār us-Salām, Cairo, 1417 (1997).

Tuḥfat ul-Mawdūdi fī Aḥkām il-Mawlūd (Gift for the Beloved about the Newborn's Rulings), Ibn ul-Qayyim, Dār ul-Bayān, Damascus, 1419 (1999).

ʿAqīqah and Slaughtering

Aḥkām uth-Thabāʾih fil-Islām (Regulations for Slaughtering in Islām), Muḥammad ʿAbdul-Qādir Abū Fās, Maktabat ul-Manār, Zarqa (Jordan), 1401 (1980).

Al-Ajwibat ud-Daqīqah ʿan Aḥkām il-Uḍḥiyati wal-ʿAqīqah (Precise Answers Concerning the Rulings of the Sarifice and *ʿAqīqah*), Saʿūd al-ʿAnazī, Dār Ibn Ḥazm, Beirut, 1420 (1999).

Al-Mufaṣṣalu fī Aḥkām il-Uḍḥiyah (the Detailed Discussion in Regard to the Sacrifice's Rulings), Ḥusām ud-Dīn ʿAfānah, Maktabatu Dandīs, Amman, 1421 (2000).

Fiqh ul-Aymān wan-Nuthūr, wa-Ḥukm ul-Islām fith-Thabāʾih (The Legislations of Oaths and Vows, and the Islāmic Ruling Regarding Slaughtering), Muḥammad Sālim ʿUbaydāt, Dār ʿAmmār, Ammn, 1412 (1992).

Thalāthu Shaʿāʾir (Three Rites of Worship), ʿUmar al-Ashqar, ad-Dār us-Salafiyyah, Kuwait, 1404 (1984).

Islāmic Names

Dawr ul-Marʾti fī Khidmat il-Ḥadīth, Āmāl Qurdāsh, Kitāb ul-Ummah, Qatar, 1420 (1999).

Taqrīb ut-Tahthīb, Ibn Ḥajar al-ʿAsqalānī, Muʾassasat ur-Risālah, Beirut, 1416 (1996).

Tarājimu Aʿlām in-Nisāʾ, Raḍwān Daʿbūl, Muʾassasat ur-Risālah, Beirut, 1419 (1998).

Tasmiyat ul-Mawlūd (Naming the Newborn), Bakr Abū Zayd, Dār ul-ʿĀṣimah, Riyadh, 1416 (1995).

Allāh's Excellent Names

Al-Qawāʿid ul-Muthlā fī Ṣifāt il-Lāhi wa-Asmāʾih il-Ḥusnā (The Ideal Rules in Regard to Allāh's Attributes and Excellent Names), Muḥammad Bin Ṣāliḥ al-ʿUthaymīn, Dār ul-Arqam, Kuwait, 1406 (1986).

An-Nahj ul-Asmā fI Sharḥi Asmāʾ Illāh il-Ḥusnā (The Most Superior Approach in the Explanation of Allāh's Excellent Names), Muḥammad al-Ḥumūd an-Najdī, Vols. 1-3, Maktabat ul-Imām ath-Thahabī, Kuwait, 1417 (1997).

Asmāʾ Ullāhi wa-Ṣifātuh fī Muʿtaqadi Ahl is-Sunnati wal-Jamāʿah (Allāh's Names and Attributes According to the Belief of *Ahl us-Sunnah wal-Jamāʿah*), ʿUmar Sulaymān al-Ashqar, Dār un-Nafāʾis, Amman, 1414 (1994).

Maʿ Allāhi Taʿālā fī Asmāʾihī wa-Ṣifātih (With Allāh, the Exalted, in His Names and Attributes), ʿAlī Aḥmad al-ʿUthmān, Dār ul-Bashīr, Cairo, 1411 (1991).

Sharḥu Asmāʾ Illāh il-Ḥusnā (Explanation of Allāh's Excellent Names), Saʿīd Bin ʿAlī al-Qaḥṭānī, Muʾassasat ul-Juraysī, Riyadh, 1409 (1989).

Tafsīru Asmāʾ il-Lāh il-Ḥusnā (Interpretation of Allāh's Excellent Names), Ibrāhīm az-Zajjāj, Dār ul-Maʾmūn, Damascus, 1403 (1983).

ARABIC TERMS

A number of Arabic terms are frequently used in Islāmic discussions, and seem to constitute a basic vocabulary that needs to be available to the readers of most books on Islām. We attempt to provide such terms, together with their definitions, in the following "Glossary" section. Other terms pertinent to the current book are included in the "Index" section, together with a page-reference indicating where they are defined in this book.

A: Glossary of Common Terms

Term	Definition
Adab	Good characters or manners; etiquettes. Plural: *Ādāb*.
Al-Fātiḥah	The first chapter of the Qur'ān.
Āmīn	Means, "O Allāh, answer my supplication."
Anṣār	"The Supporters": the residents of al-Madīnah who supported the Prophet (ﷺ) and the *muhājirūn*.
Athān	Call to the prayer.
Āyah	Literally means a miracle and a sign. The Qur'ān is a miracle in itself, and so is any portion of it. The smallest subdivision of the Qur'ānic text is thus called an *āyah*. An *āyah* is usually one sentence in length, but is sometimes longer or shorter than a complete sentence. The plural of *āyah* is *āyāt*.
Āyāt	Plural of *āyah*.
Bid'ah	Innovation in the creed or in acts of worship.
Da'wah	Call or mission.

Term	Definition
Dīn	Religion. It is usually used in reference to the religion of Islām.
Dīnār	A valuable old currency that was made of gold.
Dirham	A low-value old currency that was made of silver or copper.
Du'ā'	Supplication.
Fajr	Dawn. It usually applies to the first daily obligatory prayer, whose time extends from dawn until sunrise.
Farḍ	Obligation.
Farḍ Kifāyah	A communal obligation; if some Muslims perform it, the obligation is considered fulfilled by all; and if none does, all Muslims are considered sinful.
Farḍ 'Ayn	An individual obligation, i.e., an obligation that each individual must fulfill.
Fatwā	A religious verdict; plural: *fatāwā* or *fatāwī*.
Fiqh	The ability to understand and derive conclusions from the available evidence. It is often applied to the subject of "Islāmic jurisprudence" that deals with the practical regulations in Islām.
Fitnah	Trial, test, temptation, or affliction.
Ghayb	The world beyond our senses or perception.
Ghusl	A ritual bath required after intercourse, ejaculation, or after a women becomes clean from her menses.
Ḥadīth	Reports of the Prophet's sayings, actions, and approvals. We use *ḥadīth* (plural *ḥadīth*s) to indicate individual report(s), and *Ḥadīth* with upper case Ḥ to indicate the subject of *Ḥadīth* specialty.

Term	Definition
Ḥajj	Pilgrimage to Makkah.
Ḥalāl	Permissible.
Ḥalqah	A circle or ring. It normally refers to a study circle.
Ḥarām	Prohibited.
Ḥasan	Good or acceptable. This is usually mentioned when indicating the degree of authenticity of some reports.
Ḥijāb	Cover. It usually refers to a woman's clothing that covers all of her body except her face and hands.
Hijrah	Migration. It usually refers to migration from Makkah to al-Madīnah.
Ijmāʿ	Consensus of the scholars.
Ijtihād	Exerting *juhd* (maximum possible effort) to reach the right conclusion based on the available evidence.
Imām	A leader or distinguished Islāmic scholar. It is often applied to the leader of prayer.
Īmān	Belief or conviction.
Isnād	Chain of narrators of a *ḥadīth*.
Jāhiliyyah	The era of extreme ignorance (*jahl*) and disbelief that preceded the advent of the Prophet Muḥammad (ﷺ).
Jamāʿah	A Muslim congregation or gathering. It is often applied to the congregational prayers. *Al-Jamāʿah* (the *Jamāʿah*) refers to the original community of the *ṣaḥābah* and their true followers through the ages.
Janāzah	A funeral or a deceased's prepared body.
Jannah	The gardens of paradise.
Jihād	Striving or fighting for Allāh's cause.

Term	Definition
Jinn	An indivisible creation that Allāh created from fire and smoke, and to which belongs Satan. It is sometimes translated as "demons".
Jumuʿah	Friday. It also applies to the Friday prayer.
Kāfir	A person who practices *kufr*. Plural: "*kuffār*".
Khalīfah	Derives from *khalafa*, which means "succeeded" or "followed". It commonly refers to a Muslim ruler who succeeded the Prophet (ﷺ) in leading the Muslims. Plural: *khulafāʾ*.
Khamr	Alcoholic beverages.
Khilāfah	Successorship. It usually refers to the period of rule of a *khalīfah*.
Kufr	Disbelief or rejection of faith.
Khuṭbah	Speech or sermon.
Maghrib	Sunset. It is usually applied to the fourth daily obligatory prayer, whose time extends from sunset until the red light disappears from the horizon.
Makrūh	An act that is disapproved in Islām.
Maḥram	A person who is closely related to another in such a way as to permanently prohibit them from marrying each other. This relationship results from blood, suckling, or marriage ties. A woman's *maḥram*s are: her father, grandfather, son, grandson, brother, immediate uncle (from the mother's or father's side), father in law, son in law, foster son, foster brother, etc. Examples of non-*maḥram*s: cousins (from both sides), step brothers, brothers in law, etc.
Masjid	A place designated for *sujūd*. It usually refers to a mosque.

Term	**Definition**
Mathhab	Way or approach. It usually refers to one of the four Islāmic schools of *fiqh* established by the Four *Imāms*: Abū Ḥanīfah an-Nuʿmān Bin Thābit, Mālik Bin Anas, Muḥammad Bin Idrīs ash-Shāfiʿī, and Aḥmad Bin Ḥanbal — May Allāh bestow His mercy on them all.
Minbar	Steps (normally three) used in a *masjid* for the *imām* to stand on when delivering a *khuṭbah*.
Muhājir	A migrator - one who undertakes *hijrah*. Plural: *muhājirūn* or *muhājirīn*. It usually refers to a *ṣaḥābī* who migrated from Makkah to al-Madīnah.
Mujāhid	A person who performs *jihād*. Plural: *mujāhidūn* or *mujāhidīn*.
Munkar	Disapproved; rejected.
Muṣallā	A place designated for *ṣalāh*. Most commonly, it applies to the grounds where the prayers of *ʿīd* and *janāzah* are performed.
Mushrik	See "*shirk*".
Nafl	Extra, voluntary, or supererogatory deeds.
Qadar	Allāh's decree and measure.
Qiblah	The direction of al-Kaʿbah in Makkah.
Qudusī	Holy. A *qudusī ḥadīth* is a *ḥadīth* that the Prophet (ﷺ) relates from his Lord (ﷻ).
Rakʿah	Means a full prayer unit, because it contains only one *rukūʿ*. Plural: *rakʿāt*.
Ramaḍān	The month of fasting. It is the ninth month of the Islāmic lunar calendar.
Rukūʿ	The act of bowing in the prayer. It derives from the verb *rakaʿa* which means "bowed down".

Term	Definition
Ṣadaqah	Charity.
Ṣaḥābah	The Prophet's companions; singular: *ṣaḥābī.*
Ṣaḥīḥ	True or authentic.
Salaf	The early righteous pioneers and scholars of Islām—the *ṣaḥābah* and their true followers.
Ṣalāh	The prayer.
Salām	Peace. It also means the greeting with peace (*as-salāmu ʿalaykum*) among the Muslims.
Sanad	Same as *isnād.*
Shahādah	Testimony; it is mostly applied to the testimony of Islām: "There is no true deity but Allāh, and Muḥammad is Allāh's Messenger." Also, it is often applied to the most truthful form of physical testimony, which is martyrdom in Allāh's (ﷻ) cause.
Shahīd	A person martyred for Allāh's cause. Feminine: *Shahīdah.*
Shām	General Middle-East area of Palestine, Jordan, Syria, and Lebanon, including the major cities of Jerusalem and Damascus.
Sharʿ	It deriving from *sharaʿa*, which means "legislated". It is usually used in reference to the Islāmic Law. *Sharʿī* means a legislated or permissible matter in Islām.
Sharīʿah	Same as "*sharʿ*".
Shaykh	Literally means and old man. It is commonly used as a title of respect for a man of better Islāmic knowledge. It is also used in some Arab countries as a title of authority similar to "prince".
Shayṭān	Satan.

Term	**Definition**
Shirk	Polytheism, ascribing divinity to other than Allāh, or joining partners with Him in worship. A pagan or a person who practices *shirk* is a *mushrik.*
Ṣiyām	Fasting.
Sujūd	The act of prostration in the prayer.
Sunnah	Way, guidance, teachings, etc.
Sūrah	Qur'ānic chapter.
Tābiʻī	Literally, follower. It normally refers to a disciple of the *ṣaḥābah.* Plural: *tābiʻūn* or *tābiʻīn.*
Tafsīr	Qur'ānic commentaries and interpretations.
Takbīr	Saying, "*Allāhu Akbar* — Allāh is the greatest."
Tahlīl	Saying, "*Lā ilāha illallāh* — There is no true god except Allāh."
Taqlīd	Imitation — especially without knowledge.
Taqwā	Fearing Allāh and revering him.
Tasbīḥ	Saying, "*Subḥān Allāh* — Exalted is Allāh."
Tashahhud	Pronouncing the *Shahādah.* It is mostly applied to the part of the prayer where one sits, pronounces the *Shahādah*, invokes *ṣalāh* upon the Messenger, and supplicates.
Tayammum	A symbolic ablution performed by wiping clean dust, instead of water, over the hands (to the wrists) and face.
Taslīm	Saying *salām*, especially to conclude the prayer.
Thikr	Remembering Allāh and mentioning Him.
Ummah	Community, nation, or followers.

Term	Definition
Waḥy	Revelation or inspiration.
Wājib	Obligatory or required.
Witr	Odd numbered. The entire night prayer is sometimes called *witr* because the total number of its *rakʿāt* is odd.
Wuḍūʾ	Ablution for the prayer. It consists of rinsing the mouth, blowing the nose, washing the face, washing the forearms to the elbows, wiping over the head (including the ears), and washing the feet up to the ankles.
Zakāh	Obligatory charity.
Zinā	Adultery or fornication.
Ẓuhr	Noon. It is usually applied to the second daily obligatory prayer, whose time extends from the sun's crossing the zenith until the time when the shadows are as long as the objects.
ʿAbd	Slave or servant. In reference to Allāh (ﷻ), it usually means a devout worshiper (as in ʿAbd Ullāh). But it frequently refers to a "human being" because every human being is subdued by Allāh (ﷻ) whether one admits it or not. Plural: *ʿibād* or *ʿabīd*.
ʿAllāmah	See "*ʿālim*".
ʿĀlim	A scholar or learned man; plural: *ʿulamāʾ*. *ʿAllāmah* is an exaggerated form of *ʿālim*.
ʿAṣr	After noon. It is usually applied to the third daily obligatory prayer, whose time extends from when the shadows are as long as the objects until sunset.
ʿIbād	See "*ʿabd*".

Term	Definition
'Īd	A day of celebration in Islām. There are two annual *'īd*s (*al-fiṭr* and *al-Aḍḥā*) and one weekly *'īd* (the day of *Jumu'ah*).
'Ishā'	Night. It is usually applied to the fifth and last daily obligatory prayer, whose time extends from the disappearance of the red light from the horizon until the middle of the night (which is half way between sunset and dawn).
'Ulamā'	See "*'ālim*".

B: Index

Abū 43
Aflaḥ 49
Aḥlām 54
Aḥmad 33
Al-Fiṭr 141
Al-Ḥāshir 34
Al-Māḥī 33
Al-ʿĀqib 34
An-Naḥr 141
Arīj 54
Bahāʾ ud-Dīn 54
Barakah 50
Barrah 57
Bin 42
Bint 42
Bishārah 16
Diyāʾ ud-Dīn 54
Fakhr ud-Dīn 54
Fātin 54
Firʿawn 49
Fitnah 54
Ghādah 54
Hady 70
Hāmān 49
Hammām 31
Ḥanak 111
    Taḥnīk 111
Ḥarb 31
Ḥārith 31
Ḥassānah 58
Ḥazan 60
Hishām 58
Huyām 54
Ibn 42
Istiḥbāb 68
Jamīlah 58
Juthāmah 58
Juwayriyah 57
Khalīl 20
Khamīṣah 45
Khayr ud-Dīn 54
Khinzib 49
Khitān 108
Kunyah 43
Malak 55
Malāk 55
Muḥammad 33
Muhy id-Dīn 55
Murrah 31
Muʿawwithāt 123
Nāfiʿ 50
Nāhid 54
Najīḥ 49
Najis 143
Nasaka 64
    Nasīkah 63
Nāṣir ud-Dīn 55
Naṣr ud-Dīn 54
Nūr ud-Dīn 54
Nūr ul-Ḥaq 54
Nūr ul-Islām 54
Qayṣar 49
Qazʿ 116
Qiyās 73
Rabāḥ 49
Rāfiʿ 50
Raḥmat ul-Lāh 54
Raqā 121
    Ruqā 121
    Ruqyah 121
Sahl 60
Salāḥ ud-Dīn 54

Sayf ud-Dīn 54
Sa'd ud-Dīn 54
Shāh 71
Sharaf ud-Dīn 54
Shihāb 58
Shihāb ud-Dīn 54
Sihām 54
Siwāk 105
Taghrīd 54
Ṭāhir 144
  Ṭahārah 143
Tahni'ah 16
Tamīmah 129
Taqiyy ud-Dīn 54
Tarbiyah xv
Taṣfiyah xv
Taṣwīr 136
Tiwalah 129
Uḍḥiyah 73
Walīmah 84
Wiṣāl 54
Yasār 50
Zaynab 57
'Alā' ud-Dīn 54
'Aqqa 63
  'Aqīqah 63
  'Uqūq 63
'Aṣiyah 58
'Awrah 11
'Iddah 157
'Izz ud-Dīn 55